Ifo Survey Data in Business Cycle and Monetary Policy Analysis

Contributions to Economics

www.springeronline.com/series/1262

Further volumes of this series can be found at our homepage.

Nicole Pohl
Mobility in Space and Time
2001. ISBN 3-7908-1380-X

Mario A. Maggioni
Clustering Dynamics and the Locations of High-Tech-Firms
2002. ISBN 3-7908-1431-8

Ludwig Schätzl/Javier Revilla Diez (Eds.)
Technological Change and Regional Development in Europe
2002. ISBN 3-7908-1460-1

Alberto Quadrio Curzio/Marco Fortis (Eds.)
Complexity and Industrial Clusters
2002. ISBN 3-7908-1471-7

Friedel Bolle/Marco Lehmann-Waffenschmidt (Eds.)
Surveys in Experimental Economics
2002. ISBN 3-7908-1472-5

Pablo Coto-Millán
General Equilibrium and Welfare
2002. ISBN 7908-1491-1

Wojciech W. Charemza/Krystyna Strzala (Eds.)
East European Transition and EU Enlargement
2002. ISBN 3-7908-1501-1

Natalja von Westernhagen
Systemic Transformation, Trade and Economic Growth
2002. ISBN 3-7908-1521-7

Josef Falkinger
A Theory of Employment in Firms
2002. ISBN 3-7908-1520-9

Engelbert Plassmann
Econometric Modelling of European Money Demand
2003. ISBN 3-7908-1522-5

Reginald Loyen/Erik Buyst/Greta Devos (Eds.)
Struggeling for Leadership: Antwerp-Rotterdam Port Competition between 1870–2000
2003. ISBN 3-7908-1524-1

Pablo Coto-Millán
Utility and Production, 2nd Edition
2003. ISBN 3-7908-1423-7

Emilio Colombo/John Driffill (Eds.)
The Role of Financial Markets in the Transition Process
2003. ISBN 3-7908-0004-X

Guido S. Merzoni
Strategic Delegation in Firms and in the Trade Union
2003. ISBN 3-7908-1432-6

Jan B. Kuné
On Global Aging
2003. ISBN 3-7908-0030-9

Sugata Marjit, Rajat Acharyya
International Trade, Wage Inequality and the Developing Economy
2003. ISBN 3-7908-0031-7

Francesco C. Billari/Alexia Prskawetz (Eds.)
Agent-Based Computational Demography
2003. ISBN 3-7908-1550-0

Georg Bol/Gholamreza Nakhaeizadeh/ Svetlozar T. Rachev/Thomas Ridder/ Karl-Heinz Vollmer (Eds.)
Credit Risk
2003. ISBN 3-7908-0054-6

Christian Müller
Money Demand in Europe
2003. ISBN 3-7908-0064-3

Cristina Nardi Spiller
The Dynamics of the Price Structure and the Business Cycle
2003. ISBN 3-7908-0063-5

Michael Bräuninger
Public Debt and Endogenous Growth
2003. ISBN 3-7908-0056-1

Brigitte Preissl/Laura Solimene
The Dynamics of Clusters and Innovation
2003. ISBN 3-7908-0077-5

Markus Gangl
Unemployment Dynamics in the United States and West Germany
2003. ISBN 3-7908-1533-0

Pablo Coto-Millán (Ed.)
Essays on Microeconomics and Industrial Organisation, 2nd Edition
2004. ISBN 3-7908-0104-6

Wendelin Schnedler
The Value of Signals in Hidden Action Models
2004. ISBN 3-7908-0173-9

Carsten Schröder
Variable Income Equivalence Scales
2004. ISBN 3-7908-0183-6

Wilhelm J. Meester
Locational Preferences of Entrepreneurs
2004. ISBN 3-7908-0178-X

Russel Cooper/Gary Madden (Eds.)
Frontiers of Broadband, Electronic and Mobile Commerce
2004. ISBN 3-7908-0087-2

Jan-Egbert Sturm
Timo Wollmershäuser
Editors

Ifo Survey Data in Business Cycle and Monetary Policy Analysis

With 51 Figures
and 62 Tables

Physica-Verlag
A Springer Company

Series Editors
Werner A. Müller
Martina Bihn

Editors

Prof. Dr. Jan-Egbert Sturm
University of Konstanz
Department of Economics
P.O. Box D 131
78457 Konstanz
Germany
and
TWI – Thurgau Institute of Economics
Hauptstraße 90
P.O. Box
8280 Kreuzlingen 2
Switzerland
jan-egbert.sturm@uni-konstanz.de

Dr. Timo Wollmershäuser
Ifo Institute for Economic Research
Poschingerstraße 5
81679 Munich
Germany
wollmershaeuser@ifo.de

ISSN 1431-1933
ISBN 3-7908-0174-7 Physica-Verlag Heidelberg New York

Cataloging-in-Publication Data applied for
Library of Congress Control Number: 2004111905

Physica-Verlag is a part of Springer Science+Business Media

springeronline.com

Printed in Germany

Softcover Design: Erich Kirchner, Heidelberg

SPIN 10981900 88/3130/DK-5 4 3 2 1 0 – Printed on acid-free and non-aging paper

Foreword

A pilot flying to a distant city needs to check his position, flight path and weather conditions, and must constantly keep his plane under control to land safely. The Ifo survey data provide advance information on changing economic weather conditions and help keep the economy under control. To be sure, by their very nature they only provide short-term information. But like a plane, the economy will not be able to reach its long-term goals if it strays off course in the short term.

The Ifo survey data provide the most comprehensive and accurate, up-to-date database in Europe on the state of the business cycle, and the Ifo climate indicator, sometimes simply called "The Ifo", is the most frequently cited indicator of its kind in Europe. Both the European stock market and the euro react to our indicator. Ifo's methodology for determining the business climate indicator has been exported to more than fifty countries, most recently to Turkey and China. The Ifo people were proud to have been asked to help set up polling systems in these countries. It is said that the Chinese government relies more on their "Ifo indicator" than on their official accounting statistics.

The seven thousand firms that Ifo surveys every month not only give information about the state of their business and their expectations but answer questions on other business issues as well. The answers have been fed into a unique panel database, reaching back for decades, that contains treasures for empirical research on the business cycle. Ifo encourages researchers from all over the world to use these data for their research. For any serious research project, Ifo provides in-house facilities that give external researchers a maximum of support in analyzing the data while simultaneously protecting the anonymity of the participating firms.

This book contains examples of scholarly econometric research that is based on the Ifo data set. It contains seven fine articles on various research topics that center around business cycle problems and make use of the survey data. I very much hope that these articles will whet the appetite of econometricians around the world in applying the data for their purposes. More information on the data set can be found on our web site www.ifo.de as well as in a new handbook on the Ifo surveys that is available from the institute on request.

I am grateful to the authors of this volume for contributing to this fruitful project.

Munich, *Hans-Werner Sinn*
June 2004 *President of the Ifo Institute for Economic Research*

Preface and Overview

The Ifo Institute – short for "Information und Forschung", information and research – was founded in 1949 and is internationally renowned for its business surveys. Every month close to 7,000 enterprises are questioned on their short-term planning and their appraisals of the actual and future business situation. The confidence indicator frequently referred to as the Ifo Business Climate Index is derived from the responses to this Ifo Business Survey. While the Index attracts a lot of attention by practitioners (especially financial market analysts), the use and empirical exploitation of this and other components of Ifo business surveys is – amongst academics – still relatively scarce.

The present volume is a collection of papers presented at a conference entitled "The Academic Use of Ifo Survey Data" which took place at the Ifo Institute on December 5 and 6, 2003. It aims to promote the use of Ifo survey data by the scientific community by giving examples of timely research questions which can be addressed by qualitative survey data like the monthly Ifo Business Survey. As will be shown, this type of real-time data can be very informative when it comes to e.g. forecasting real economic activity or exploring monetary policy transmission.

The book is organized as follows. After a brief review of the survey activity of the Ifo Institute given by Gernot Nerb, the head of Ifo's Business Survey department, the volume centres on two topics: (I) the analysis of business cycles; and (II) the analysis of monetary policy.

The first part – dealing with business cycle analysis – is made up of five papers. Stefan Mittnik and Peter A. Zadrozny's paper illustrates and evaluates a Kalman-filtering method for forecasting German real GDP at monthly intervals. GDP data is usually published at quarterly intervals but analysts and decision makers often want monthly GDP forecasts. Quarterly GDP could be regressed on monthly indicators, which would pick up monthly feedbacks from the indicators to GDP, but would not pick up implicit monthly feedbacks from GDP onto itself or the indicators. An efficient forecasting model which aims to incorporate all significant correlations in monthly-quarterly data should, however, include all significant monthly feedbacks. Mittnik and

Zadrozny do this with VAR(2) models of quarterly GDP and up to three monthly indicator variables which are estimated using a Kalman-filtering-based maximum-likelihood estimation method. The monthly indicators are industrial production and current and expected business conditions as measured by the Ifo Institute's business surveys. The main result is that the mixed-frequency method produces monthly GDP forecasts for the first two months of a quarter ahead which are more accurate than one-quarter-ahead GDP forecasts based on the purely-quarterly data.

The paper by Ulrich Woitek investigates the cyclicality between real wages and the business cycle in Germany and the US. Using a threshold vector autoregressive model to condition the relationship between real wages and business cycle fluctuations on the phase of the cycle, he demonstrates that the former behaves differently during an upswing as compared to a downswing. If there is an asymmetry in the relationship between real wages and the business cycle, significant correlations might cancel out if calculated without conditioning on the phase of the cycle. In the case of the US, both manufacturing output and employment are analyzed as cycle measures. In the case of Germany, the business cycle is additionally measured by the Ifo Business Climate Index. In general, the evidence for countercyclical wages appear to be stronger in Germany than for the US.

Thomas A. Knetsch addresses the data revision problems for German inventory investment, an important variable in business cycle analysis. As commonly known, the preliminary data published in the German national accounts is rather unreliable. By applying standard techniques of time series analysis, he shows that there is considerable co-movement of the reference series and three Ifo series taken from the Ifo Business Survey which document manufacturers', retail and wholesale traders' assessments of stockholdings. Knetsch constructs composite indices of inventory fluctuations by means of codependent cycle analysis (i.e. a method based on canonical correlations) and static factor modelling. Using recursive estimates, the different variants are assessed with respect to the stability of the weighting schemes and their ability to produce reliable forecasts of the "real" inventory fluctuations. Knetsch finds clear evidence that these composite indices outperform the preliminary official releases of the national accounting statistics.

The paper by Jan Jacobs and Jan-Egbert Sturm also deals with the ability of Ifo survey indicators to explain data revisions. Like the data on inventory investment, the official index of German industrial production is also prone to several revisions following its first release in the official bulletin of the statistical agency. Using two indicators taken from the Ifo Business Survey, one on the current business situation, and the other on the development of industrial production compared to the previous month, Jacobs and Sturm set-up a model of the revision process of industrial production. Their model exploits the property that Ifo indicators are not revised in subsequent months. They conclude that the two Ifo indicators play a significant role in explaining data revisions, but counterintuitively the Ifo business situation indicator outperforms the Ifo production indicator.

The final paper in Part I of this volume by Henk Kranendonk, Jan Bonenkamp and Johan Verbruggen describes the methodology and presents the empirical results of the leading indicator approach used by the CPB Netherlands Bureau for Economic Policy Analysis to prepare short-term forecasts for the Dutch economy. The system of the CPB leading indicator is composed of ten separate composite indicators, seven for expenditure categories ("demand") and three for the main production sectors ("supply"). Special attention is paid to the role and significance of indicators from the Ifo Business Survey. Especially the business expectations of German manufacturers for the next six months play a prominent role in the CPB long-leading indicator. The authors conclude that their approach performs quite well in describing the cyclical nature of GDP; turning points are predicted adequately, and the different indicators produce a sensible story underlying the business cycle.

The theme of Part II is the analysis of monetary policy. The first of three papers in this Part is written by Michael Ehrmann and is concerned with the transmission of monetary policy impulses. According to both, the balance sheet channel and the bank lending channel small firms are more likely to be affected by a monetary tightening than large firms because of credit market imperfections. For his empirical analysis Michael Ehrmann uses Ifo Business Survey data on the current business conditions and the development of the demand situation of more than 3,000 firms belonging to the West German manufacturing industry. By sorting this data into five size classes, ranging from firms with 1 to 49 employees to firms with more than 1,000 employees, the paper finds support for the hypotheses formulated in capital market imperfection theories. The business conditions of small firms are more sensitive to monetary policy shocks than those of large firms, also when accounting for demand differences. In addition, these effects are reinforced in business cycle downturns.

The paper by Elmer Sterken analyzes the role of forward-looking indicators for describing German monetary policy. He focuses his analysis on the information content of the Ifo Business Climate Index and of housing and equity prices. While the Ifo Business Climate Index serves as a real-time indicator of the output gap, asset price changes are assumed to reflect changes in expectations of all future economic variables. Sterken shows that the use of both the Ifo Business Climate Index and asset prices improves the performance and interpretation of a vector autoregression model of German monetary transmission. On the one hand, the Bundesbank responded more intensively to changes in the Ifo Business Climate Index than to changes in GDP. On the other hand, housing prices help to give a more accurate description of the recent history of German monetary policy, whereas equity price shocks turned out to be rather irrelevant.

The final paper by Sandra Waller and Jakob de Haan investigates the views of private sector economists on the credibility, transparency and independence of seven major central banks. In contrast to the other papers presented in this volume, Waller and de Haan formulated a one-time set of special questions within the framework of the Ifo's quarterly World Economic Survey to which more than 200 economists from all over the world respond. In line with a survey conducted by Alan Blinder among central bankers, they asked participants in the Ifo World Economic Survey to answer questions on the importance and determinants of credibility. The results of both surveys are very comparable. Credibility is considered to be important to attain price stability at low cost, while the best ways to earn credibility are a history of honesty and a high level of central bank independence. According to the respondents of the Ifo World Economic Survey, the Federal Reserve is the most credible, transparent and independent central bank. The ECB is not perceived as highly credible or transparent, even though the respondents consider it to be very independent.

Konstanz, Munich,
June 2004

Jan-Egbert Sturm
Timo Wollmershäuser

Contents

Survey Activity of the Ifo Institute

Gernot Nerb

Ifo Institute for Economic Research, Poschingerstraße 5, 81679 Munich, Germany
nerb@ifo.de

1 Ifo Business Survey: More Than a Substitute Statistic

Business surveys are at the heart of the Ifo Institute's activities – both in terms of comments on current trends as well as research studies. The great success of survey-based economic research was not foreseeable in the initial phase of the Ifo Business Survey, which was launched in the fall of 1949 and by the end of the 1950s had been expanded to include business and investment surveys in the most important areas of the economy.[1] Currently the Ifo institute conducts the surveys appearing in Table 1.

The introduction of these surveys occurred pragmatically with the goal of closing the considerable gaps in the official statistics in the post-war period and, in addition, of supplying timely information for areas that are surveyed by the official statistics, but with considerable delays and frequent subsequent revisions. From the early 1970s at the latest, more and more academics, economic forecasters as well as the users of economic information in business and government recognized the special value of business survey results beyond that of a mere statistic substitute. The initial belief that prevailed in the 1960s and early 1970s that accurate short- and long-term forecasts should be possible with the help of modern computers and econometric models was disappointed. This was not primarily because of external shocks and monetary crises, as model designers like to point out when their forecasts are wrong. The more important finding was that economic behavior of entrepreneurs and consumers is not stable over time and that problems can arise especially in short-term forecasting if one relies schematically on behavior equations derived from past data.

[1] See Strigel (1989), pp. 6ff.

Table 1. Important Ifo-Panels 2003

Survey	p*	Number of Received Questionnaires			Representation ca. %			Repres. Base
		Germany	G.-West	G.-East	Germany	G.-West	G.-East	
Business Survey								
Manufacturing	m	3800	3000	800	35	35	25	Empl.
Trade	m	1700	1250	450		10	10	Sales
Construction	m	1100	800	300		15	15	Sales
Services**	m	1200						
EDP Services (Electronic Data Processing)	q	350			50			Sales
Architects	q	2300						
Insurance Companies	q	220			80			Premium ins.
Leasing Companies	y	350			90			Invest.
Innovation***	s	2800/ 1400	2200/ 1080	600/ 320	25/ 11	25/ 12	14/ 8	Empl.
Investment	s		2300	2200		50	50	Invest.
Economic Survey International	q	ca. 90 Countries						

* Periodicity: m = monthly, q = quarterly, s = 2x a year, y = 1x a year
** Survey started in April 2001; panel still under construction
*** Numbers of reports refer to: main survey using special questionnaires (near middle of the year) supplementary survey on regular Business Survey forms (near end of the year).

2 The Empirical Collection of Assessments and Expectations Supported by Economic Theory

Entrepreneurial plans, expectations and assessments have gained central importance in recent economic theory, and the Ifo business and investment survey data have proved to be a treasure trove for empirical economic research. It has been increasingly acknowledged that economic behavior research that lacks empirical microeconomic underpinnings is questionable. It is now widely accepted that the only promising way to adequately consider entrepreneurial plans, expectations and assessments in economical analysis and forecasting is to resort to authentic survey data. This conclusion is also supported by the so-called theory of rational expectations. This school of thought, which strongly influenced economics and politics in the 1970s and early 1980s, assumes that entrepreneurial plans and expectations are, as a rule, clearly targeted and display no systematic distortions since they take into consideration all important information from managers in the "correct manner". If surprises occur despite everything, this is immediately expressed in prices. For this reason, prices are the key indicator for imbalances between supply and demand.

If this finding were correct, it would be sufficient for empirical economic research to pose several so-called "ultimate questions", that is, for example, investment and production plans and otherwise to observe price data to detect sudden changes in enterprize plans. For the assessment data collected in the Ifo Business Survey on the business situation, on order reserves and inventories

– as for consumer attitudes as reflected in consumer surveys – there would no longer be any real justification.

Numerous studies have shown, however, that the plans of entrepreneurs and consumers as a rule are not entirely rational, in keeping with the theory.[2] There are a number of explanations for the only partial agreement of plans and implementation. Contrary to the assumptions of the theory of rational expectations, the costs are quite high for the procurement and utilization of information and the costs and risks of implementing what is considered right are also high. Because of cost-benefit considerations, information is only partially used, by the enterprizes and by consumers, or adjustment processes are not carried out or only after some delay. But even if economic subjects were willing to assume these costs, there would still be deviations in ex-post and ex-ante values – independent of price changes – since the implicit "forecasting model" of the enterprizes and consumers into which the information would have to be injected is not unalterable but changes over time.

3 Replies to Assessment Questions Often More Useful Than Concrete Information on Plans

On the whole the empirical results of all relevant studies support a "weak" version of the theory of rational expectations. The literature refers to this as "semi-rational" expectations.[3]

For survey research, the result is that the so-called "receptive-critical" questions, such as the assessment of the current and future business situations as well as order reserves and inventories, are of special importance for business cycle analysis and forecasting.[4] On this basis of these questions, early insight can be gained regarding the changing risk appraisals of the enterprizes, from which in turn corresponding inferences can be made as to economic behavior in terms of investment, production and employment decisions.

Such findings are valid analogously also for consumer research. George Katona, the doyen of consumer surveys, always argued for "soft" questions in consumer surveys ("attitudes" instead of "plans") since such survey results in an aggregated form allow us to recognise changes in consumer behaviour, such as a fall in the savings rate in the wake of increasing economic confidence.[5] In this connection, attention should also be directed to the so-called "time series/cross section paradox," according to which aggregated responses to confidence questions – e.g. the consumption climate constructed from five macro-series – in time series analyses produce better results in consumer fore-

---

[2]See Nerb (1989), pp. 72ff.

[3]See Häberle (1982), pp. 199ff.

[4]For the distinction between "receptive-critical" and "final" statements, see Poser (1969), pp. 64 ff.

[5]See Katona (1951), in particular Chap. 3.

casting than exact purchase plans, although on the micro-level the plans appeared better suited for forecasting individual purchase decisions than general attitude variables.[6] A partial explanation is that the so-called "intenders", i.e. consumers with concrete purchase plans, are the ones with a high probability of a subsequent purchase. The problem in this case, however, was that about half of the later purchases were made by "non-intenders", i.e. households that had not expressed any prior, concrete purchase intentions but made spontaneous purchases. In the case of automobiles, this portion was approximately 50%, and for other consumer durables, the portion of spontaneous purchasers was even higher. For this reason, attitude questions (e.g.: "How would you assess your present financial circumstances in comparison to a year ago?") are more useful to business-cycle researchers than concrete purchase plans, since the former provide initial indications for a changing purchasing inclination among customers, the majority of whom are irresolute. What ultimately matters for the business-cycle researcher is correctly forecasting aggregate amounts and not the decisions of isolated individuals. As a result of these considerations most consumer surveys only contain attitude questions and no longer collect information on concrete purchasing plans. A further consequence is that the emphasis of most studies on the prognostic suitability of data from consumer surveys should be placed on the macro-level and not on the micro-level.

In the case of enterprize decisions, for example investments, the assumption is more likely than for consumer purchase decisions that planning and not spontaneous behaviour is involved. This explains also the relatively good forecasting suitability of the Ifo investment planning data. Nevertheless, empirical studies show that especially in the case of small and medium-sized enterprizes (SMEs), investment decisions are often made on short notice and investment plans are also sometimes quickly changed. For this reason, the Ifo Business Climate has proved to be a suitable indicator for the monthly extrapolation of the large-scale Ifo Investment Survey that is conducted only twice a year – in the spring and autumn. Generally it has proved expedient to interpret the information on enterprize and consumer plans – e.g., investment, production, employment and purchase plans – as variants of attitude questions and not in the sense of strong rational expectations as fixed intent with high likelihood of occurrence.

To sum up: Judgemental questions (based ordinal scales) are the cornerstone of the Ifo surveys. Apart from statistical reasons (smaller sampling error at given sample size in the case of ordinally scaled data compared with data measured on a metric scale; less seasonal distortions) lessons from the "time series-cross section paradox" favor judgemental questions measured on ordinal scales compared with change questions (both with regard to previous or future period) on metric scales.

[6] For the "time series/cross section paradox", see, for example, Nerb (1975), pp. 69 ff.

4 The Business Climate as an Example of a Survey-Based Early Indicator

The results of two questions of the Ifo Business Survey have proved to be especially important for forecasting and analyzing economic activity. One is the question of the assessment of the current business situation, the other is the appraisal of the business outlook for the next six months. The business climate is calculated as the geometric average from the balances of these two questions (see Fig. 1).

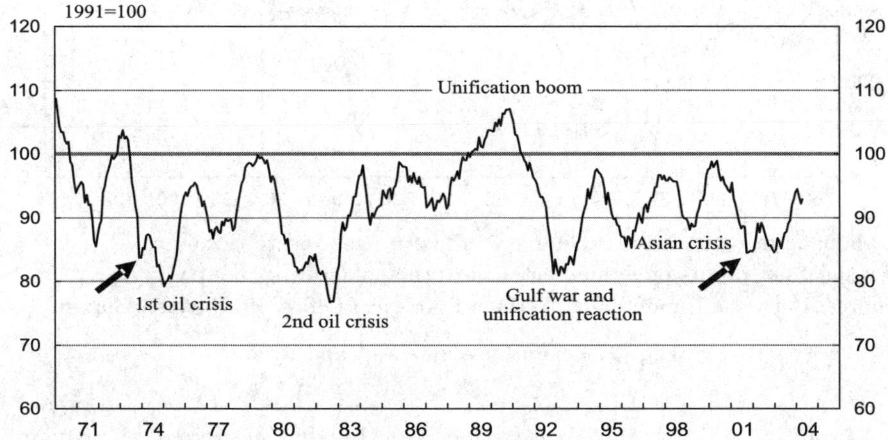

[1] Manufacturing industry, construction, wholesale and retail trade.
Source: Ifo Business Survey

Fig. 1. Ifo Business Climate: Trade and Industry[1] – Western Germany

The obvious question is why the business climate with its two components displays such good forecasting qualities. The main reason is presumably because it primarily measures the actual and the expected earnings performance. This can be demonstrated by a comparison of the business climate with profit performance as published by the Bundesbank on the basis of financial statement analyzes, however, with a time lag of approximately two years (Fig. 2). This finding is in accord with earlier studies of Ifo Institute with regard to the determinants of the assessments and expectations on business conditions. As the so-called "test of the test" showed, profit appraisal plays a decisive role alongside the demand trend. One possible objection is: Why not ask a direct question regarding profit? The reason this is not done is German reluctance to make direct statements regarding profits. Moreover, at the time the business survey is conducted there are no detailed profit figures for the just-completed month so that a more general question like "business conditions" appears more suitable than a direct question regarding profits.

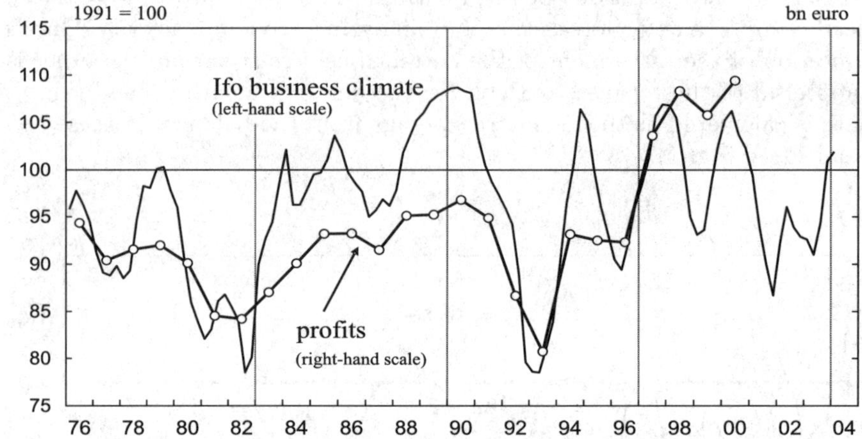

[1] Manufacturing industry excluding food, beverages and tobacco.
[2] Annual net profits of german enterprises (manufacturing indutry), real.
Source: Deutsche Bundesbank, German Statistical Office, Ifo Business Survey.

Fig. 2. Ifo Business Climate[1] and Profits[2]

Profit appraisals and expectation are the driving forces of economic growth. This is the quintessence of the work of Wesley Claire Mitchell, the founder of the National Bureau of Economic Research (NBER) in the USA, whose work is still very helpful for practical economic forecasting. An economic expansion is based on increasing demand which in turn is based on higher profit expectations. This leads, sooner or later, to bottlenecks and increasing input prices, which puts pressure on profit margins. Cost-cutting measures such as short-time working and dismissals prevail in economic downturns. A central aspect of Mitchell's ideas is that in the early upswing the cost trend of the movement of prices lags behind, which enables profits and profit expectations to increase. Already before the upper cyclical turning point, experience shows that this relationship between costs and price reverses, which is initially expressed by more unfavourable appraisals of the current profit situation.

An additional reason for the suitability of the Ifo Business Climate as an early indicator lies in its relatively smooth progression over time. The quality of an early indicator depends – in addition to the length of its leads – also on how clearly turning points are signalled and on how stable the leads are. The so-called MCD measure gives an indication of the clarity of an indicator in signalling turning points:[7] it shows how long, on average, we must wait before we can be sure in the statistical sense that a change in this indicator is not coincidental but that a trend change is being signalled. In such a comparison, incoming orders perform considerably worse than the Ifo Business Climate and also the Ifo business expectations. Because of the uneven progression of the time series for incoming orders, the MCD measure is around 7; in the case of the two Ifo time series, the period of insecurity is considerably shorter (MCD measure between 1 and 2). In addition, incoming orders in the official statistics are published approximately two to three weeks later than the Ifo series, and also incoming orders numbers in the official statistics – in contrast to the Ifo series – are often subject to considerable subsequent revisions. For this reason, a subsequent comparison of these series renders a very incomplete picture on how the data was perceived in a concrete situation.

A recent detailed analysis of the behaviour of the Ifo Business Climate at turning points – applying also the Bayes Theorem reconfirmed that the "Three-Times-Rule" is well suited to forecast changes of the direction of the economic development in Germany.[8] According to this rule we have to wait for three consecutive changes of the Ifo Business Climate in a new direction before we should predict a cyclical turning point.

5 The Ifo Business Cycle Clock and the Formation of Company Categories as Practical Examples of Applying Business Survey Results for Cyclical Analysis and Forecasting

As mentioned above, the development of the profit margin is still of central importance for assessing the current economic situation and appraising the short-term outlook. This is very well illustrated in the so-called Ifo Business Cycle Clock (Fig. 3). Along the horizontal axis are the balances for the question on the current business situation and on the vertical axis the balances for the question on the business expectations. An upswing in economic activity is characterised by the current business situation being estimated, on balance, as unfavourable while the business expectations are already in the positive field. If the upswing gains more strength, the responses on the current situation also move into the positive zone (boom phase quadrant). A slowdown of the economy usually becomes apparent in a worsening of business expectations while the assessments of the current business situation are still positive.

[7]The MCD measure indicates the lowest support area for which the sum of the economic changes is identical or larger than those of the irregular ones. In the case of an MCD value of 7, which is typical for the incoming orders index of the Official Statistics, a 7 moving average is recommended, which leads to a loss of 4 months at the most recent area.

[8]See Hott et al. (2004).

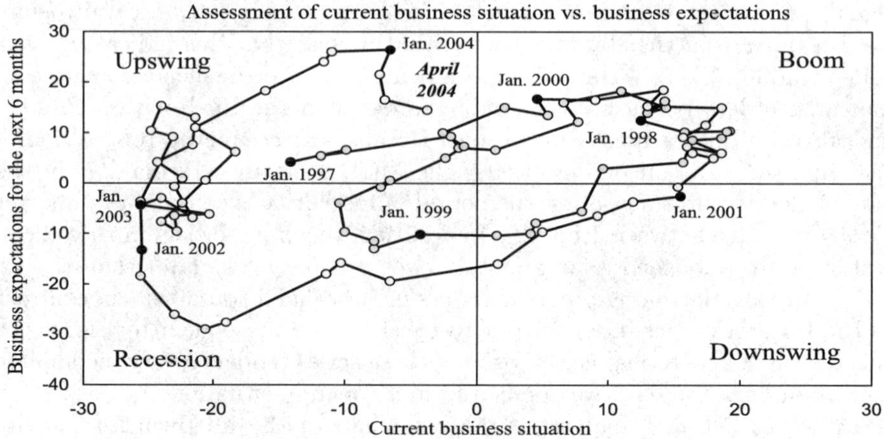

[1] Excluding food, beverages and tobacco. Balances, seasonally adjusted data.
Source: Ifo Business Survey.

Fig. 3. Ifo Business-Cycle Clock for Germany – Manufacturing Industry[1]

The variant presented above of a two-dimensional analysis – business situation and business expectations – can be expanded even more. One possibility is a breakdown of companies according to considerably more criteria than just one or two. The inspiration for this multivariate approach came from disequilibrium models.

The central idea of disequilibrium models is convincing and simple at the same time: Prices and wages do not change fast and sufficiently enough to prevent imbalances between supply and demand. This applies to goods markets as well as to the labour market. Depending on what kind of imbalance predominates at the micro-level, we can speak of a macroeconomic supply and demand gap. The first disequilibrium models were developed at the beginning of the 1980s by Barro and Grossmann (1971). For empirical economic research, these models were not very suitable, however, since they were aggregated too much and only allowed very general conclusions to be drawn on the state of the economy. This reservation also applies to Malinvaud's studies, Malivaud and Younes (1977), although Malinvaud's great merit is having worked out the economic-policy relevance of this research method. The effect of the traditional economy-policy measures depends, according to his studies, on the initial situation of the economy, e.g. whether unemployment is basically a demand-side, Keynesian type or whether it is "classical" unemployment caused by real wages that are too high and that result in too little job-creating investment. In the first case the multiplier-effect would come into play in the case of government demand-stimulation; on the other hand, in the case of "classical" unemployment no multiplier effect would appear. Reduction in real wages in the Keynesian case would have a negative employment effect; in the "classical" unemployment case, it would have a positive employment effect.

The economic reality, however, is much more differentiated than the simple labels of "Keynesian demand-conditioned unemployment" or "classical unemployment" would indicate. The further development of the disequilibrium models thus correctly sets out from the microeconomic underpinnings of this approach.

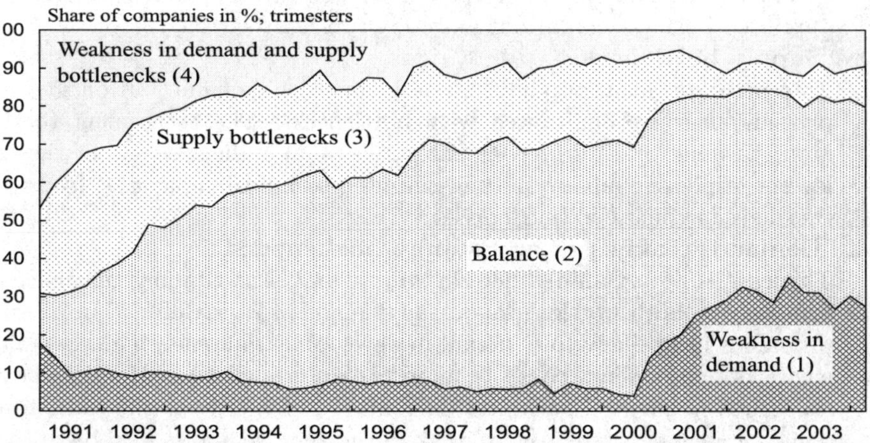

[1] Total manufacturing industry
Source: Ifo Business Survey.

Fig. 4. Regime Classification of Industrial Companies – Eastern Germany[1]

Here, the suitability of business survey data is evident, since they are meant to measure deviations from the normal state, however defined (e.g. whether finished goods inventories are higher or lower than normal; whether technical capacities are too large or too small in light of expected demand). A pioneering achievement in this area was done by Lambert (1984). His model produces results that are considerably closer to reality and more relevant for economic policy than the "first generation" disequilibrium models since in his model the transition from one predominant state of disequilibrium to another is not abrupt but more gradual. Lambert does not work with "black & white templates" but takes into consideration the variety of grey tones that are found in reality. This is not the place for a detailed discussion of the Lambert model. Instead, stimulated by Lambert's work, we have produced a typology of industrial firms according to following categories of economic activity (see Fig. 4 and 5):

1. **"Demand weakness"**

   The main problem here is that demand is too weak to adequately utilise available production potential. There are no supply bottlenecks; for this

reason with an increase in demand and production, an (appreciable) acceleration of price increases would also not be expected.
In practical terms the allocation is done so that all enterprizes are included that responded to the quarterly question on current production constraints by ticking "too little demand".

2. **"No economic difficulties (Balance)"**
This group includes enterprises that have reported no production constraints, neither on the supply nor on the demand side, and who have also appraised business conditions as good or at least satisfactory.
3. **"Supply bottlenecks"**
Enterprises in this group have no problems with demand, but on the supply side they are confronted with bottlenecks. The assignment to this group is done by filtering out enterprises that indicated one of the following responses: labour shortage, limited technical capacities, feedstock shortages, or financial bottlenecks.
4. **"Demand weaknesses and supply bottlenecks"**
This case is not examined here in more detail. An economy that is characterised by both bottlenecks on the demand side as well as on the supply side is most likely to be found in developing and emerging economies, where, due to currency controls, imports of intermediate products and capital goods frequently encounter difficulties and where, at the same time, domestic demand is relatively weak – e.g. due fiscal austerity because of high external and internal indebtedness – and were exports cannot restore equilibrium because of weak qualitative international competitiveness.

The allocation to these categories can be refined even more. For example, in Groups 1 and 3 a more detailed breakdown can be achieved with the help of the variable "technical capacities in the next 12 months".

1.1. **"Marked demand weakness"**
In addition to the current demand deficits, the enterprises anticipate excess capacities in the next 12 months.

1.2. **"Temporary demand weakness"**
Here production is constrained in the survey month by inadequate demand. But in the medium-term (next 12 months) firms do not expect any capacity utilisation problems.

3.1. **"Marked supply bottlenecks"**
In addition to the current constraints on production from supply-side bottlenecks, technical capacities are regarded as too small, also for the coming 12 months.

3.1. **"Temporary supply bottlenecks"**
Here firms have sufficient technical capacities in the medium term, but they currently lack specialists lack or are experiencing delivery bottlenecks

This new way of presenting business survey results – as a supplement to the conventional breakdown according to industries and enterprize sizes – is especially well suited to the study of enterprize behaviour. It combines cyclical and structural elements. This becomes especially clear in the graphics for east Germany (see Fig. 5):

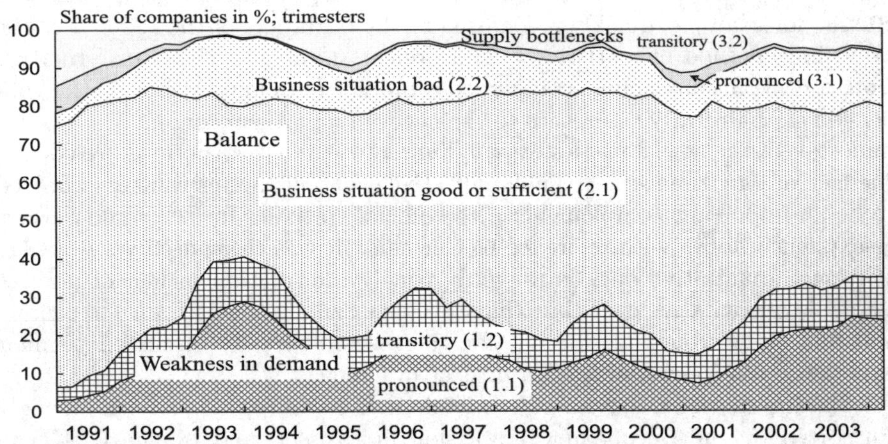

[1] Total manufacturing industry
Source: Ifo Business Survey.

Fig. 5. Regime Classification of Industrial Companies - Western Germany[1]

At the beginning of the 1990s, when the Ifo Institute introduced the Business Survey in east Germany, only a small portion of the industrial firms was in the "equilibrium category". A high portion of the enterprises showed considerable problems on the supply side. In the course of the last ten years, the portion of east German industrial firms in the "equilibrium" category has clearly increased. Noticeable is also the clear drop of portion of firms with "supply and demand problems". Precisely this category poses a major problem for economic policy, since the combination of structural problems that are shown on the supply side and the cyclical problems that become clear primarily on the demand side can only be treated with a whole bundle of measures, and this only over a longer period of time.

6 Transferability of the Survey-Based Methods of Economic Activity Research to Non-Western Cultures

A great advantage of qualitative economic-activity surveys patterned after the Ifo Business Survey lies in the flexibility of their approach. In assessing their current business situation, their order backlogs or their inventories of unsold finished goods, to name only some survey items, the enterprises weigh the individual influencing factors according to the importance they have at the time of the survey. Precisely in times of major structural change this is a considerable advantage over traditional quantitative surveys. This goes a long way in explaining the world wide spread of the economic activity surveys based on the Ifo model. Economic-policy authorities in Eastern Europe and Russia, for example, quickly recognised at the beginning of the 1990s that the prevailing method of statistics was no longer suitable in the transformation from a centrally managed economy to a market economy. Although the conversion of quantitative statistics to the needs of a market economy was swiftly undertaken, the new statistics were of limited use due to structural breaks and the lack of long time series. The qualitative economic activity surveys proved to be an important complement to the official statistics for the same reasons as explained above with reference to Germany. It was recognised very quickly that such qualitative data is not only timely information in lieu of not yet available quantitative data, but that this data can also be used for forecasting and analysing economic activity, for the reasons already discussed. Similar experience was gained in the Ifo project in China.

The international spread of economic activity surveys has been strongly supported by the European Commission in Brussels and by the OECD in Paris. Both organisations played a considerable role in developing a harmonised core-questionnaire programme. The institutions in the various countries that conduct economic activity surveys were advised to incorporate these questions verbatim to facilitate international data comparability. Since both institutions support these surveys financially, they were able to exert pressure to achieve this harmonisation.

Experience has shown that economic activity surveys patterned on the Ifo Business Survey can be conducted in all countries in which decision-making freedom exists in the private sector. In command economies in which production is based on government specifications and in which prices have no controlling function but are fixed by the government, business surveys have little value.

The main beneficiaries of economic activity survey results are the participating enterprises, who receive the detailed results, or at least the results broken down for their industry, as a service for their collaboration. Also, economic policy-makers and the central banks receive authentic assessments and expectations from the private sector, which is important in order to obtain a realistic and current picture of the situation of the economy and to be able to appraise the effects of their measures at an early stage.

7 More Recent Developments

7.1 Extension of Ifo Business Surveys to the Service Sector

Despite the high and further growing share in GDP, there was in the past a dispute amongst economists about the importance of the tertiary sector for cyclical analysis. However, recent experience shows that services have gained importance not solely with respect to a growth, but also to a cyclical perspective. For that reason the EU commission has started already in 1997 to set up a monthly business survey of service companies. Ifo has contributed to this project first by providing quarterly results for selected service branches (electronic data processing, architects and leasing) and since early 2000 with monthly results of a newly set-up panel in the service sector.

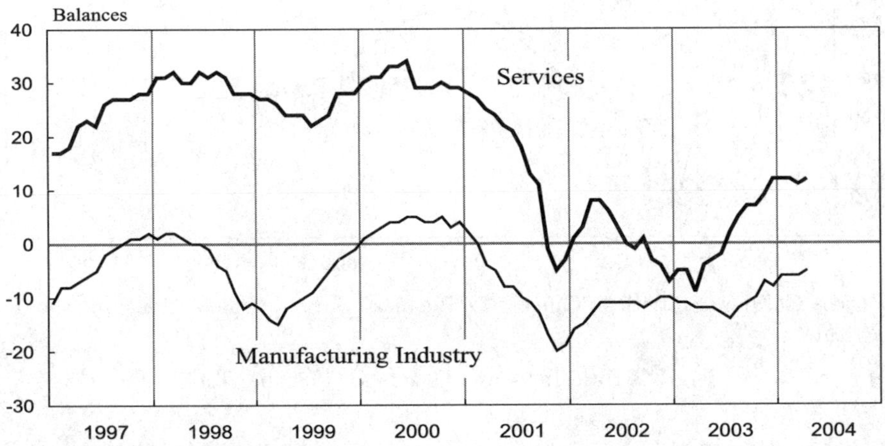

Source: European Comission.

Fig. 6. Services Confidence Indicator in Comparison to the Climate Indicator in Manufacturing (EU15)

How strongly at the EU level the confidence indicator in the service sector was affected by the cyclical downturn in 2001/02 is demonstrable in Fig. 6. Also the initial phase of the recent upturn which get in in 2003 appears to be in the service sector more pronounced than in manufacturing industry. For all these reasons the Ifo Institute puts much effort in enlarging the panel in the monthly service sector business survey which comprises in early 2004 about 1200 companies.

7.2 Use of Business Survey Results for Monetary Policy

The usefulness of a combination of business survey data from manufacturing industry and the service sector to construct an overall real time indicator for capacity utilization which can serve as a proxy for the output gap at the macroeconomic level has been demonstrated in a recent paper, Grzeda and Nerb (2004). This real time measure of the output gap can be used in Taylor Rule or VAR models to assess monetary policy and to forecast the development of short-term interest rates.

7.3 Use of Business Survey Results for Industrial Branch Forecasts

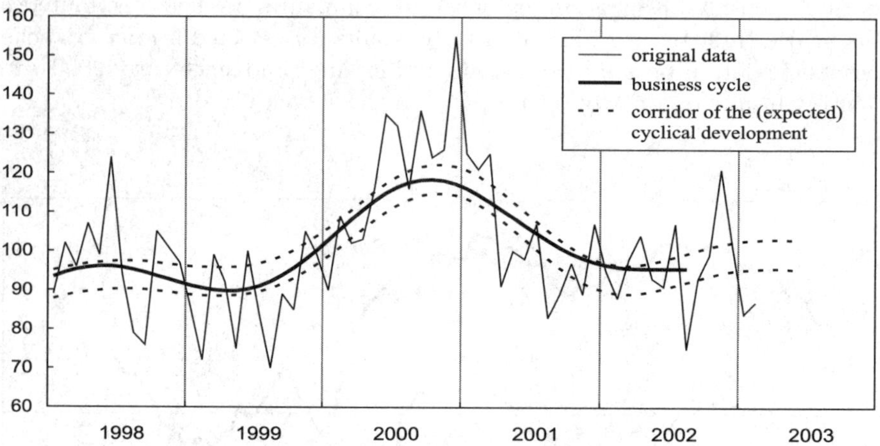

Source: German Statistical Office, Ifo Business Survey. Calculations by the Ifo Institute.

Fig. 7. Total Incoming Orders for Machine Tools

Every month on the basis of the most recent Ifo business survey results forecasts of the incoming orders of 23 industrial branches are produced and sent to the companies providing monthly answers to the business survey questions. An example of this type of forecast is presented in Fig. 7 for machine tools. It is planned to enlarge the scope of branch forecasts in coming years and to test more sophisticated estimation methods.

7.4 New Publication on Ifo Business Surveys

At the end of 2004 a new book in German will be published by the Ifo Institute which contains in depth contributions to almost all important aspects of the Ifo business surveys, see Goldrian (2004) in the references.

References

BARRO, J., AND H. GROSSMANN (1971): "A General Disequilibrium Model of Income and Employment," *The American Economic Review*, 61(1), 82–93.

GOLDRIAN, G. (2004): "Handbuch der umfragebasierten Konjunkturforschung," Schriftenreihe des ifo instituts, Ifo Institut, Munich.

GRZEDA, R., AND G. NERB (2004): "Modelling Short-term Interest Rates in the Euro Area Using Business Survey Data," in *Journal of Business Cycle Measurement and Analysis*. OECD and CIRET, Paris.

Häberle, L. (1982): "Wirtschaftspolitik bei rationalen Erwartungen, Konsequenzen einer kritischen Analyse der Theorie rationaler Erwartungen für die Wahl wirtschaftspolitischer Strategien," *Reihe Untersuchungen des Instituts für Wirtschaftspolitik, Universität Köln,*, 49, 199ff.

Hott, C., A. Kunkel, and G. Nerb (2004): "On the Accuracy of Turning Point Prediction with the Ifo Business Climate," to be published as Ifo Discussion Paper in 2004.

Katona, G. (1951): *Psychological Analysis of Economic Behaviour.* McGraw-Hill, New York.

Lambert, J.-P. (1984): *Disequilibrium Macromodels Based on Business Survey Data. Theory and Estimation for the Belgian Manufacturing Sector.* L'Universite Catholique de Louvain, Louvain-la-Neuve.

Malivaud, E., and Y. Younes (1977): "Some New Concepts for the Microeconomic Foundations of Macroeconomics," in *Microeconomics Foundations of Macroeconomics.* Harcourt.

Nerb, G. (1975): "Konjunkturprognose mit Hilfe von Urteilen und Erwartungen der Konsumenten und der Unternehmer," in *Schriftenreihe des Ifo Instituts für Wirtschaftsforschung*, ed. by D. &. Humblot, Berlin-München.

——— (1989): "Sind Erwartungen Rational," in *Handbuch der Ifo-Umfragen*, chap. Die Entwicklung der ifo-Umfragen seit 1949. Karl-Heinrich Oppenländer and Günter Poser, Berlin-Muenchen.

Poser, G. (1969): "Der Beitrag der Konsumforschung zur Diagnose und Prognose konjunktureller Entwicklungen," *CIRET-Studie, Ifo Institut*, 15, 64ff.

Strigel, W. H. (1989): "Die Entwicklung der Ifo-Umfragen seit 1949," in *Handbuch der Ifo Umfragen*, p. 6ff. Karl-Heinrich Oppenländer and Günter Poser, Berlin-Muenchen.

Part I

Business Cycle Analysis

Forecasting Quarterly German GDP at Monthly Intervals Using Monthly Ifo Business Conditions Data*

Stefan Mittnik[1] and Peter Zadrozny[2]

[1] University of Munich, Akademiestr. 1, 80799 Munich, Germany, Ifo Institute for Economic Research, Munich, Germany and Center for Financial Studies, Frankfurt, Germany finmetrics@stat.uni-muenchen.de

[2] Bureau of Labor Statistics, 2 Massachusetts Ave., NE, Washington, DC 20212, USA zadrozny_p@bls.gov

1 Introduction

This paper illustrates and evaluates a Kalman-filtering method for forecasting German real GDP at monthly intervals. Like the US real GDP, German real GDP is produced and publicly released at quarterly intervals, although both US and German economic analysts and business decision-makers often want monthly GDP forecasts. Quarterly GDP could be regressed on monthly indicators organized quarterly. Thus, one could: (i) organize all observations on variables at quarterly intervals, with GDP automatically being quarterly and monthly indicators being made quarterly as first-, second-, and third-month quarterly observations; (ii) regress quarterly GDP on the monthly indicators organized quarterly; and, (iii) compute monthly GDP forecasts as the estimated regression evaluated at particular values of the monthly indicators. This description is purposely simple for illustrating the general point that a regression can pick up feedbacks of monthly variables onto quarterly variables, but it cannot pick up implicit intra-quarterly monthly feedbacks from quarterly to monthly variables. To avoid this problem, we use a Kalman-filtering method developed by Zadrozny (2000) for any number of variables observed at any mixture of frequencies and illustrated in a similar context of forecasting quarterly US real GNP at monthly intervals using a monthly indicator. The method can account for any possible feedbacks, from any variable at any frequency to any other variable at the same or other frequency. The method involves estimating a multivariate time-series model of all variables considered. The model operates at the highest observed frequency, monthly in this

*The opinions expressed in the paper are the authors' and do not reflect any official positions of the Bureau of Labor Statistics

case, and, thus, produces forecasts of any variable at monthly intervals, regardless of the interval at which the variable is observed. Here, data are set up at the highest monthly frequency so that unobserved intra-quarterly monthly values of quarterly GDP are marked as missing. Maximum likelihood estimation (MLE) is used to estimate VAR(2) models. The Kalman filter is used in two ways. First, the Kalman filter is used to compute the likelihood function, under Gaussian or normality assumptions, which is maximized with respect to unknown model parameters. Second, given an estimated model, the Kalman filter is used to produce forecasts of variables, at the higher monthly frequency at which the model operates, any number of months ahead. In both cases, the Kalman filter is applied in a "missing data" form in order to "properly skip over" missing values. Details of these computations are discussed by Zadrozny (2000). The method allows models as general as vector autoregressive moving-average (VARMA) models, although previous and current experience indicates that purely VAR models often suffice for forecasting a variable with the help of other variables, when no restrictions on coefficients, indicated by statistical analysis or economic reasoning, are imposed on the forecasting model.

2 Description of Data

The data, obtained from the Ifo Institute in Munich, Germany, comprise quarterly German real GDP and three monthly indicators of the German economy: German real industrial production (PRD), current German real business conditions (CUR) and expected (6 months in the future) German real business conditions (EXP). The business conditions variables are produced by the Ifo Institute from its own surveys of German business firms. The monthly data cover January 1970 to December 2003 and the quarterly GDP data cover the same period, quarter 1 1970 to quarter 4 2003.

The four variables and their filtered values are displayed in Figs. 1–9 in the appendix. Figures 1–3 are monthly time plots and Figs. 4–9 are quarterly time plots. In the monthly graphs, the monthly variables are displayed as continuous lines, with no missing values, and quarterly GDP is displayed as a broken or dashed line, with missing intra-quarterly monthly values. Because each quarter's GDP is fully assigned to the third month of the quarter, GDP is treated as unobserved or missing in the first two intra-quarterly months of a quarter.

There are no missing values after the data are aggregated into quarterly form, so all displayed lines in the quarterly graphs are continuous. GDP is automatically in quarterly form. There are two ways, called "stock" and "flow", for aggregating monthly values to quarterly values. "Stock" means monthly values are skip sampled in the third month of each quarter, so that the value in the third month of a quarter becomes the quarterly value and the values in the first two months of the quarter are discarded. "Flow" means monthly values are aggregated into quarterly form by averaging the monthly values in a quarter.

Also, monthly PRD is detrended and deseasonalized in two possible ways, called "AD filtered" and "AD/AMA filtered," to be discussed. Thus, the four ways considered for converting monthly-quarterly data to purely-quarterly data are called stock-AD-filtered, stock-AD/AMA-filtered, flow-AD-filtered, and flow-AD/AMA-filtered.

The variables are graphed in original and filtered forms. Henceforth, we use subscript t to denote months, e.g., PRD_t means PRD in month t, and for now let L^k denote the monthly lag operator applied k times in succession to a monthly variable, e.g., $\mathrm{L}^{12}\mathrm{PRD}_t = \mathrm{PRD}_{t-12}$. We know that the annual differencing operator, defined for monthly time intervals as $\mathrm{AD(L)} = 1 - \mathrm{L}^{12}$, is the product of a single monthly difference, $\mathrm{MD(L)} = 1 - \mathrm{L}$, times a single annual sum, $\mathrm{AS(L)} = 1 + \mathrm{L} + \ldots + \mathrm{L}^{11}$, or $\mathrm{AD(L)} = \mathrm{MD(L)AS(L)}$. Frequency analysis shows that multiplying a variable by MD(L) eliminates its linear deterministic (polynomial) and linear stochastic (unit-root autoregressive) trends and multiplying the variable by AS(L) eliminates its deterministic (harmonic) seasonality, although a variable can have additional stochastic seasonality which cannot be removed by AS(L). This appears to be the case with PRD_t, which is discussed below.

Figure 1 displays the four variables in original monthly form. We see that GDP_t follows an upward trend with additional, relatively small, seasonal variations about the trend. PRD_t also follows an upward trend, with relatively larger seasonal variations about the trend, plus more easily seen cyclical variations. CUR_t and EXP_t both display no apparent trends or seasonality, only cyclical variations. Because in original form the variables are compatible only as GDP_t with PRD_t and CUR_t with EXP_t, there is little hope of obtaining MLE of a VAR model of the four variables in original form, namely GDP_t, PRD_t, CUR_t, and EXP_t. Therefore, to obtain MLE of a VAR model of the four variables, we first linearly filtered GDP_t and PRD_t to eliminate their trends and seasonality, so that the resulting four variables display only cyclical variations and are compatible.

As seen in the figures, the main difference between monthly data versus quarterly data and quarterly-stock data versus quarterly-flow data is smoothness versus noisiness, where "noisiness" means unpredictable high-frequency random variation and "smoothness" means absence of noisiness. As expected, monthly data are noisier than quarterly data and quarterly-stock data are noisier than quarterly-flow data. We expect smoother data to produce better GDP forecasts. Summary Table 9 shows that smoother quarterly data produce better long-term GDP forecasts than noisier monthly data, but that choosing stocks instead of flows or AD instead of AD/AMA filtering has insignificant effect on GDP forecast accuracy.

3 Transformation of Data

We filtered GDP_t and PRD_t, respectively, using the single quarterly difference, QD(L) = 1 - L^3, and MD(L), graphed the results, and visually determined that QD(L) and MD(L) remove trends from GDP_t and PRD_t. Because GDP_t is observed only in the third month of a quarter, the shortest time interval over which it can be differenced to remove trend is the quarter. Then, in effect, we filtered QD(L)GDP_t and MD(L)PRD_t using AS(L). Actually, we restarted the filtering and directly annually differenced GDP_t and PRD_t using AD(L), which amounts to the same operation. Then, we graphed the results and visually determined that AD(L) removes trends and seasonality from GDP_t and PRD_t. Although we do not display the intermediate QD(L)- and MD(L)-filtered results, Fig. 2 displays the final monthly AD-filtered GDP_t and PRD_t, denoted AD(GDP_t) and AD(PRD_t), and the original unfiltered CUR_t and EXP_t. Because AD(GDP_t), AD(PRD_t), CUR_t, and EXP_t display only cyclical variations, in this mixed form the four variables are compatible and suitable for estimating a VAR model.

AD filtered means GDP_t and PRD_t are filtered using only AD(L) and CUR_t, and EXP_t are unfiltered. Initial model estimation resulted in PRD_t residuals with a significantly negative autocorrelation coefficient at the annual lag, indicating AD(L) does not remove all seasonality from PRD_t. Therefore, we extended AD(L) to an "airline model", with an additional estimated annual (seasonal) first-order moving-average term, to remove any remaining significant stochastic seasonality from PRD_t. We denote airline-model filtered PRD_t by AD/AMA(PRD_t), where AMA refers to annual moving average. The term "airline model" comes from Box and Jenkins (1976) and is often the "default" model in a search for the best ARIMA seasonal-adjustment model.

We extended monthly AD(PRD_t) to monthly AD/AMA(PRD_t) as follows. We supposed AD(PRD_t) is generated by the seasonal-adjustment model

$$\mathrm{AD}(\mathrm{PRD}t) = \left(1 - \phi_1\mathrm{L} - \phi_2\mathrm{L}^2 - \phi_3\mathrm{L}^3\right)^{-1}\left(1 + \theta\mathrm{L}^{12}\right)\varepsilon_t,$$

where the nonseasonal AR(3) component $\left(1 - \phi_1\mathrm{L} - \phi_2\mathrm{L}^2 - \phi_3\mathrm{L}^3\right)^{-1}$ accounts for cyclicality, the seasonal MA(1) component $1 + \theta\mathrm{L}^{12}$ accounts for stochastic seasonality, and ε_t is a white-noise disturbance distributed $\mathrm{NIID}(0, \sigma_\varepsilon^2)$.

Note that both the univariate seasonal-adjustment models and the multivariate VAR models for GDP forecasting were estimated using mean-adjusted and standardized data (divided by standard deviation after mean adjustment). The data and the estimated AR(3) component are stationary, which means that $1 - \phi_1\lambda - \phi_2\lambda^2 - \phi_3\lambda^3 = 0$ implies $|\lambda| > 1$, and the seasonal MA(1) is estimated as invertible, which means that $|\theta| < 1$.

AD/AMA(PRD_t) is defined as $\left(1 + \theta\mathrm{L}^{12}\right)^{-1}$ AD(PRD_t) and is approximated by four terms:

$$\mathrm{AD/AMA(PRD}_t) = \text{ missing},$$

for $t = 1, \ldots, 48$, and

$$\begin{aligned}\mathrm{AD/AMA(PRD}_t) = \mathrm{PRD}_t - \left(1+\hat{\theta}\right)\mathrm{PRD}_{t-12} + \hat{\theta}\left(1+\hat{\theta}\right)\mathrm{PRD}_{t-24} \\ - \hat{\theta}^2\left(1+\hat{\theta}\right)\mathrm{PRD}_{t-36} + \hat{\theta}^3\left(1+\hat{\theta}\right)\mathrm{PRD}_{t-48},\end{aligned}$$

for $t = 49, \ldots, 408$, where monthly $\hat{\theta} = -.5033$ is estimated jointly with the AR parameters, using MLE.

Similarly, we extended quarterly $\mathrm{AD(PRD}_s)$ to quarterly $\mathrm{AD/AMA(PRD}_s)$, using the analogous model

$$\mathrm{AD(PRD}_s) = \left(1 - \phi_1\mathrm{L} - \phi_2\mathrm{L}^2 - \phi_3\mathrm{L}^3\right)^{-1}\left(1+\theta\mathrm{L}^4\right)\varepsilon_s,$$

where subscript s denotes quarters and L now denotes the quarterly lag operator. $\mathrm{AD/AMA(PRD}_s)$ is defined as $\left(1+\theta\mathrm{L}^4\right)^{-1}\mathrm{AD(PRD}_s)$ and is approximated by four terms:

$$\mathrm{AD/AMA(PRD}_s) = \text{ missing},$$

for $s = 1, \ldots, 16$, and

$$\begin{aligned}\mathrm{AD/AMA(PRD}_s) = \mathrm{PRD}_s - \left(1+\hat{\theta}\right)\mathrm{PRD}_{s-4} + \hat{\theta}\left(1+\hat{\theta}\right)\mathrm{PRD}_{s-8} \\ - \hat{\theta}^2\left(1+\hat{\theta}\right)\mathrm{PRD}_{s-12} + \hat{\theta}^3\left(1+\hat{\theta}\right)\mathrm{PRD}_{s-16},\end{aligned}$$

for $s = 17, \ldots, 136$, where $\hat{\theta} = -.6769$ using quarterly stock data and $\hat{\theta} = -.5041$ using quarterly flow data.

Both monthly and quarterly AD-filtered data comprise AD(GDP), AD (PRD), CUR, and EXP and monthly and quarterly AD/AMA-filtered data comprise AD(GDP), AD/AMA(PRD), CUR, and EXP. Because AD/AMA (PRD) is smoother than AD(PRD), as seen for example in the quarterly figures, Figs. 4–9, we might expect more accurate GDP forecasts using AD/AMA(PRD). But, because this was not always the case, we did not further extend the AD/AMA model and filter to a more detailed seasonal-adjustment model and filter, cf., Flaig (2003). Thus, present forecasting results indicate some seasonal adjustment is necessary to put all variables in compatible cyclical form in order to estimate a forecasting model, but Table 9 shows that a more thorough seasonal adjustment does not necessarily improve short- or long-term forecasts. Of course, a government statistical agency responsible for producing seasonally adjusted data is obliged to produce thoroughly adjusted data, whatever the consequences in subsequent applications.

Because log-form data are often more homogeneous (have more constant variances or homoskedasticity), hence, are often easier to fit, we also considered log-form data. Because non-missing original values of GDP_t and PRD_t

values are positive, these variables were transformed directly to natural logs. However, because values of CUR_t and EXP_t are negative, zero, or positive fractions, they were indirectly transformed into logs as follows. For example, consider CUR_t and suppose d_t, u_t, and i_t denote the fractions of survey respondents who, respectively, said current business conditions declined, are unchanged, or improved. Then, $\mathrm{CUR}_t = i_t - d_t$, such that u_t is ignored. However, because

$$d_t + u_t + i_t = 1$$

and assuming $u_t = 0$,

$$i_t/d_t = (1 + \mathrm{CUR}_t)/(1 - \mathrm{CUR}_t) > 0,$$

so that $\ln\left[(1 + \mathrm{CUR}_t) / (1 - \mathrm{CUR}_t)\right]$ is well defined and can be considered the "log" of CUR_t and similarly for EXP_t. Thus, we computed AD-filtered $\ln(\mathrm{GDP}_t)$ and $\ln(\mathrm{PRD}_t)$, as in the unlogged cases, and unfiltered $\ln(\mathrm{CUR}_t)$ and $\ln(\mathrm{EXP}_t)$. Resulting graphs of monthly, original and filtered, log-form data were very close to those in Figs. 1–3. Also, monthly model estimates were very similar, regardless whether the data were log transformed or not. Thus, we did not conduct further analysis with the log-form data.

4 Estimation of VAR Models

In principle, we searched for the best combination of monthly indicators for forecasting GDP (we now denote filtered GDP and PRD more simply as "GDP" and "PRD", without AD or AD/AMA). In practice, we restricted the search to three of seven possibilities: models of GDP, PRD, CUR, and EXP; models of GDP, PRD, and CUR; and, models of GDP and PRD. First, we dropped EXP because it is considered the less informative Ifo variable and is somewhat redundant statistically, given CUR. Then, we dropped CUR to see what difference using any Ifo variables makes in forecasting GDP. Finally, we kept PRD because it is often the first choice of a monthly indicator when forecasting GDP.

We aimed for "adequate" estimated VAR models, by which we mean the following. As usual, our ideal was models with minimum numbers of parameters and zero-mean, constant-variance, and independently distributed residuals. For each of the three variable sets, we estimated unrestricted VAR(1) models, whose residuals showed significant serial correlations, and, then, estimated unrestricted VAR(2) models, whose residuals showed mostly insignificant correlations except for a few higher-lag correlations which could not be accounted for with lower-order VAR models. Thus, we accepted estimated VAR(2) models as adequately fitting the three sets of variables. In reaching this conclusion, we inspected graphs of residual own- and cross-serial correlations, evaluated p values of Ljung–Box Q statistics, Ljung and Box (1978), and evaluated information criteria. Although Ljung–Box Q statistics were developed to test for significant residual own-serial correlations, we also used them to test for significant residual cross-serial correlations. We did not test for significance of individual estimated parameters or remove any.

For the eighteen final estimated VAR(2) models, in Table 1 we report only R_e^2 (the usual R-squared called "estimation R squared", which is distinguished in Sect. 5 from $R_{f,h}^2$, called "forecasting R squared"). We do not report estimated parameters because, as usual in VAR models, they are very imprecise and, thus, provide little reliable information about feedbacks among variables. We also computed implied estimated AR characteristic roots which were all expectedly and firmly stationary. Although R_e^2 does not account for degrees of freedom used in estimation, only pertains to individual variables, and does not pertain to complete estimated models, nevertheless, higher values of R_e^2 are generally associated with more accurate GDP forecasts as seen by comparing Table 1 with Tables 2–9. We used "in sample" data from January 1970 to December 1993 to estimate models and "out of sample" data from January 1994 to December 2003 to produce and evaluate GDP forecasts.

We implemented the MLE using a FORTRAN 77 program, compiled the program using the Lahey–Fujitsu FORTRAN 95 complier version 5.6, and executed the program on a personal computer with a Pentium 4 central processor, running at about 2 gigahertz speed and controlled by the Windows XP operating system. Using a 10^{-8} convergence criterion, estimating the largest models, with 4 variables and 42 parameters, took about 4000 iterations or less than 20 minutes from start to finish. We started all iterations by setting parameter values to .01. If iterations stalled (reached a point in parameter space where the likelihood function appeared flat in all directions so that no further moves were made, even though convergence was not achieved), we restarted them at the last parameter values. Sometimes we restarted the iterations several times before achieving convergence. Thus, the MLE was not automatic and needed intervention.

5 Evaluation of GDP Forecasts

For the GDP forecasts, we define normalized root mean squared forecast error for h-period-ahead forecasts as

$$\mathrm{NRMSFE}_h = \sqrt{\left(\sum_{t=1}^{T} e_{t|t-h}^2\right) / T} \div \text{out-of-sample standard deviation of GDP},$$

where $e_{t|t-h} = \mathrm{GDP}_t - \mathrm{GDP}_{t|t-h}$ = error of forecasting GDP_t in period $t-h$, for out-of-sample periods $t = 1, \ldots, T$, missing values of $e_{t|t-h}$ are dropped from the summation, and T is reduced correspondingly. For every variable, we define estimation R-squared as the usual

$$R_e^2 = 1 - \frac{\text{in-sample variance of a variable's residual in an estimated model}}{\text{in-sample variance of the variable}}$$

and define forecasting R-squared as

$$\mathrm{R}^2_{f,h} = 1 - \mathrm{NRMSFE}^2_h, \quad \text{for } h \geq 1.$$

First, generally, $\mathrm{R}^2_{f,h} \leq \mathrm{R}^2_e$ and, equivalently, $\mathrm{NRMSFE}_h \geq \sqrt{1 - \mathrm{R}^2_e}$, for $h \geq 1$. $\mathrm{R}^2_{f,h} \cong \mathrm{R}^2_e$ and $\mathrm{NRMSFE}_h \cong \sqrt{1 - \mathrm{R}^2_e}$, for $h \geq 1$, suggest that the data generating process has changed not at all or insignificantly between the in- and out-of-sample periods, so that out-of-sample forecasts should be maximally accurate. Alternately, $\mathrm{R}^2_{f,h} << \mathrm{R}^2_e$ and $\mathrm{NRMSFE}_h >> \sqrt{1 - \mathrm{R}^2_e}$, for $h \geq 1$, suggest that the data generating process has changed significantly between in- and out-of-sample periods, where $<<$ and $>>$ denote "much less than" and "much greater than".

Second, an efficient forecast, which fully exploits available information, is orthogonal to its forecast error, so that $\mathrm{R}^2_{f,h} > 0$ and $\mathrm{NRMSFE}_h < 1$, for $h \geq 1$. Because the last conditions are necessary, but not sufficient, for efficiency, $\mathrm{R}^2_{f,h} \leq 0$ and $\mathrm{NRMSFE}_h \geq 1$, for $h \geq 1$, imply that a forecast is inefficient, but $\mathrm{R}^2_{f,h} > 0$ and $\mathrm{NRMSFE}_h < 1$, for $h \geq 1$, do not imply that the forecast is efficient.

Tables 1–7 show that R^2_e is significantly greater than any $\mathrm{R}^2_{f,h}$, which suggests that the data generating process of the German economy changed significantly after 1993. This is what we expect as a result of the immediate political and evolving economic unification of Germany in 1990. We produced nonrecursive forecasts based on fixed models estimated using fixed in-sample data. Recursive forecasts based on models reestimated using recursively updated in-sample data should reduce the differences between R^2_e and $\mathrm{R}^2_{f,h}$. Table 9 shows that monthly-long-term GDP forecasts are inefficient, certainly relative to quarterly-long-term GDP forecasts. Thus, we disregard these forecasts and further evaluate only the remaining three cases.

We can compare forecasts "internally" by comparing in-sample R^2_e and out-of-sample $\mathrm{R}^2_{f,h}$ based on the same estimated model of interest, or, we can compare forecasts "externally" by comparing out-of-sample $\mathrm{R}^2_{f,h}$ and NRMSFE_h for the model of interest and competing "external" models. External comparisons are costly to the extent that competing models must be developed, although both comparisons should be made. For simplicity, we focus on internal comparisons and report external comparisons only in terms of Theil U statistics for essentially costless "naive" forecasts.

By definition,

$$\text{Theil U} = \frac{\mathrm{NRMSFE}_h \text{ of the forecast of interest}}{\mathrm{NRMSFE}_h \text{ of the naive forecast}},$$

where the naive forecast is the last observed value of the variable of interest at least h periods ago Doan (2000). A Theil U value < 1 implies that the forecasts of interest are better than the naive forecasts. As hoped, this occurs in almost all cases in Tables 2–7. Although we focus on NRMSFE_h and $\text{R}^2_{f,h}$, conclusions based on Theil U would be the same.

We used the following test to determine whether using the Ifo variables, CUR and EXP, results in better monthly or quarterly GDP forecasts. In the undiscarded, monthly short-term and quarterly cases in Table 9, we let ρ denote the total number of variables in the 50% best-forecasting models divided by the total number of variables in the 50% worst-forecasting models. Thus, $.636 \leq \rho \leq 1.571$; because using 2, 3, or 4 variables means using 0, 1, or 2 Ifo variables, higher values of ρ imply that using Ifo variables produces better GDP forecasts; and, if ρ is uniformly distributed, its bottom quartile spans $[.636, .870]$, its middle quartiles span $[.870, 1.338]$, and its top quartile spans $[1.338, 1.571]$. Thus, if ρ is in the lowest quartile, the middle quartiles, or the highest quartile, we conclude, respectively, that using Ifo variables significantly reduces, insignificantly changes, or significantly improves GDP-forecast accuracy.

We used analogous tests to determine which filtering and aggregation methods produced better GDP forecasts. We assigned 0 to AD filtering, 1 to AD/AMA filtering, 0 to stock aggregation, and 1 to flow aggregation (analogous tests follow from reverse assignments). For each classification, we let φ denote the sum of the numerical values in the 50%-best-forecasting models divided by 3 in monthly cases or divided by 6 in quarterly cases. Then, $0 \leq \varphi \leq 1$ and, if φ is uniformly distributed, its bottom quartile spans $[0.0, .25]$, its middle quartiles span $[.25, .75]$, and its top quartile spans $[.75, 1.0]$. Thus, for a particular classification, if φ is in the lowest quartile, the middle quartile, or the highest quartile, we conclude, respectively, that choosing the zero option significantly improves GDP forecasting accuracy, choosing either option insignificantly affects GDP forecasting accuracy, and choosing the unit option significantly improves GDP forecasting accuracy.

Recall that we are forecasting AD-filtered GDP. We could transform the forecasts of filtered GDP back to the original form of GDP by unnormalizing the forecasts using the standard deviation and mean of filtered GDP and undifferencing the result. Frequently, the backtransformed original-form forecasts are more accurate, because the restored trends and seasonalities are purely deterministic, hence, perfectly predictable.

6 Conclusions

NRMSFE_h and $\text{R}^2_{f,h}$ of the filtered GDP forecasts in Tables 2–7 are summarized in Table 9 and imply the following six general conclusions.

1. **Monthly GDP forecasts are feasible**
   Estimating a monthly VAR model of quarterly-observed German GDP and monthly-observed indicators of the German economy, using Kalman-filtering-based MLE to produce monthly GDP forecasts, is feasible only if

the variables are in compatible cyclical form and not too many parameters are estimated. We estimated unrestricted VAR(2) models of 2–4 variables, with 15–42 parameters, using 408 monthly and 96 quarterly in-sample periods. Estimating monthly models using monthly-quarterly data seems essential for producing accurate monthly GDP forecasts, especially short-term forecasts, because, even though we can transform quarterly models estimated with purely-quarterly data into monthly models, generally, such transformed models are not expected to produce accurate monthly forecasts.

2. **Monthly models produce better short-term GDP forecasts**
   Monthly models 1–3 produce better short-term GDP forecasts (1–3 months ahead) than the best quarterly-short-term GDP forecasts (1 quarter ahead) produced by model 14. Both monthly- and quarterly-short-term GDP forecasts are not inefficient ($\text{NRMSFE}_h < 1$). The greater accuracy of the monthly-short-term GDP forecasts should provide sufficient motivation for estimating monthly models, using quarterly-observed GDP and monthly-observed indicators, for producing monthly-short-term GDP forecasts.

3. **Quarterly models produce better long-term GDP forecasts**
   Every monthly model produced inefficient monthly-long-term GDP forecasts (average NRMSFE_h of 1–24 months ahead > 1) which should be disregarded. Every quarterly model produced not inefficient, hence, at least tentatively acceptable, quarterly long-term GDP forecasts (average NRMSFE_h of 1–8 quarters ahead < 1).

4. **Ifo variables improve quarterly short-term GDP forecasts**
   After disregarding monthly-long-term GDP forecasts, we have monthly short-term, quarterly short-term, and quarterly long-term cases in Table 9. In these cases, ρ is, respectively, 1.125, 1.400, and 1.118, which implies that using the Ifo variables insignificantly improves monthly short-term or quarterly long-term GDP forecasts, but significantly improves quarterly short-term GDP forecasts (use of ρ is explained in Sect. 5).

5. **Aggregation and filtering choices insignificantly affect GDP forecasts**
   In the monthly-short-term case in Table 9, the filtering $\varphi = 0$, which implies that AD filtering produces significantly better GDP forecasts, and the aggregation φ is irrelevant. In the quarterly cases, the aggregation $\varphi = .500$ and .667, and the filtering $\varphi = .500$ and .333, which implies that how we aggregate or filter has no significant effect on GDP forecasts (use of φ is explained in Sect. 5). Thus, choosing AD filtering makes a difference — improves GDP forecasts — only in the monthly-short-term case.

6. **Extensions to mixed-frequency forecasting with larger models**
We might want to estimate larger models, with more variables and more parameters, but the present experience suggests that the present models are at the limit of what MLE can handle, especially with mixed-frequency data. To estimate larger models with mixed-frequency data, we should not use MLE, but should use a noniterative finite-step estimation method. For example, Chen and Zadrozny (1998) developed and illustrated the extended Yule–Walker (XYW) method, a linear 2-step GMM method, Hansen (1982), for estimating a VAR model with mixed-frequency data. Being linear and 2-step, the XYW method can be implemented automatically and should be able to handle much larger models than MLE can handle. Mittnik (1990a, 1990b, 1992) developed and illustrated a linear 2-step method for estimating a state-space model with single-frequency data and using the estimated model for forecasting. Extending this method to mixed-frequency data could be more attractive, because, although the two methods have comparable numerical properties, state-space models are more general. Often, a low-dimensional state-space model can fit data well, which even a many-lag VAR model cannot.

A Appendix

A.1 Figures

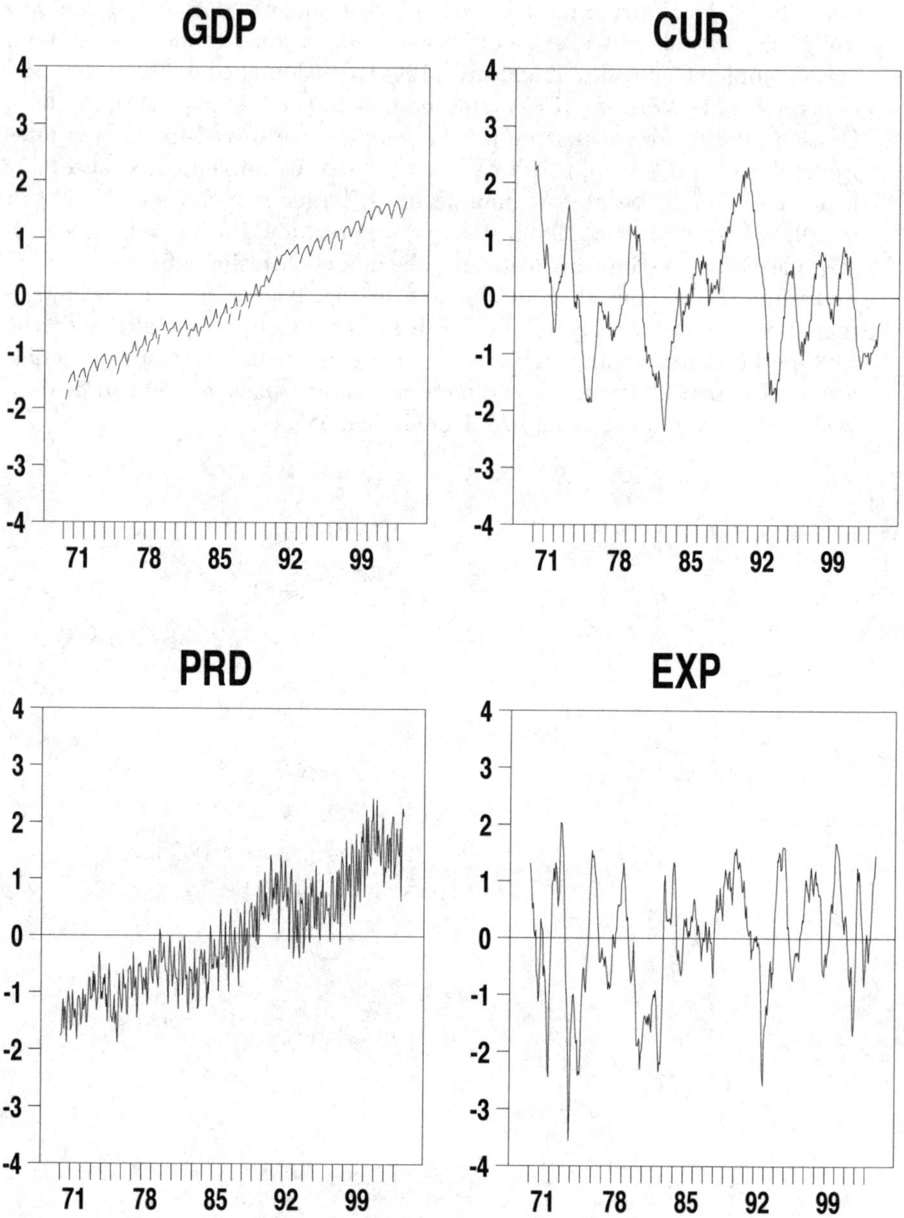

Fig. 1. Monthly, Original Variables

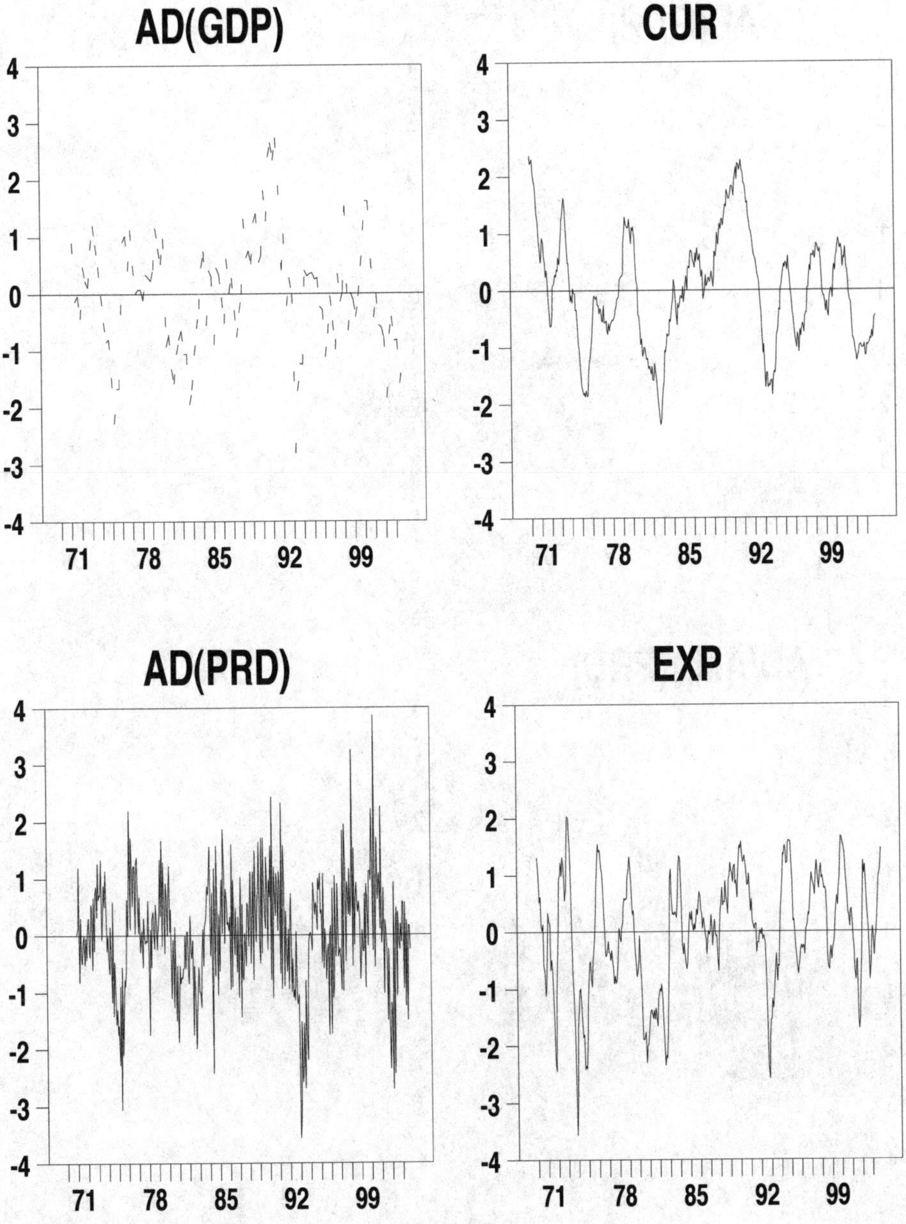

Fig. 2. Monthly, AD Filtered

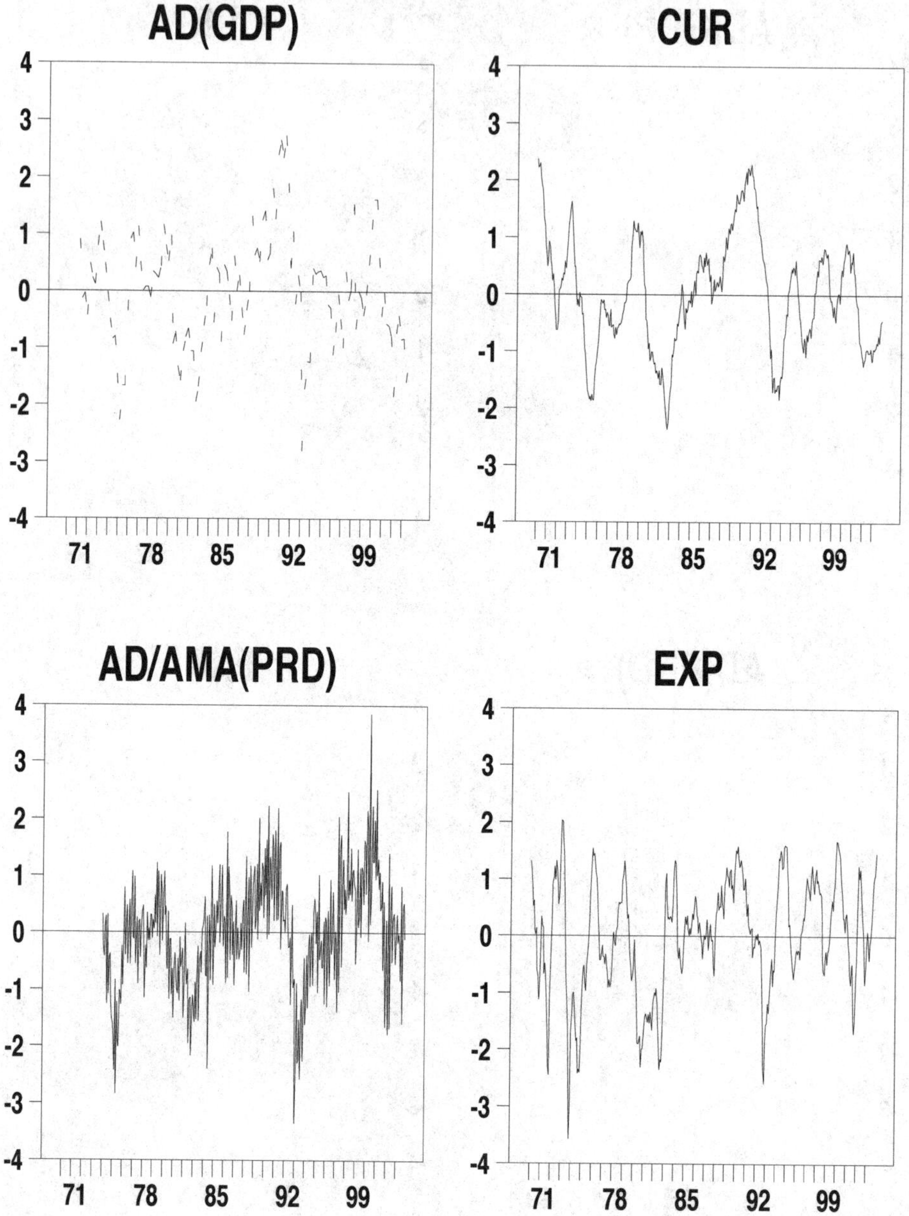

Fig. 3. Monthly, AD/AMA Filtered

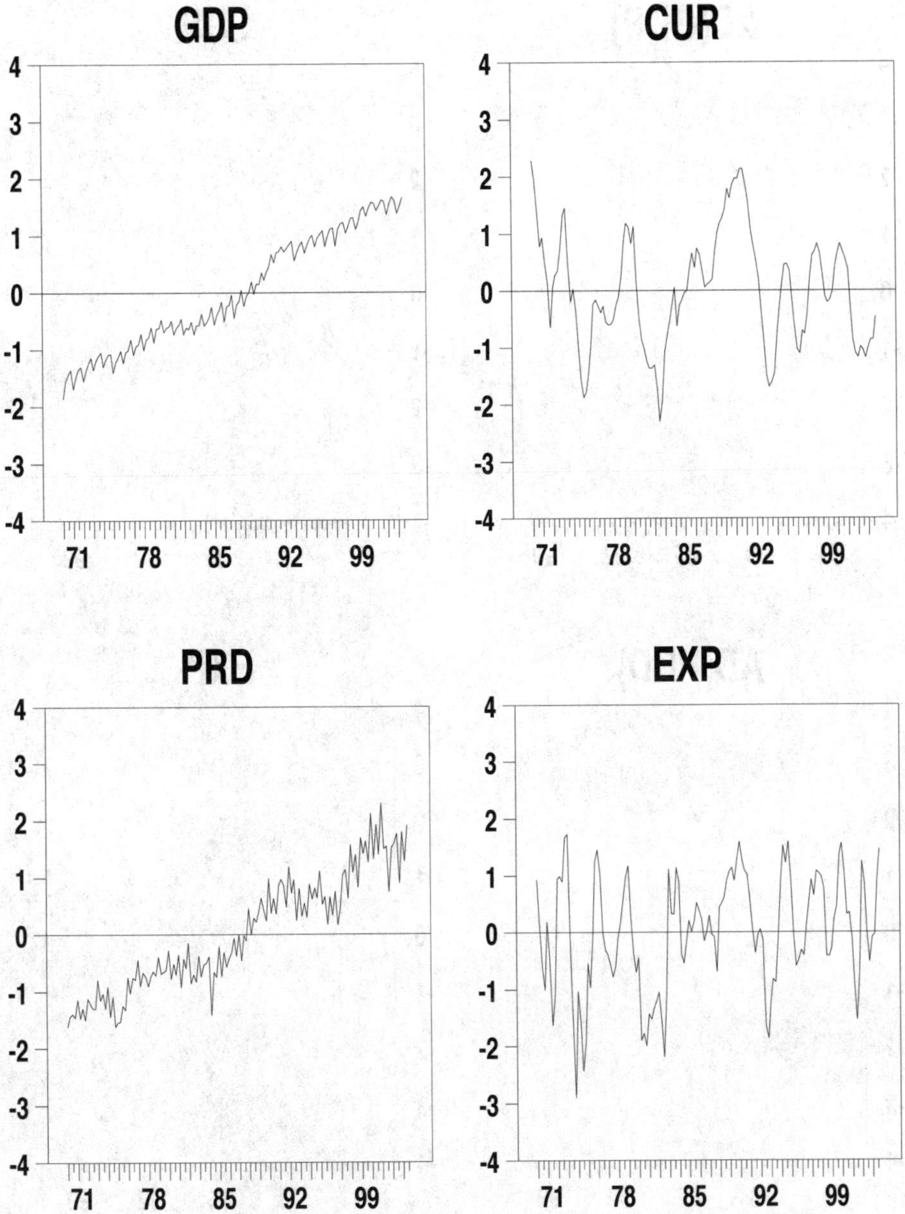

Fig. 4. Quarterly, Stocks, Original Variables

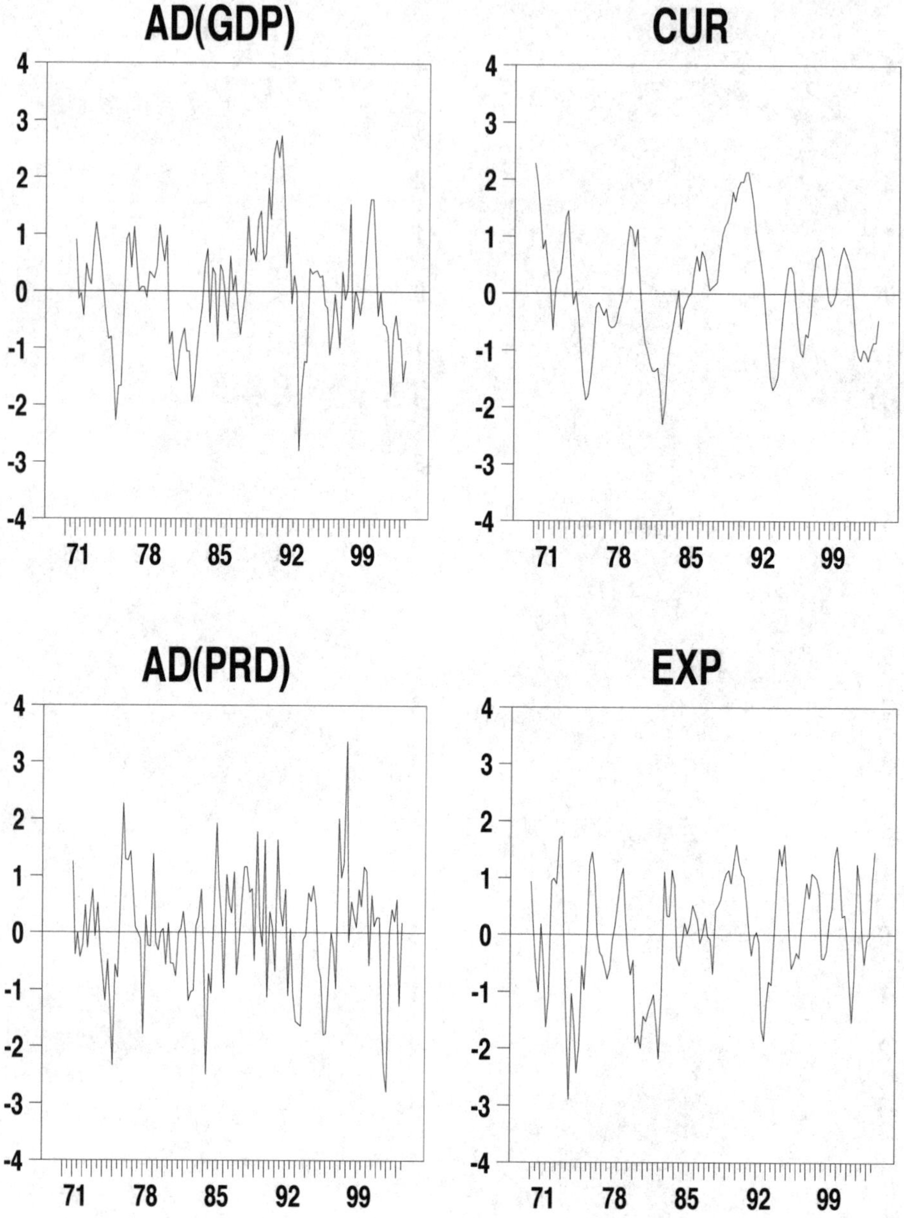

Fig. 5. Quarterly, Stocks, AD Filtered

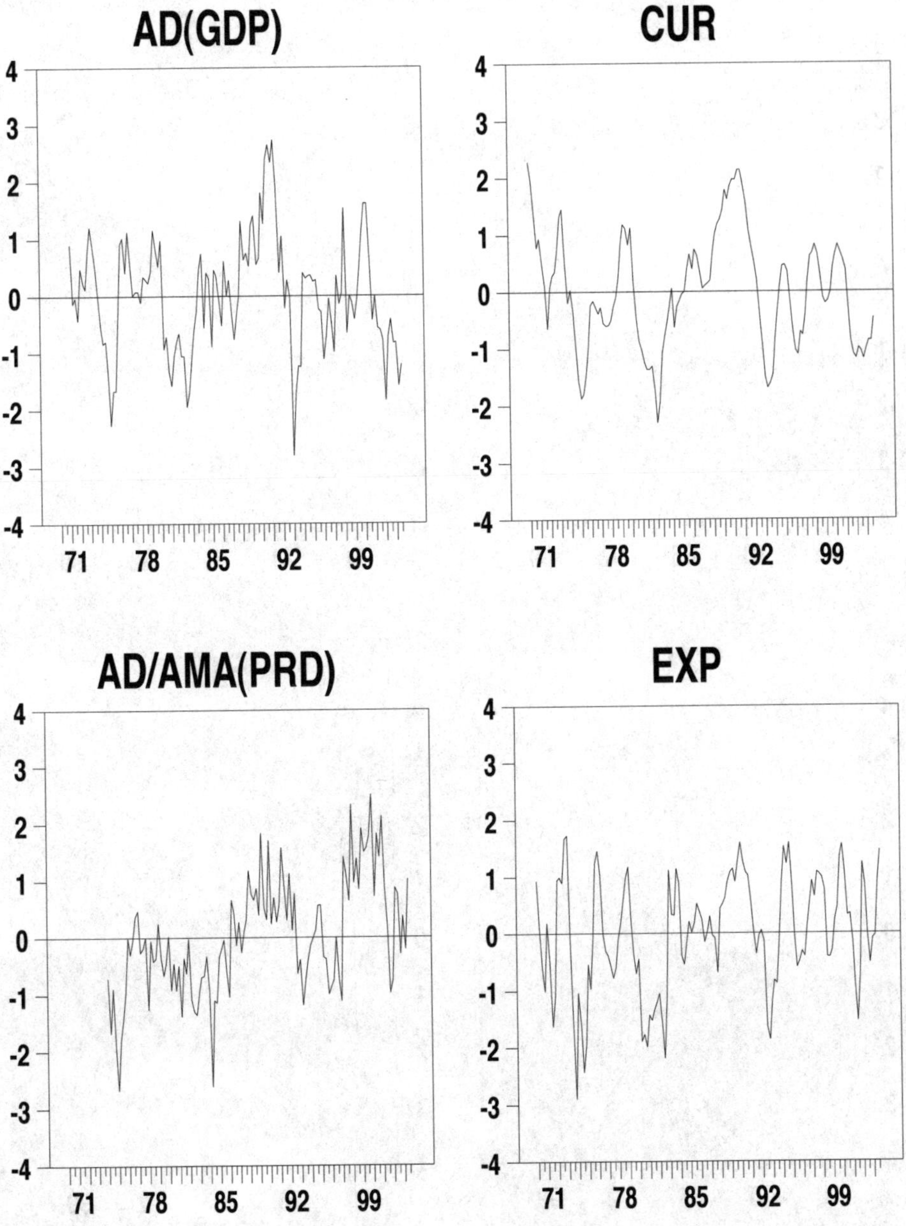

Fig. 6. Quarterly, Stocks, AD/AMA Filtered

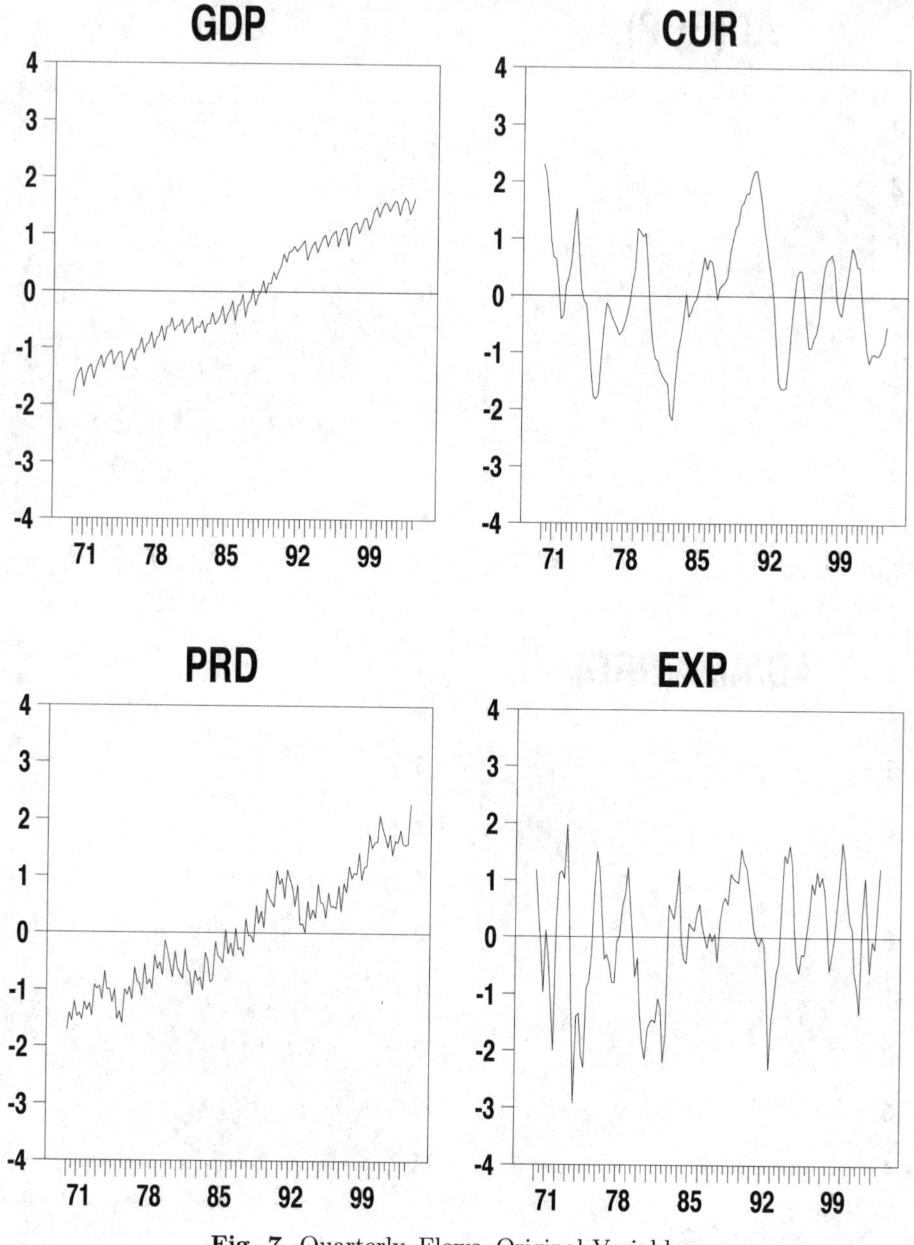

Fig. 7. Quarterly, Flows, Original Variables

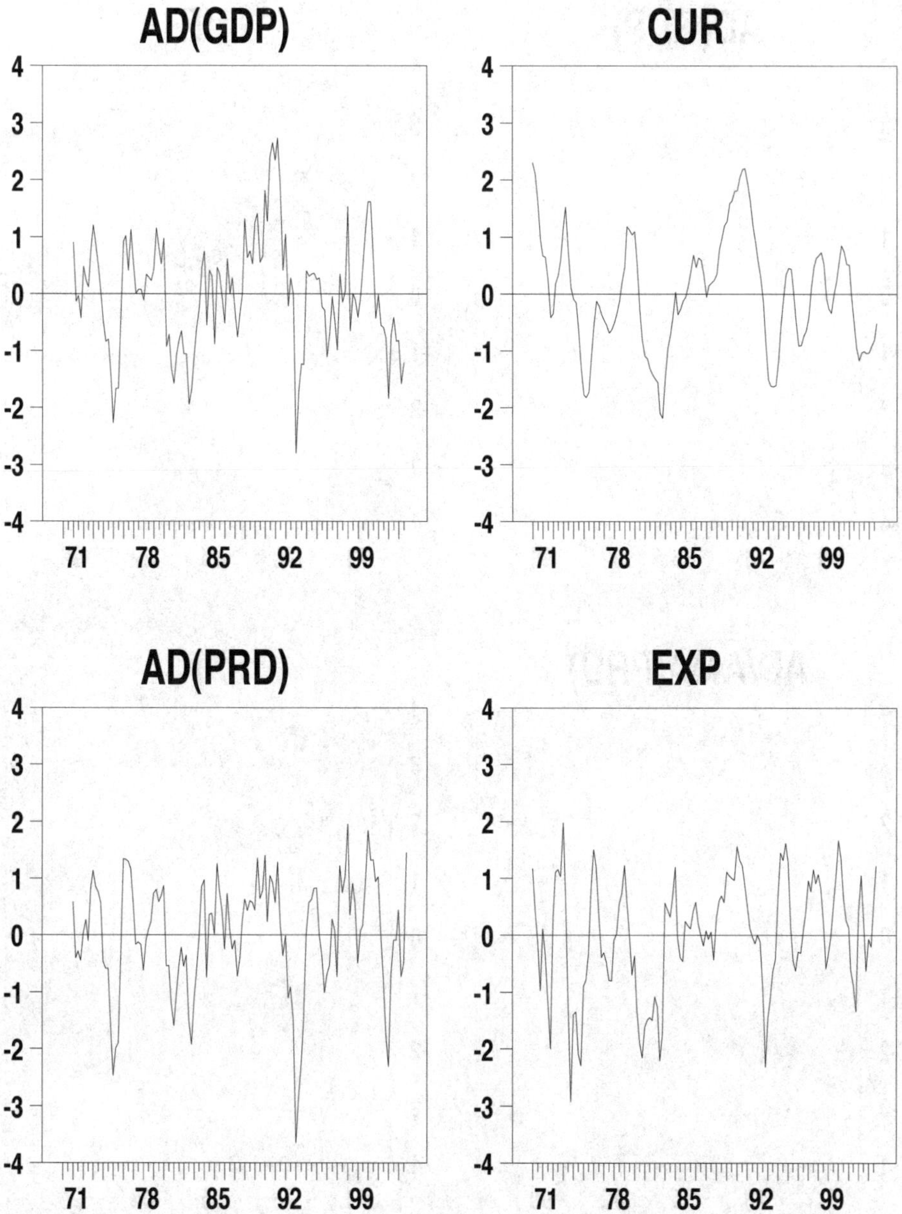

Fig. 8. Quarterly, Flows, AD Filtered

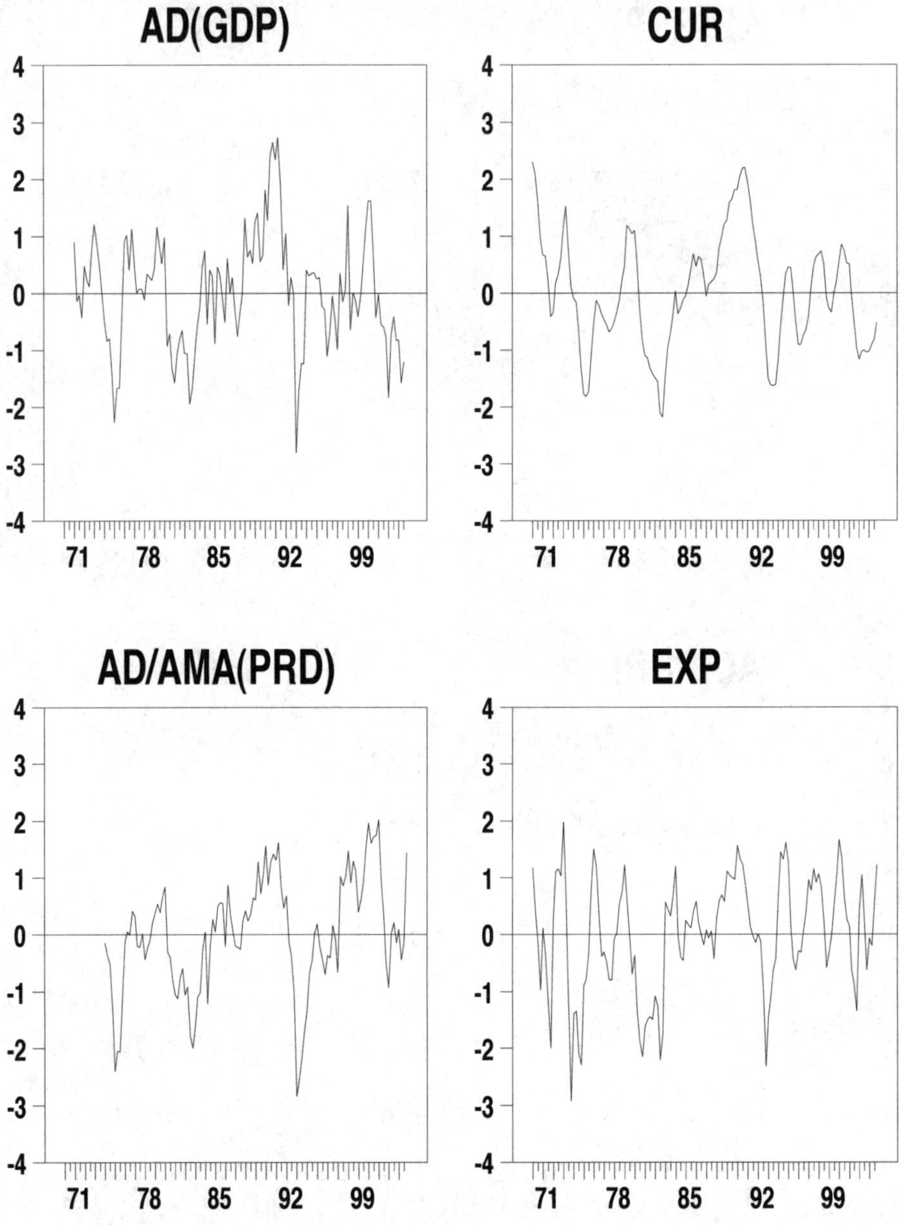

Fig. 9. Quarterly, Flows, AD/AMA Filtered

A.2 Tables

Tables 1–9 display estimation R-squared $\left(\mathrm{R}_e^2\right)$, forecasting R-squared $\left(\mathrm{R}_{f,h}^2\right)$, normalized root mean squared forecast error (NRMSFE_h), and Theil U statistics, for $h \geq 1$ forecast periods ahead, all defined in Sect. 5.

Table 1. R_e^2 of Estimated VAR(2) Models

	Model	GDP	PRD	CUR	EXP
1	mon, 4 vars, AD	.804	.522	.966	.904
2	mon, 3 vars, AD	.812	.478	.958	—
3	mon, 2 vars, AD	.850	.488	—	—
4	mon, 4 vars, AD/AMA	.783	.608	.966	.903
5	mon, 3 vars, AD/AMA	.780	.592	.959	—
6	mon, 2 vars, AD/AMA	.516	.567	—	—
7	qrt, 4 vars, stocks, AD	.735	.239	.882	.606
8	qrt, 3 vars, stocks, AD	.663	.201	.867	—
9	qrt, 2 vars, stocks, AD	.592	.145	—	—
10	qrt, 4 vars, stocks, AD/AMA	.734	.553	.882	.606
11	qrt, 3 vars, stocks, AD/AMA	.663	.530	.867	—
12	qrt, 2 vars, stocks, AD/AMA	.592	.499	—	—
13	qrt, 4 vars, flows, AD	.725	.715	.912	.626
14	qrt, 3 vars, flows, AD	.685	.682	.900	—
15	qrt, 2 vars, flows, AD	.606	.600	—	—
16	qrt, 4 vars, flows, AD/AMA	.721	.822	.911	.632
17	qrt, 3 vars, flows, AD/AMA	.690	.802	.901	—
18	qrt, 2 vars, flows, AD/AMA	.597	.739	—	—

Table 2. GDP Forecast Accuracy, Monthly, AD Filtered

Model 1: VAR(2) of 4 Variables AD(GDP), AD(PRD), CUR, EXP

Months ahead	$NRMSFE_h$	$R^2_{f,h}$	Theil U
1	.723	.477	.724
2	.802	.357	.796
3	.852	.274	.846
4	.947	.103	.787
5	.993	.014	.824
6	1.02	-.404	.846
9	1.22	-.488	.900
12	1.36	-.850	.795
18	1.30	-.690	.756
24	1.16	-.346	.671
average 1–24 months	1.18	-.392	.781

Model 2: VAR(2) of 3 Variables AD(GDP), AD(PRD), CUR

Months ahead	$NRMSFE_h$	$R^2_{f,h}$	Theil U
1	.731	.466	.725
2	.846	.284	.839
3	.917	.159	.910
4	1.02	-.040	.847
5	1.12	-.254	.934
6	1.15	-.323	.958
9	1.39	-.932	1.02
12	1.54	-1.37	.896
18	1.46	-1.13	.852
24	1.33	-.769	.771
average 1–24 months	1.32	-.742	.872

Model 3: VAR(2) of 2 Variables AD(GDP), AD(PRD)

Months ahead	$NRMSFE_h$	$R^2_{f,h}$	Theil U
1	.711	.494	.705
2	.799	.362	.792
3	.920	.154	.913
4	.959	.080	.797
5	.962	.075	.799
6	1.02	-.040	.846
9	1.07	-.144	.785
12	1.17	-.369	.684
18	1.25	-.563	.656
24	1.11	-.232	.644
average 1–24 months	1.08	-.166	.719

Table 3. GDP Forecast Accuracy, Monthly, AD/AMA Filtered

Model 4: VAR(2) of 4 Variables AD(GDP), AD/AMA(PRD), CUR, EXP

Months ahead	$NRMSFE_h$	$R^2_{f,h}$	Theil U
1	.820	.328	.813
2	.816	.334	.810
3	.821	.326	.814
4	.932	.131	.774
5	.993	.014	.792
6	.981	.038	.815
9	1.18	-.392	.873
12	1.31	-.716	.763
18	1.27	-.613	.740
24	1.12	-.254	.649
average 1–24 months	1.15	-.323	.761

Model 5: VAR(2) of 3 Variables AD(GDP), AD/AMA(PRD), CUR

Months ahead	$NRMSFE_h$	$R^2_{f,h}$	Theil U
1	.814	.337	.808
2	.870	.243	.863
3	.882	.222	.875
4	.966	.067	.802
5	1.07	-.145	.888
6	1.06	-.124	.882
9	1.23	-.513	.906
12	1.34	-.796	.783
18	1.33	-.769	.774
24	1.19	-.416	.691
average 1–24 months	1.21	-.464	.804

Model 6: VAR(2) of 2 Variables AD(GDP), AD/AMA(PRD)

Months ahead	$NRMSFE_h$	$R^2_{f,h}$	Theil U
1	.935	.126	.927
2	1.02	-.040	1.01
3	.997	.006	.989
4	1.11	-.232	.923
5	1.23	-.513	.936
6	1.13	-.277	.939
9	1.10	-.210	.808
12	1.06	-.124	.617
18	1.09	-.188	.634
24	1.07	-.145	.623
average 1–24 months	1.07	-.145	.729

Table 4. GDP Forecast Accuracy, Quarterly, Stocks, AD Filtered

Model 7: VAR(2) of 4 Variables AD(GDP), AD(PRD), CUR, EXP

Quarters ahead	$NRMSFE_h$	$R^2_{f,h}$	Theil U
1	.812	.341	.872
2	.822	.324	.730
3	.846	.284	.648
4	.876	.233	.512
6	.928	.139	.512
8	.977	.045	.510
average 1–8 quarters	.889	.210	.600

Model 8: VAR(2) of 3 Variables AD(GDP), AD(PRD), CUR

Quarters ahead	$NRMSFE_h$	$R^2_{f,h}$	Theil U
1	.765	.415	.821
2	.751	.436	.687
3	.764	.416	.610
4	.788	.379	.482
6	.837	.299	.482
8	.877	.231	.480
average 1–8 quarters	.807	.349	.565

Model 9: VAR(2) of 2 Variables AD(GDP), AD(PRD))

Quarters ahead	$NRMSFE_h$	$R^2_{f,h}$	Theil U
1	.845	.286	.907
2	.837	.299	.759
3	.842	.291	.674
4	.856	.267	.533
6	.889	.210	.533
8	.919	.155	.530
average 1–8 quarters	.871	.241	.625

Table 5. GDP Forecast Accuracy, Quarterly, Stocks, AD/AMA Filtered

Model 10: VAR(2) of 4 Variables AD(GDP), AD/AMA(PRD), CUR, EXP			
Quarters ahead	$NRMSFE_h$	$R^2_{f,h}$	Theil U
1	.811	.342	.870
2	.790	.376	.729
3	.823	.323	.647
4	.858	.264	.512
6	.931	.133	.511
8	.991	.018	.509
average 1–8 quarters	.883	.220	.599

Model 11: VAR(2) of 3 Variables AD(GDP), AD/AMA(PRD), CUR			
Quarters ahead	$NRMSFE_h$	$R^2_{f,h}$	Theil U
1	.780	.392	.837
2	.760	.422	.700
3	.768	.410	.622
4	.786	.382	.492
6	.838	.298	.492
8	.888	.211	.489
average 1–8 quarters	.812	.341	.576

Model 12: VAR(2) of 2 Variables AD(GDP), AD/AMA(PRD)			
Quarters ahead	$NRMSFE_h$	$R^2_{f,h}$	Theil U
1	.844	.288	.906
2	.825	.319	.758
3	.828	.314	.673
4	.842	.291	.532
6	.881	.224	.532
8	.918	.157	.530
average 1–8 quarters	.863	.255	.624

Table 6. GDP Forecast Accuracy, Quarterly, Flows, AD Filtered

Model 13: VAR(2) of 4 Variables AD(GDP), AD(PRD), CUR, EXP			
Quarters ahead	$NRMSFE_h$	$R^2_{f,h}$	Theil U
1	.786	.382	.844
2	.752	.434	.706
3	.752	.434	.627
4	.769	.409	.496
6	.848	.281	.496
8	.913	.166	.493
average 1–8 quarters	.814	.337	.581

Model 14: VAR(2) of 3 Variables AD(GDP), AD(PRD), CUR			
Quarters ahead	$NRMSFE_h$	$R^2_{f,h}$	Theil U
1	.734	.461	.787
2	.709	.497	.659
3	.712	.493	.585
4	.748	.440	.463
6	.842	.291	.463
8	.918	.157	.460
average 1–8 quarters	.793	.371	.542

Model 15: VAR(2) of 2 Variables AD(GDP), AD(PRD)			
Quarters ahead	$NRMSFE_h$	$R^2_{f,h}$	Theil U
1	.825	.319	.885
2	.800	.360	.741
3	.805	.352	.658
4	.827	.316	.520
6	.874	.236	.520
8	.912	.168	.517
average 1–8 quarters	.849	.279	.609

Table 7. GDP Forecast Accuracy, Quarterly, Flows, AD/AMA Filtered

Model 16: VAR(2) of 4 Variables AD(GDP), AD/AMA(PRD), CUR, EXP

Quarters ahead	$NRMSFE_h$	$R^2_{f,h}$	Theil U
1	.762	.419	.818
2	.736	.458	.685
3	.767	.412	.608
4	.823	.323	.481
6	.901	.188	.481
8	.905	.181	.478
average 1–8 quarters	.834	.304	.563

Model 17: VAR(2) of 3 Variables AD(GDP), AD/AMA(PRD), CUR

Quarters ahead	$NRMSFE_h$	$R^2_{f,h}$	Theil U
1	.819	.329	.879
2	.850	.278	.736
3	.869	.245	.653
4	.872	.240	.517
6	.882	.222	.516
8	.923	.148	.514
average 1–8 quarters	.874	.236	.605

Model 18: VAR(2) of 2 Variables AD(GDP), AD/AMA(PRD)

Quarters ahead	$NRMSFE_h$	$R^2_{f,h}$	Theil U
1	.818	.331	.877
2	.803	.355	.734
3	.809	.346	.652
4	.828	.314	.516
6	.877	.231	.516
8	.920	.154	.513
average 1–8 quarters	.851	.276	.604

Table 8. GDP Forecast Accuracy, Rankings of All Models, Monthly

Monthly Short Term:
$NRMSFE_h$ and $R^2_{f,h}$ of GDP Forecasts 1 Month ahead

Rank	$NRMSFE_h$	$R^2_{f,h}$	Variables	Model
1	.711	.494	2 vars, AD	3
2	.723	.477	4 vars, AD	1
3	.731	.466	3 vars, AD	2
4	.814	.337	3 vars, AD/AMA	5
5	.820	.328	4 vars, AD/AMA	4
6	.935	.126	2 vars, AD/AMA	6

Monthly Long Term:
Average $NRMSFE_h$ and $R^2_{f,h}$ of GDP Forecasts 1–24 Mons. ahead

Rank	$NRMSFE_h$	$R^2_{f,h}$	Variables	Model
1	1.07	-.145	2 vars, AD/AMA	6
2	1.08	-.166	2 vars, AD	3
3	1.15	-.323	4 vars, AD/AMA	4
4	1.18	-.392	4 vars, AD	1
5	1.21	-.464	3 vars, AD/AMA	5
6	1.32	-.742	3 vars, AD	2

Table 9. GDP Forecast Accuracy, Rankings of All Models, Quarterly

Quarterly Short Term:
$NRMSFE_h$ and $R^2_{f,h}$ of GDP Forecasts 1 Quarter ahead

Rank	$NRMSFE_h$	$R^2_{f,h}$	Variables	Model
1	.734	.461	3 vars, flows, AD	14
2	.762	.419	4 vars, flows, AD/AMA	16
3	.765	.415	3 vars, stocks, AD	8
4	.780	.392	3 vars, stocks, AD/AMA	11
5	.786	.382	4 vars, flows, AD	13
6	.811	.342	4 vars, stocks, AD/AMA	10
7	.812	.341	4 vars, stocks, AD	7
8	.818	.331	2 vars, flows, AD/AMA	18
9	.819	.329	3 vars, flows, AD/AMA	17
10	.825	.319	2 vars, flows, AD	15
11	.844	.288	2 vars, stocks, AD/AMA	12
12	.845	.286	2 vars, stocks, AD	9

Quarterly Long Term:
Average $NRMSFE_h$ and $R^2_{f,h}$ of GDP Forecasts 1–8 Qrts. ahead

Rank	$NRMSFE_h$	$R^2_{f,h}$	Variables	Model
1	.793	.371	3 vars, flows, AD	14
2	.807	.349	3 vars, stocks, AD	8
3	.812	.341	3 vars, stocks, AD/AMA	11
4	.814	.337	4 vars, flows, AD	13
5	.834	.304	4 vars, flows, AD/AMA	16
6	.849	.279	2 vars, flows, AD	15
7	.851	.276	2 vars, flows, AD/AMA	18
8	.863	.255	2 vars, stocks, AD/AMA	12
9	.871	.241	2 vars, stocks, AD	9
10	.874	.236	3 vars, flows, AD/AMA	17
11	.883	.220	4 vars, stocks, AD/AMA	10
12	.889	.210	4 vars, stocks, AD	7

References

BOX, G., AND G. JENKINS (1976): *Time Series Analysis, Forecasting and Control.* Holden–Day, San Francisco, CA.

CHEN, B., AND P. ZADROZNY (1998): "An Extended Yule-Walker Method for Estimating Vector Autoregressive Models with Mixed-Frequency Data," in *Advances in Econometrics: Messy Data–Missing Observations, Outliers, and Mixed-Frequency Data*, ed. by T. Fomby, and R. Hill, vol. 13, pp. 47–73. JAI Press, Greenwich, CT.

DOAN, T. (2000): *RATS Reference Manual*, Version 5. Estima, Evanston, IL.

FLAIG, G. (2003): "Seasonal and Cyclical Properties of Ifo Business Test Variables," *Journal of Economics and Statistics*, 223, 556–570.

HANSEN, L. (1982): "Large Sample Properties of Generalized Method of Moments Estimators," *Econometrica*, 50, 1029–1054.

LJUNG, G., AND G. BOX (1978): "On a Measure of Fit in Time Series Models," *Biometrika*, 65, 297–303.

MITTNIK, S. (1990a): "Forecasting with Balanced State Space Representations of Multivariate Distributed Lag Models," *Journal of Forecasting*, 9, 207–218.

——— (1990b): "Macroeconomic Forecasting Experience with Balanced State Space Models," *International Journal of Forecasting*, 6, 337–348.

——— (1992): "Forecasting International Growth Rates with Leading Indicators: A System-Theoretic Approach," *Computers and Mathematics with Applications*, 24, 31–41.

ZADROZNY, P. (2000): "Estimating a Multivariate ARMA Model with Mixed-Frequency Data: An Application to Forecasting U.S. GNP at Monthly Intervals," Working paper, Bureau of Labor Statistics, Washington, DC.

Real Wages and Business Cycle Asymmetries

Ulrich Woitek*

Department of Economics, University of Munich, Ludwigstr. 28 Vgb III, 80539 Munich, Germany and CESifo u.woitek@lrz.uni-muenchen.de

1 Introduction

In their paper on the cyclicality of real wages, Abraham and Haltiwanger (1995) point out that empirical evidence on whether real wages co-move with the business cycle is inconclusive.[1] Among the potential explanations for this finding they list measurement problems like the choice of the price index and composition bias: because there are changes in labour quality over the business cycle (low-skilled employment is more sensitive to business fluctuations), aggregate wage measures are not as volatile as wage measures on the individual level. In fact, using data from the Panel Study of Income Dynamics, Solon, Barsky, and Parker (1994) find that US real wages are strongly procyclical. More recently, Liu (2003) reaches a similar conclusion in a cross-country study on the US, Canada and the United Kingdom. Another explanation is that the real wage is influenced by factors which can either lead to a pro- or a countercyclical response. This has recently been examined by Fleischmann (1999), who shows in a structural VAR framework that the reaction of real wages to technology and oil price shocks is procyclical, while the response to labor supply and aggregate demand shocks is countercyclical.

The cyclicality of real wages has important implications for business cycle theory, as illustrated in Table 1 from Malley, Muscatelli, and Woitek (forth-

*I would like to thank Bernd Süßmuth, Stefan Mittnik and participants of the workshop "Academic Use of Ifo Survey Data" for helpful comments and suggestions.

[1]Building on Neftci (1978), Sargent (1978) shows that postwar US employment and real wages move countercyclically. Using a wholesale price index instead of the consumer price index, Geary and Kennan (1982) find that the relationship is insignificant. Bils (1985) analyzes panel data from the National Longitudinal Survey and finds that real wages are procycical. Other studies on the aggregate level cited by Abraham and Haltiwanger (1995) are Bodkin (1969) (procyclical real wage with consumer price index, countercyclical real wage with producer price index), Otani (1978) (procyclical real wage), Chirinko (1980) (countercyclical real wage), and Sumner and Silver (1989) (countercyclical real wage before the 1970s, procyclical after).

coming). The table contains stylized expected patterns from competing models of the cycle. Following a positive technology shock ϵ, the standard real

Table 1. Expected Pattern of Responses to Technology Schocks

Model	ϵ	Y	L	w/p
RBC	+	+	+	+
Sticky Nominal Wages	+	+	+	0
Sticky Prices	+	+	-	-

Source: Malley, Muscatelli, and Woitek (forthcoming).

business cycle model, e.g. Kydland and Prescott (1982), Long and Plosser (1983) and King and Plosser (1984), predicts a positive response of output Y, labor L, and the real wage w/p. In other words, output and real wages move together. For New Keynesian type models with wage and price rigidities, e.g. Goodfriend and King (1997), Rotemberg and Woodford (1997), Gali (1999), the outcome is different. In a model with sticky nominal wages, real wages do not change much in response to a technology shock. For the sticky price/imperfect competition model, we would expect a negative relationship between output and the real wage.[2]

For studies on the aggregate level, the common wisdom seems to be that "*correcting for all of the measurement problems, estimation problems, and composition problems does not lead to a finding of systematically procyclical or countercyclical real wages*" (Abraham and Haltiwanger (1995), p. 1262). However, one can show that using frequency domain techniques instead of calculating correlation coefficients,[3] and focussing the analysis on business cycle frequencies, real wages in the US are strongly procyclical (Hart, Malley and Woitek 2002). The approach adopted in this paper is different: if we accept the possibility that the real wage is influenced by factors which can either lead to a pro- or a countercyclical response, we can also expect different dynamics dependent on the phase of the business cycle, leading to an asymmetric relationship between the real wage and the cycle measure.

It is a well-known fact that business cycles are asymmetric. In the US, the average business cycle length after 1960 is about 75 months. An upswing takes on average 64 months, while the average downswing of the cycle is

[2]Analyzing data from the NBER–CES/Census manufacturing industry productivity database, Malley, Muscatelli, and Woitek (forthcoming) find more support for RBC type models, implying a positive relationship between output and the real wage.

[3]The result in Abraham and Haltiwanger (1995) is based on correlation coefficients between real wages in manufacturing and employment/output, for different filtering techniques, and quarterly and annual frequencies.

much shorter (11 months).[4] This difference between expansion and contraction phases can also be seen when looking at business cycle measures for Germany (Fig. 1).

As pointed out by Koop and Potter (1999), the number of macroeconometric studies allowing for non-linearities is relatively low.[5] They explain the reluctance to use these techniques with the perceived weakness of the statistical evidence, the potential danger of data mining and the lack of economic significance.[6] However, phenomena like the downward rigidity of nominal wages make it reasonable to suspect asymmetries in the relationship between the real wage and the cycle.

The approach adopted here is to estimate a threshold vector autoregressive model (TVAR), conditional on the phase of the business cycle,[7] using a grid-search based estimation strategy proposed by Tong (1990). For each of the two subsamples, one obtains a VAR for which the implied cross correlation coefficients are calculated. The two data sets under analysis are for the US and for Germany, to compare two economies with very different labor market characteristics. The paper is structured as follows: Section 2 describes the data set; the methodology is explained in detail in Sect. 3; Section 4 discusses the results and Sect. 5 conludes.

2 Data

To calculate correlations between the business cycle and the real wage, we need to find appropriate measures for both. As pointed out by (Abraham and Haltiwanger 1995), differences in measurement potentially lead to different results with respect to real wage cyclicaltity. Therefore, given data availability, alternative measures are tried to check robustness. In the case of the US, both manufacturing output and employment are analyzed as cycle measures, in the case of Germany (west), the business cycle is also measured by the Ifo business climate index (see below).

The US data on wages and prices are monthly data from the Bureau of Labor Statistics, the observation period is 1956:01–1997:12.[8] Average hourly

[4]See the US Business Cycle Expansions and Contractions (NBER) at http://www.nber.org/cycles.html/.

[5]As examples, Koop and Potter (1999) cite the Markov-switching model proposed by Hamilton (1989), and the studies by Beaudry and Koop (1993), and Pesaran and Potter (1997). Other examples are DeLong and Summers (1986), Potter (1995) and Rothman (1991).

[6]Another reason is certainly the fact that macroeconomic time series are notoriously short.

[7]For a similar approach to study the dynamics of output and unemployment in the US, see Altissimo and Violante (2001).

[8]Production workers in natural resources and mining and manufacturing, construction workers in construction and nonsupervisory workers in the service-providing industries (source: http://www.bls.gov).

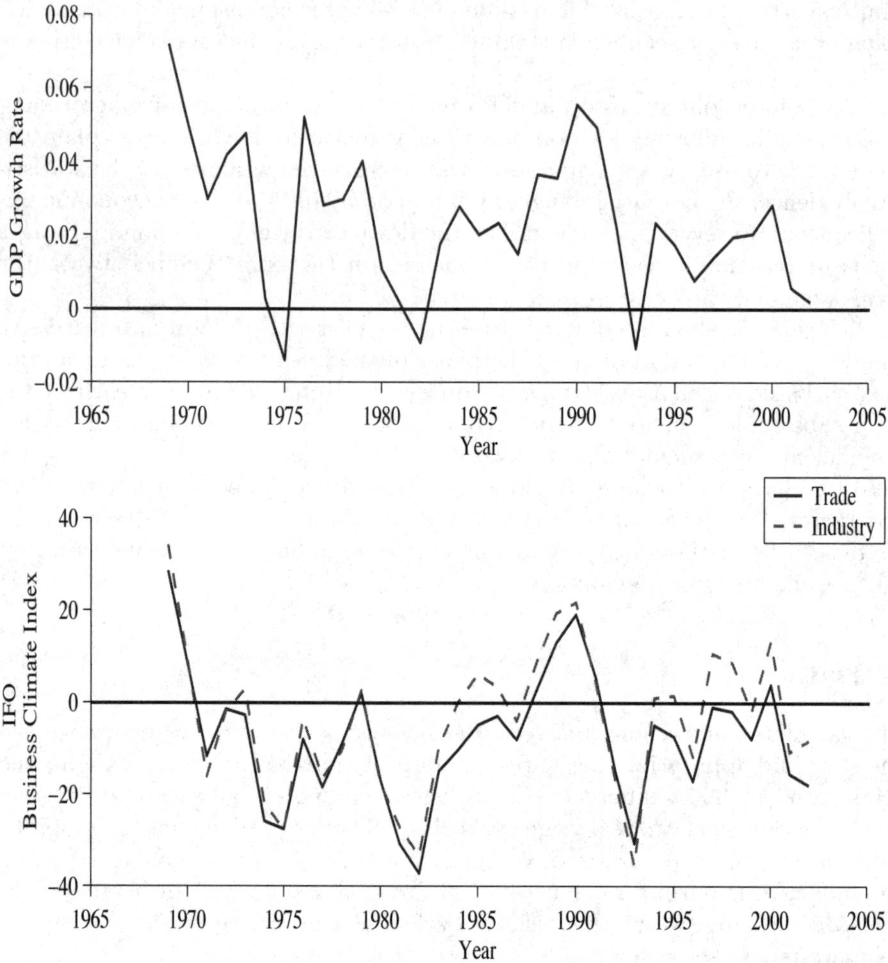

Notes:
Sources: (1) GDP (West Germany), 1969–2002, GGDC Total Economy Database, University of Groningen (http://www.eco.rug.nl/ggdc), in 1999 US dollars. (2) Ifo business climate index, 1969–2002, Trade: wholesale and retail, Industry: manufacturing and construction. The index is based on a monthly survey of about 7000 enterprises on their assessment of the business climate (http://www.ifo.de, see also Sect. 2 for further details).

Fig. 1. The German Business Cycle, 1969–2002

earnings A and average hourly earnings excluding overtime W are deflated using either the producer (PPI) or the consumer price index (CPI). These real wage measures are compared with cycles in employment and an index for manufacturing output (source: http://www.nber.org).

The Ifo business climate index is based on a monthly survey of about 7000 enterprises on their assessment of the business climate. Both the assessment of the current climate as well as the expectations for the next six months are collected. The answers are converted to a seasonally adjusted index (base year: 1991), which can fluctuate between -100 (all firms are pessimistic) and +100 (all firms are optimistic). Both the current climate index ($IFO1$) and the expectations index ($IFO2$) are analyzed, in addition to the aggregate business climate index, which the Ifo institute calculates as a geometric average of the of the current and the expectations index ($IFO3$). The observation period is 1986:01–2003:07 (monthly data).[9]

To compare the results across different cycle measures, manufacturing output (Y) is also analyzed. The data are from the Bundesbank data base (1950:01–1998:02: CDRom Deutsche Bundesbank – 50 Jahre Deutsche Mark. Monetäre Statistiken 1948–1997. 1991.01–2002.12: Bundesbank Time Series Data Base (http://www.bundesbank.de), series UX01NA). The wage measures are gross earnings in manufacturing and mining per employee (W_1) and per hour (W_2) (Observation period: 1991:01–2002:12, source: Bundesbank Time Series Data Base (http://www.bundesbank.de), series US07RB, US08RB) To deflate gross earnings, the consumer price index (CPI) is used (1950:01–1998:02: CDRom Deutsche Bundesbank – 50 Jahre Deutsche Mark. Monetäre Statistiken 1948–1997.1991.01–2002.12: Bundesbank Time Series Data Base (http://www.bundesbank.de), series UUFA01.)

Since the observation period is rather short, the robustness of the results for west Germany is checked by analyzing a second data set (quarterly data).[10] The observation period is 1964:01–1996:04, the data are manufacturing output (Y), employment (N), an index of hourly earnings in manufacturing (W, 1985=100) and the consumer price index (CPI, 1991=100, source: OECD Statistical Compendium, 2003–1, Main Economic Indicators. The employment data are from the CDRom Deutsche Bundesbank – 50 Jahre Deutsche Mark. Monetäre Statistiken 1948–1997).

3 Method

The results in Sect. 4 are based on a Threshold VAR (TVAR) model for the business cycle measure (percentage changes in output Y, employment N, or business cycle index IFO) and the percentage change in the real wage RW:

---

[9]I am grateful to the Ifo Institute for providing me with the data.

[10]Note that the second data set does not cover more observations. However, since the time span is longer (1964–1996), it covers more realisations of the business cycle.

$$\mathbf{X_t} = \begin{pmatrix} Y_t \\ RW_t \end{pmatrix} = \begin{cases} \mathbf{c}_1 + \sum_{j=1}^{p_1} \mathbf{A}_j \mathbf{X}_{t-j} + \boldsymbol{\epsilon}_t & \text{if } X_{1,t-d} \leq 0; \\ \mathbf{c}_2 + \sum_{j=1}^{p_2} \mathbf{B}_j \mathbf{X}_{t-j} + \boldsymbol{\eta}_t & \text{else} \end{cases}. \tag{1}$$

Whenever the growth rate representing the cycle at time $t - d$ is less than or equal to zero, the economy is deemed to be in a recession, and the first model is active. If the growth rate is positive, the second model describes the dynamic interaction between cycle and real wage. Note that d is set to zero because of the small sample size for West Germany.

The TVAR model in (1) is estimated adopting the strategy set out in Tong (1990). For a fixed threshold lag d and fixed VAR orders p_1 and p_2, the parameter matrices

$$\mathbf{A} = \left(\mathbf{c}_1 \ \mathbf{A}_1 \ldots \mathbf{A}_{p_1}\right), \qquad \mathbf{B} = \left(\mathbf{c}_1 \ \mathbf{B}_1 \ldots \mathbf{B}_{p_2}\right)$$

and the error variance-covariance matrices $\hat{\boldsymbol{\Sigma}}_1$ and $\hat{\boldsymbol{\Sigma}}_2$ are estimated using least squares. The VAR orders are determined by minimizing the Akaike information criterion (AIC), given d:[11]

$$AIC_{j,d} = N_j \ln |\tilde{\boldsymbol{\Sigma}}_j| + 2n(p_j + 1), \qquad j = 1, 2,$$

where n is the row dimension of $\mathbf{X}_t$, and N_j is the effective sample size. The matrix $\tilde{\boldsymbol{\Sigma}}_j$ is the LS estimator with degrees of freedom adjustment Lütkepohl (1991)

$$\tilde{\boldsymbol{\Sigma}}_j = \frac{N_j - p_j n - 1}{N_j} \hat{\boldsymbol{\Sigma}}$$

Let

$$NAIC_d = \frac{(AIC_{1,d} + AIC_{2,d})}{N_1 + N_2}$$

denote the average of the two minimum AIC values obtained for a given d. Minimizing $NAIC_d$ w.r.t. d gives the minimum AIC estimates for the TVAR. Because the purpose of this exercise is to examine differences in the cross-correlations dependent on the phase of the business cycle, the parameter space is restricted to stationary solutions. To ensure that the estimated system is stationary, we calculate the roots of the characteristic polynomial $|\mathbf{F}_j - \lambda \mathbf{I}| = 0$, where $\mathbf{F}_j$ is the companion matrix of the parameter matrices of the two models, and check whether the moduli are inside the unit circle Lütkepohl (1991).

Once the representative model is found, the cross corellation matrices can be obtained from the covariance matrices $\boldsymbol{\Gamma}(\tau)$ calculated using the Yule-Walker equations

[11] For the US data, the maximum lag is set to 10. Due to the small size of the west German sample, the maximum lag is set to 5, both for the quarterly and the monthly frequency.

$$\boldsymbol{\Gamma}(0) = \sum_{j=1}^{p_1} \mathbf{A}_j \boldsymbol{\Gamma}(-j) + \boldsymbol{\Sigma}_1;$$

$$\boldsymbol{\Gamma}(0) = \sum_{j=1}^{p_2} \mathbf{B}_j \boldsymbol{\Gamma}(-j) + \boldsymbol{\Sigma}_2;$$

and for $\tau > 0$,

$$\boldsymbol{\Gamma}(\tau) = \sum_{j=1}^{p_1} \mathbf{A}_j \boldsymbol{\Gamma}(\tau - j);$$

$$\boldsymbol{\Gamma}(\tau) = \sum_{j=1}^{p_2} \mathbf{B}_j \boldsymbol{\Gamma}(\tau - j).$$

The first p_j covariance matrices needed as starting values for the recursion are derived from the VAR(1) representation of the two models Lütkepohl (1991). As Tong (1990) points out in Theorems 5.7 and 5.8, approximate standard errors can be obtained from standard regression theory, conditional on the threshold lag d and the VAR orders p_1 and p_2. Significance of the cross-correlations is established by calculating standard errors from a parametric bootstrap of the two models (2000 replications).

4 Results

The correlation coefficents implied by the models fitted to the three data sets are displayed in Tables 2 and 3. More detailed estimation results can be found in Table 4. This table contains the two VAR orders p_1 and p_2, as well as the effective sample sizes N_1 and N_2. The maximum absolute eigenvalues and the maximum period length calculated from the roots of the characteristic polynomial help to judge differences in the dynamics during different phases of the business cycle. For example, when using output as measure for the cycle in the US case, the average maximum cycle length during an upswing is estimated as 67.8 months, while it is 26.3 months during a downswing. Especially the result for the downswing is very close to the business cycle duration in the US. As discussed above, the NBER calculates an average duration of the contraction phase of 11 months for the period after 1960. This is almost exactly half the cycle length estimated for the downswing. With German monthly output data, the average maximum cycle length in an upswing is 68.9 months and 23 months in a downswing, which is very close to the outcome for the US. Using the monthly Ifo indices as cycle measure results in shorter cycles (33.1 months in an upswing, 20 months in a downswing). In the case of the US, the maximum absolute eigenvalues do not depend on the phase of the business cycle. On average, we obtain 0.95 in an uspwing and 0.97 in a downswing. For the German monthly output series, the averages are lower, but also very close (0.88 in an upswing and 0.86 in a downswing). Using the Ifo indices produces different results: one obtains an average of 0.94 in an upswing and 0.85 in a downswing.

Turning to the correlations, the first striking difference between real wage cyclicality in Germany and the US is that for Germany, there is much less evidence of asymmetric correlations. In the US, both average hourly earnings and average hourly earnings excluding overtime show procyclical behavior in an upswing if output is used as a measure for the cycle and if the nominal wage is deflated using the CPI. With PPI as deflator, real wages fluctuate countercyclically during a downswing. With employment as cycle measure, there is some evidence of weak procyclical fluctuations when looking at average hourly earnings. With the exception of average hourly earnings excluding overtime deflated with PPI, which are countercyclical during a downswing, all the other results point towards acyclical fluctuations.

Given the stylized model predictions from Table 1, one can conclude that the relationship between business cycles and real wages in the US are best characterized by models with sticky nominal wages, while there is also some evidence of RBC type fluctuations.[12] A sticky price model which predicts a countercyclical relationship fits only for wages excluding overtime deflated with PPI during a contraction of the economy.

Table 2. Correlation between Real Wage and Business Cycle Measures (USA)

	Y		N	
	Upswing	Downswing	Upswing	Downswing
A/CPI	0.52	0.14	0.23	0.28
	(0.08)	(0.08)	(0.10)	(0.10)
A/PPI	0.20	−0.47	−0.04	−0.06
	(0.11)	(0.11)	(0.12)	(0.11)
W/CPI	0.34	−0.06	0.08	−0.16
	(0.10)	(0.08)	(0.13)	(0.08)
W/PPI	0.08	−0.65	−0.15	−0.35
	(0.13)	(0.12)	(0.13)	(0.09)

Notes:
A: average hourly earnings, W: average hourly earnings excluding overtime, CPI: consumer price index, PPI: producer price index, Y: output, N: employment. The figures in brackets are bootstrap standard errors.

With the results for West Germany, the case for a countercyclical relationship is much stronger: 50 per cent of the real wage/cycle measure pairs show a negative correlation. In two cases, there is a significant positive correlation,

[12] This is in line with the results reported in Malley, Muscatelli, and Woitek (forthcoming).

but just during a contraction. Based on these results one can conclude that Germany is better characterized by New Keynesian type models than the US. This conclusion is obviously in line with the institutional differences between the two labour markets.

Table 3. Correlation between Real Wage and Business Cycle Measures (West Germany)

Quarterly Data	Y		N	
	Upswing	Downswing	Upswing	Downswing
E_1/CPI	0.20	−0.38	0.07	−0.17
	(0.16)	(0.10)	(0.19)	(0.10)
Monthly Data	$E2/CPI$		$E3/CPI$	
	Upswing	Downswing	Upswing	Downswing
Y	−0.01	0.41	−0.31	−0.02
	(0.12)	(0.07)	(0.13)	(0.09)
$IFO1$	−0.40	0.07	−0.79	−0.37
	(0.11)	(0.11)	(0.08)	(0.10)
$IFO2$	−0.18	0.46	−0.68	−0.19
	(0.13)	(0.11)	(0.12)	(0.13)
$IFO3$	−0.35	−0.24	−0.50	−0.29
	(0.12)	(0.12)	(0.12)	(0.11)

Notes:
Y: output; $IFO1$: current climate index, $IFO2$: expectations index; $IFO3$: composite index; CPI: consumer price index; E_1: hourly earnings (quarterly data); E_2: earnings per employee (monthly data); E_2: earnings per hour (monthly data). The figures in brackets are bootstrap standard errors.

5 Conclusions

This paper analyzes the cyclicality between real wages and the business cycle by looking at data sets for the US and for Germany. Using a threshold vector autoregressive model to calculate correlation coefficients dependent on the phase of the cycle, it is demonstrated that the result does not only depend on measurement problems, estimation method and composition bias, but also on whether the economy is in an upswing or a downswing: if there is asymmetry in the relationship between the real wage and the cycle, significant correlations might cancel out if calculated without conditioning on the phase of the cycle. In general, the evidence for countercyclical real wages is stronger for Germany than for the US, but taken together, there is no systematic pattern.

An interesting extension would be to look not just for differences in the cyclicality of the real wage conditional on the phase of the business cycle, but to see whether there are changes over time. It is striking that studies with observation periods up to the 1970s find countercyclical results (e.g. Sargent (1978), Neftci (1978)), while more recent work concludes that the evidence for procyclical real wages is much stronger. Identifying the transition from one regime to the other and comparing it across countries could help in further understanding the interaction between the real wage and the business cycle.

A Appendix

Table 4. Estimation Results, USA and West Germany

Business Cycle	Real Wage	p_1	p_2	$\|\lambda_1\|$	$\|\lambda_2\|$	P_1	P_2	N_1	N_2
USA, Monthly Data									
Y	A/CPI	10	7	0.93	0.89	67.23	20.75	460	59
	A/PPI	10	9	0.93	0.98	65.59	30.47	460	47
	W/CPI	10	7	0.93	0.91	71.92	21.78	460	59
	W/PPI	10	9	0.94	0.99	66.43	32.13	460	47
N	A/CPI	10	10	0.97	0.99	68.88	31.63	387	115
	A/PPI	10	8	0.97	0.99	73.94	61.69	387	131
	W/CPI	10	10	0.96	0.99	71.87	36.15	387	115
	W/PPI	10	8	0.98	0.99	75.48	71.75	387	131
Germany, Quarterly Data									
Y	E_1/CPI	3	3	0.89	0.73	14.27	23.15	137	18
N	E_1/CPI	3	3	0.84	0.92	24.63	10.48	111	44
Germany, Monthly Data									
Y	E_2/CPI	3	3	0.88	0.85	3.06	20.86	106	29
	E_3/CPI	3	3	0.87	0.87	134.82	25.20	106	29
$IFO1$	E_2/CPI	5	3	0.93	0.89	37.91	18.28	84	59
	E_3/CPI	5	3	0.94	0.89	36.75	16.88	84	59
$IFO2$	E_2/CPI	5	3	0.98	0.89	34.45	27.11	76	67
	E_3/CPI	5	3	0.99	0.88	34.43	27.51	76	67
$IFO3$	E_2/CPI	5	2	0.89	0.77	26.23	16.07	87	61
	E_3/CPI	5	3	0.92	0.79	28.93	13.90	87	57

Notes:
Y: output; N: employment; $IFO1$: current climate index, $IFO2$: expectations index; $IFO3$: composite index.
CPI: consumer price index, PPI: producer price index.
A: average hourly earnings (USA),
W: average hourly earnings excluding overtime (USA);
E_1: hourly earnings (west Germany, quarterly data); E_2: earnings per employee (west Germany, monthly data); E_2: earnings per hour (west Germany, monthly data).
p_1, p_2: VAR orders; $|\lambda_1|, |\lambda_2|$ maximum absolute eigenvalue; P_1, P_2: maximum period length; N_1, N_2: effective sample sizes.

References

ABRAHAM, K. G., AND J. C. HALTIWANGER (1995): "Real Wages and the Business Cycle," *Journal of Economic Literature*, XXXIII, 1215–1264.

ALTISSIMO, F., AND G. L. VIOLANTE (2001): "The Non-Linear Dynamics of Output and Unemployment in the U.S.," *Journal of Applied Econometrics*, 16, 461–486.

BEAUDRY, P., AND G. KOOP (1993): "Do Recessions Permanently Change Output?," *Journal of Monetary Economics*, 31, 149–164.

BILS, M. (1985): "Real Wages over the Business Cycle: Evidence from Panel Data," *Journal of Political Economy*, 93, 666–689.

BODKIN, R. G. (1969): "Real Wages and Cyclical Variations in Employment: A Re-Examination of the Evidence," *Canadian Journal of Economics*, 2, 353–374.

CHIRINKO, R. S. (1980): "The Real Wage Rate over the Business Cycle," *Review of Economics and Statistics*, 62, 459–461.

DELONG, J. B., AND L. SUMMERS (1986): "Are Business Cycles Symmetrical?," in *The American Business Cycle: Continuity and Change*, ed. by R. J. Gordon. University of Chicago Press, Chicago.

FLEISCHMANN, C. A. (1999): "The Cause of Business Cycles and the Cyclicality of Real Wages," Finance and Economics Discussion Series 1999-53, Board of Governors of the Federal Reserve System (U.S.).

GALI, J. (1999): "Technology, Employment, and the Business Cycle: Do Technology Shocks Explain Aggregate Fluctuations?," *American Economic Review*, 89, 249–271.

GEARY, P. T., AND J. KENNAN (1982): "The Employment-Real Wage Relationship: An International Study," *Journal of Political Economy*, 90, 854–871.

GOODFRIEND, M., AND R. G. KING (1997): "The New Neoclassical Synthesis and the Role of Monetary Policy," *NBER Macroeconomics Annual*, 12, 231–282.

HAMILTON, J. D. (1989): "A New Approach to the Economic Analysis of Nonstationary Time Series and the Business Cycle," *Econometrica*, 57, 357–384.

HART, R. A., J. R. MALLEY, AND U. WOITEK (2002): "Manufacturing Earnings and Cycles: New Evidence," Working Paper 2002-16, University of Glasgow, Department of Economics.

KING, R. G., AND C. I. PLOSSER (1984): "Money, Credit, and Prices in a Real Business Cycle," *American Economic Review*, 24, 363–380.

KOOP, G., AND S. M. POTTER (1999): "Dynamic Asymmetries in U.S. Unemployment," *Journal of Business and Economics Statistics*, 17, 298–312.

KYDLAND, F. E., AND E. C. PRESCOTT (1982): "Time to Build and Aggregate Fluctuations," *Econometrica*, 50, 1345–1370.

LIU, H. (2003): "A Cross-Country Comparison on the Cyclicality of Real Wages," *Canadian Journal of Economics*, 36, 923–948.

LONG, J. B., AND C. I. PLOSSER (1983): "Real Business Cycles," *Journal of Political Economy*, 91, 36–69.

LÜTKEPOHL, H. (1991): *Introduction to Multiple Time Series Analysis.* Springer, Berlin, Heidelberg, New York, Tokio.

MALLEY, J. R., V. A. MUSCATELLI, AND U. WOITEK (forthcoming): "Real Business Cycles or Sticky Prices? The Impact of Technology Shocks on US Manufacturing," *European Economic Review.*

NEFTCI, S. N. (1978): "A Time Series Analysis of the Real Wages-Employment Relationship," *Journal of Political Economy*, 86, 281–291.

Otani, I. (1978): "Real Wages and Business Cycles Revisited," *Review of Economics and Statistics*, 6, 301–304.

Pesaran, M. H., and S. M. Potter (1997): "A Floor and Ceiling Model of U.S. Output," *Journal of Economic Dynamics and Control*, 21, 661–698.

Potter, S. M. (1995): "A Nonlinear Approach to U.S. GNP," *Journal of Applied Econometrics*, 10, 109–125.

Rotemberg, J., and M. Woodford (1997): "An Optimisation Based Econometric Framework for the Evaluation of Monetary Policy," *NBER Macroeconomics Annual*, 12, 297–345.

Rothman, P. (1991): "Further Evidence on the Asymmetric Behavior of Unemployment Rates over the Business Cycle," *Journal of Macroeconomics*, 13, 291–298.

Sargent, T. J. (1978): "Estimation of Dynamic Labor Demand Schedules under Rational Expectations," *Journal of Political Economy*, 86, 1009–1044.

Solon, G., R. Barsky, and J. A. Parker (1994): "Measuring the Cyclicality of Real Wages: How Important is Composition Bias?," *Quarterly Journal of Economics*, 109, 1–26.

Sumner, S., and S. Silver (1989): "Real Wages, Employment and the Phillips Curve," *Journal of Political Economy*, 97, 706–720.

Tong, H. (1990): *Non-linear Time Series. A Dynamical System Approach.* Oxford University Press, Oxford.

Evaluating the German Inventory Cycle Using Data from the Ifo Business Survey

Thomas A. Knetsch*

Deutsche Bundesbank, Economics Department, Wilhelm-Epstein-Str. 14, 60431 Frankfurt am Main, Germany thomas.knetsch@bundesbank.de

1 Introduction

Amongst business cycle analysts, the German national accounts statistics of inventory investment are regarded as being unreliable as far as preliminary data releases are concerned. However, especially around cyclical turning points, judgement on current and future trends in inventories often plays an important role in the diagnosis of recent economic developments as well as in short-term macroeconomic forecasting.

In fact, the pro-cyclical movement of inventory investment in business cycles is a result which is well established both in economic theory and in empirical studies.[1] From the theoretical perspective, the key reference is still Metzler's (1994) inventory accelerator mechanism, which is based on the traditional production-smoothing/buffer-stock hypothesis of inventory behavior.[2] Empirical evidence proves the destabilizing effect of inventory investment on aggregate output.[3] In applied business cycle research, inventory fluctuations

*The author would like to thank Erich Langmantel for a stimulating discussion as well as Jörg Breitung, Jörg Döpke, Hermann-Josef Hansen, Heinz Herrmann and the participants of the CESifo workshop for valuable comments and suggestions. Of course, the author is fully responsible for all remaining shortcomings. The paper expresses the author's personal opinion, which does not necessarily reflect the views of the Deutsche Bundesbank.

[1]Recent survey articles stressing this result are Ramey and West (1999) and Blinder and Maccini (1991).

[2]Since the early 1980s, the production-smoothing/buffer-stock hypothesis has been called into question. A strand of literature, perhaps initiated by Blinder (1981), argues in favor of the so-called (S,s) approach to inventory behavior which stresses the stock-out problem: whenever inventory stocks are expected to reach a critical lower margin s, firms are going to replenish stockholdings up to the upper limit S. On the micro level, the implications of this hypothesis are quite different.

[3]An early comprehensive study of the impact of inventory fluctuations on business cycle movements is Abramovitz (1950). Apart from the above-cited references,

are seen as being central to the explanation of minor business cycles.[4] Furthermore, it is argued that destocking is an important phenomenon during recessions.

Against this background, it is surprising that the statistical basis for an analysis of inventory investment is extraordinarily weak in the German national accounts. Since the conversion to the European System of Accounts 1995 (ESA 95), the primary basis for the compilation of changes in inventories, i.e. annual data on inventory stocks in sectoral division, has no longer been published. In the preliminary releases of quarterly national accounts, inventory changes are (to a large extent) measured as a residual when reconciling the production and the expenditure concept of GDP. As a consequence of this approach, preliminary data on inventory investment are tremendously prone to revision and thus highly unreliable.[5]

It is therefore important to base the judgement on the current stance of the inventory cycle on alternative sources. On a monthly basis, the Ifo Institute publishes survey data on the assessment of inventory stocks in manufacturing as well as in the retail and wholesale trade sector. Although the survey on manufacturers' inventories only captures stocks of finished goods, (virtually) all sectors holding significant proportions of inventories are considered in this data set. Furthermore, survey data is available in a timely manner and free of revisions.

However, in order to obtain an aggregate measure of inventory fluctuations, one has to address the issue of amalgamating information from different sources. In order to construct a composite index of inventory fluctuations, we will apply different methodologies. The composite index may be given by the codependent cycle of the three Ifo series at hand, which is identified by analyzing canonical correlations. Alternatively, the common factor might be obtained by means of classical static factor analysis. In an investigation based on recursive estimates of the composite indices, the methods are compared with respect to the stability of the weighting schemes.

We will further show that, regardless of which composite index is considered, the use of Ifo survey data helps to explain the difference between the first and the "final" release of inventory investment in the national accounts statistics. Moreover, simple indicator-based forecasting models clearly outperform the first announcement of the Statistisches Bundesamt in predicting the "true" picture of the inventory fluctuations. Hence there might be an ongoing debate on the best way of extracting the common factor from the Ifo series. However, it turns out to be rather clear that, as regards the aggregate in-

detailed inquiries of inventory fluctuations are presented in Blinder and Holtz-Eakin (1986) for the United States as well as in Knetsch (2004) and Döpke and Langfeldt (1997) for Germany.

[4] See Zarnowitz (1985) and Moore and Zarnowitz (1986), for instance.

[5] Even for the United States where primary statistics of inventories are much more detailed, inventory investment figures are often revised substantially. See Howrey (1984).

ventory fluctuations of the German economy, the Ifo business survey provides information which is most reliable in a real-time forecasting exercise.

The remainder of the paper is organized as follows. In Sect. 2, we first study the time series properties of our reference, the seasonally adjusted series of real inventory investment drawn from the German national accounts. We also illustrate to which extent this series has been revised in recent years. Then, we present time series characteristics of the three Ifo indicator series including a discussion on their comovement with the reference, both in the time and the frequency domain. In Sect. 3, we construct a composite index of inventory fluctuations by extracting the common factor from the Ifo series by means of canonical correlation and static factor analysis. In Sect. 4, an evaluation of the methods is presented which is based on recursive estimates. In this context, two criteria are of interest: the stability of the weighting schemes in the case of re-estimation with an updated data set and the predictive content for "true" inventory cycle movements. Finally, Sect. 5 presents a conclusion.

2 Time Series Properties of the Reference and the Ifo Indicator Series

The first part of this section is devoted to a discussion of the seasonally and working-day adjusted time series properties of inventory investment in real terms as published in the national accounts. We will argue that the series shows cyclical features which are usually attributed to inventory fluctuations. Therefore, the national accounts data on inventory investment serve as our reference series in the sense that it generally approximates the inventory cycle of the German economy.

At the end of sample, however, the series is tremendously prone to revision. Hence, in order to assess the current stance of the inventory cycle or to forecast its prospective path, it is necessary to rely on different data sources. We will show that the inventory series published in the Ifo business survey are good candidates in this respect because they fulfill the important indicator property of a high correlation with the reference. In the second part of the section, this strong empirical connection is documented by using standard time series techniques.

2.1 The Time Series of Inventory Investment

Figure 1 shows the plot of the time series of inventory investment in the sample between the first quarter of 1970 and the second quarter of 2003. Whereas the data prior to 1991 refer to West Germany, the whole series is measured using the ESA 95 principles.[6]

[6]In that respect, this paper differs from Knetsch (2004), in which the West German series measured according to the previous accounting standards was chained up

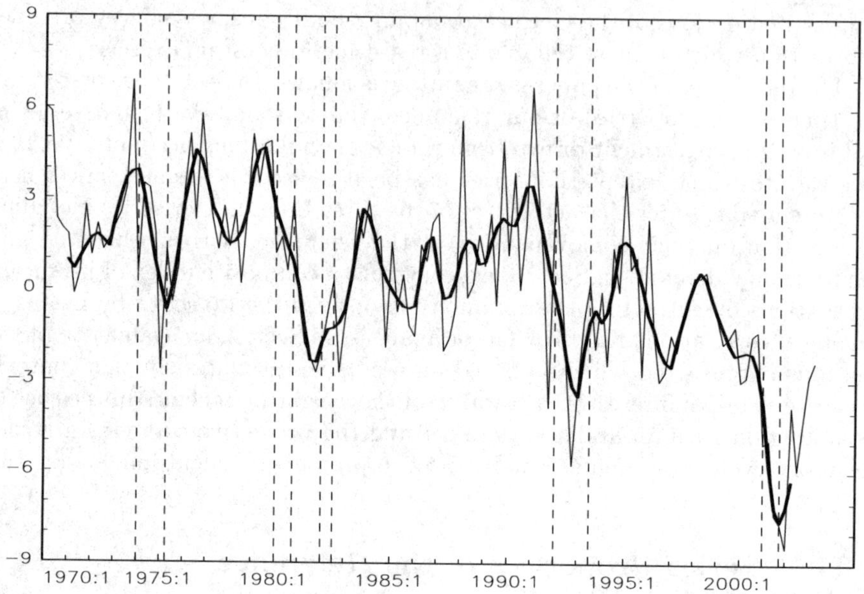

Inventory investment is seasonally and working-day adjusted and measured in billions of 1995 euro. Source: National accounts published in August 2003. The original series is plotted by the solid line and the filtered series by the thick line. Vertical lines indicate the beginning and the end of the recession periods (technically defined).

Fig. 1. Series of Inventory Investment

Because of dominating erratic variations,[7] it is convenient to filter the series using an optimal low-pass filter which only lets oscillations longer than $1\frac{1}{2}$ years pass.[8] Simply by counting the peaks and troughs of the filtered series, we observe eight full inventory cycles in 30 years which leads (in a purely arithmetical sense) to an average periodicity of $3\frac{3}{4}$ years. In the traditional

with the series for (unified) Germany measured according to the ESA 95 principles. In the series used here, there is only a statistical break owing to the unification but no longer a break owing to the change in the accounting standards at the same date. Further information on the statistical breaks during the 1990s is given in Appendix A.2.

[7]The erratic fluctuations are (to some extent) a result of the seasonal and calendar adjustment procedure applied: since the aggregates of the production and the expenditure side of GDP are separately adjusted for seasonal and calendar effects, statistical discrepancies are almost certain to arise. By convention, the remaining seasonal and calendar effects are attributed to the series of inventory investment in order to meet the GDP accounting identity.

[8]The filter lag length is 4. For the construction of this type of filter, see Baxter and King (1999), for instance.

classification of cycle movements, such a duration fits to the class of so-called "Kitchin cycles" (i.e. about three to four years) which are usually attributed to inventory fluctuations.[9]

Further important stylized facts concern the relationship of inventory changes to aggregate fluctuations.[10] In macroeconomics, it is common knowledge that inventories are a destabilizing factor in business cycles. During recessions, we usually observe that firms reduce inventory stocks by a sizeable amount. A look at Fig. 1 shows that there is strong destocking during all cyclical downturns in Germany since 1970.[11]

By visual evidence, we therefore conclude that the series of inventory investment as published in the national accounts shows features typically attributable to aggregate inventory behavior which is known from economic theory and which is supported by empirical results from countries (such as the United States) where the statistical basis for compiling the figures of inventory investment is less weak than in Germany. Although we claim that national accounts data on inventory investment are generally appropriate as a proxy of aggregate inventory behavior in a historical perspective, we will show right now that the use of those figures for the purpose of current business cycle diagnosis and short-term forecasting is rather dangerous.

Figure 2 highlights the fact that the data on inventory investment are very susceptible to revision. It is worth mentioning that those revisions are for the most part a consequence of the poor quality of the original data.[12] The reasons for that are evident: As a product of the evaluation of the inquiries about the cost structures of firms, data on inventory stocks in sectoral division are only ascertained in annual periodicity and with a considerable time lag.[13] Since the conversion to ESA 95, these data have no longer been published. In the preliminary releases of quarterly national accounts, however, inventory changes are (to a large extent) determined as a residual of GDP (compiled according to the production concept) and the sum of the expenditure aggregates.[14] Since these quantities are measured with uncertainty, preliminary figures of inventory investment also include statistical discrepancies. After two years or so,

---

[9]The cycle classification is sketched in Moore and Zarnowitz (1986), for instance.

[10]For a closer look at the stylized facts of the German inventory cycle, see Knetsch (2004), for instance.

[11]For simplicity, recessions are dated using the mechanical rule that seasonally adjusted real GDP declines in at least two consecutive quarters.

[12]Another source of revisions is the seasonal adjustment procedure. However, revisions induced by that are thought to be of limited extent compared to changes in raw data.

[13]For the compilation of inventory investment based on sectoral inventory stocks, see Statistisches Bundesamt (2003), pp.295–304.

[14]As mentioned in Braakmann (2003), for the preparation of new quarterly figures, the Statistisches Bundesamt has recently started using the Ifo business survey on the assessment of inventory stocks to cross-check the general adequacy of the figure which comes out of the residual accounting and which is called inventory investment.

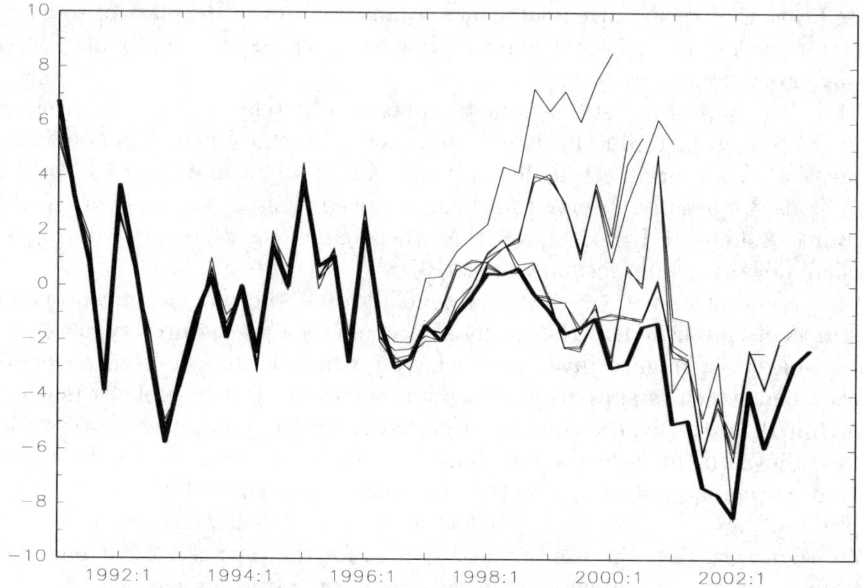

The last 14 releases of seasonally adjusted changes in inventories (in billions of 1995 euro) are plotted with regard to the publications of the national accounts from May 2000 through August 2003. The current release is plotted by the thick line.

Fig. 2. Data Revisions with Respect to Inventory Investment

when detailed statistical information (such as the results of the value-added tax statistics and the inquiries about the cost structures of firms) are incorporated into the system of national accounts, the inventory investment figures are more or less free of that kind of mismeasurement.

For the above-mentioned purposes, waiting for two years is not a feasible option. Hence, we search for other data sources which enable us to proxy the German inventory cycle with timeliness and reliability.

2.2 The Ifo Indicator Series

In its business survey, the Ifo Institute asks the participating firms to assess inventory stocks. Firms in manufacturing as well as in the retail and wholesale trade sector are invited to give their view on whether inventories are regarded as being too small, sufficient/normal (in seasonal terms), or too big. The individual qualitative answers are aggregated by weighting the proportion of positive and negative replies. For interpretational reasons, the scale of the aggregates is inverted because an increasing proportion of firms reporting too small inventory stocks indicates a rising expansive pressure on upstream

Table 1. Cross-Correlation Between Indicators and Inventory Investment

Indicator	lag			coin.	lead		
	−3	−2	−1	0	+1	+2	+3
Manufacturers' Invent.	.06	.18$^{(\star)}$	.28**	**.36****	.35**	.23*	.09
Retail Traders' Invent.	.24*	.29**	.28**	.35**	.33**	**.40****	.31**
Wholesale Traders' Invent.	−.03	.06	.16	.24*	.31*	**.37****	.25*

Correlations between the indicators and the respective lead or lag of the series of inventory investment are reported. **,* ,$^{(\star)}$ means rejection of the null hypothesis of no cross-correlation at the 1%, 5% and 10% level, respectively. Standard errors are calculated using Newey and West (1987) heteroskedasticity and autocorrelation consistent covariance; lag truncation is 4. The largest correlation is printed in bold.

sectors in the value-added chain and vice versa.[15] On a monthly basis, the Ifo institute publishes indicators for manufacturers' assessment of inventory stocks of finished goods and for the assessments of stockholdings in retail and wholesale trade. Whereas the former indicator includes East German firms, the latter two only correspond to the West German trade sector.

To avoid problems which potentially arise from different scales, the three series used are standardized such that they possess zero means and unit variances. In Fig. 3, the quarterly averages of the Ifo series are plotted in the sample between the first quarter of 1970 and the second quarter of 2003.[16] In general, all series show a cyclical pattern, although it is not always clear-cut. Whereas the series of manufacturers' inventories is (surprisingly) smooth, depicting cycles of appropriate duration and clear turning points, the series of retail and wholesale traders' inventories are much more erratic. Apart from some short-term fluctuations, at least the series attached to wholesale trade is clearly oscillating at inventory cycle frequencies.

It is interesting to have a look at the cross-correlations between the Ifo series and inventory investment for the following reasons. First, only if the Ifo series are correlated with the reference to a sufficiently large extent, can they serve as indicators for the inventory cycle. Second, in order to simplify the interpretation of the results of the statistical methodologies which will be applied in the subsequent section, it is worth knowing whether or not there are phase shifts between the series.

In Table 1, we report the estimates of cross-correlations between the Ifo series and inventory investment in the sample from the first quarter of 1970 through the final quarter of 2001.[17] Since the results show significant cross-

[15] Further details on the Ifo business survey are given by Oppenländer and Poser (1989).

[16] We plot the time series on the basis of quarterly averages for the sake of better visibility of (potential) cycling at business cycle frequencies.

[17] The final observations are dropped from the analysis for two reasons. First, we

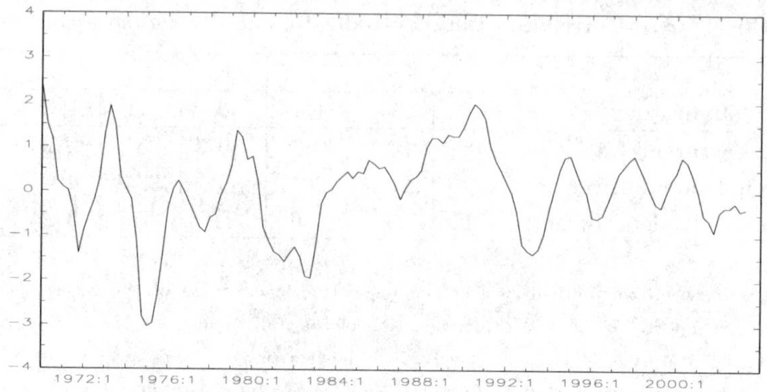

Fig. 3. (a) Assessment of Manufacturers' Inventory Stocks

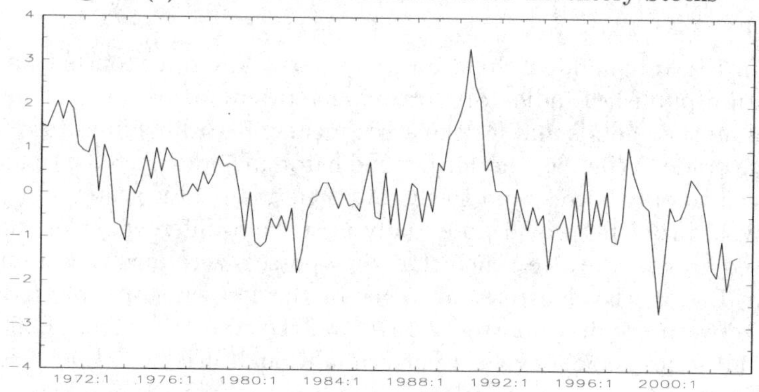

Fig. 3. (b) Assessment of Retail Traders' Inventory Stocks

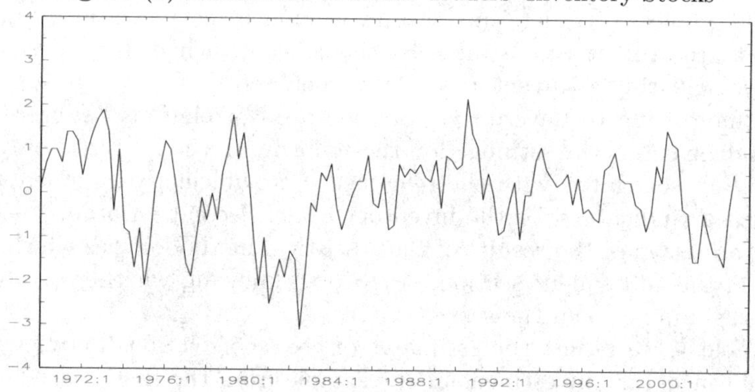

Fig. 3. (c) Assessment of Wholesale Traders' Inventory Stocks

A positive value indicates that, in the aggregate, inventory stocks are regarded as being "favorable" which means that the proportion of "too big" judgements (relative to the sum of "too big" and "too small" answers) is below average. A negative value indicates an "unfavorable" stance in that sense.

Fig. 3. Ifo Indicator Plots

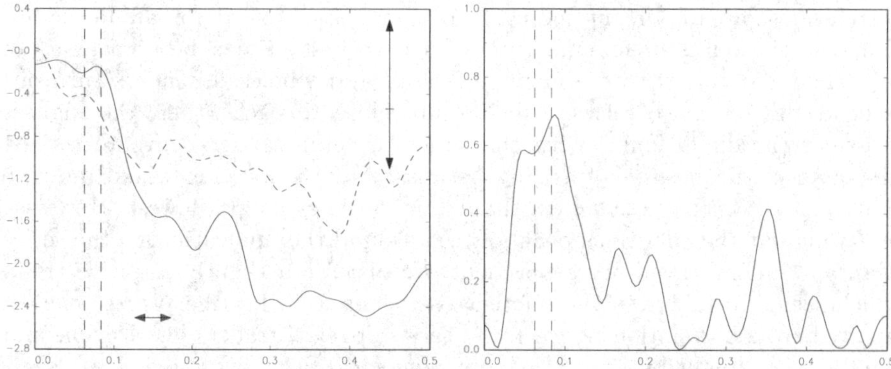

Fig. 4. (a) Assessment of Manufacturers' Inventory Stocks

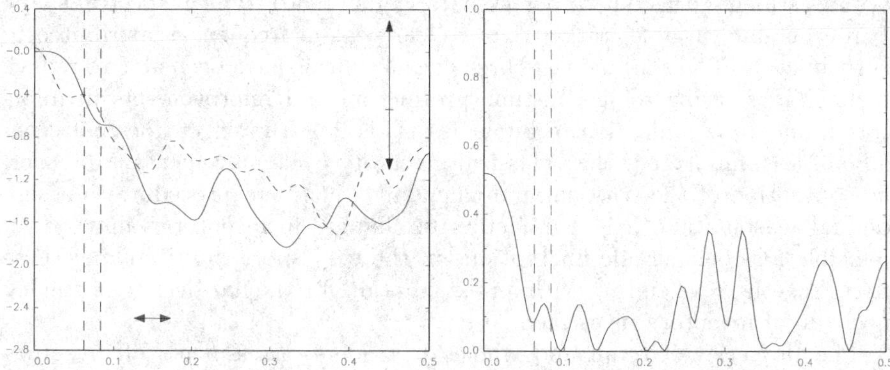

Fig. 4. (b) Assessment of Retail Traders' Inventory Stocks

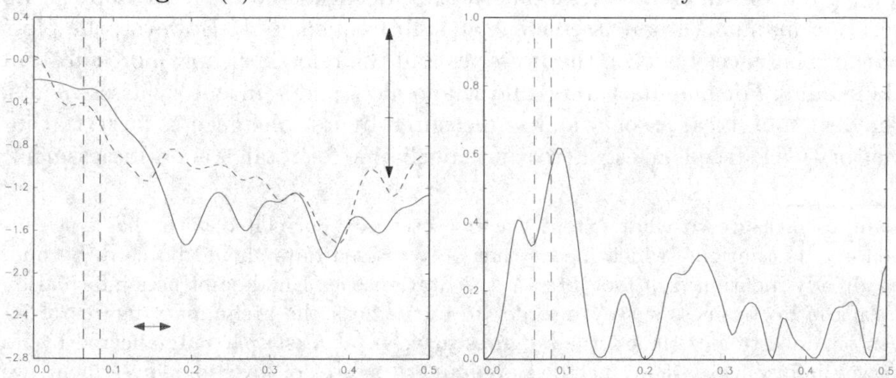

Fig. 4. (c) Assessment of Wholesale Traders' Inventory Stocks

On the left-hand side, the graphs depict the log spectra of the respective Ifo series (solid line) and inventory investment (broken line). On the right-hand side, the graphs show the coherence between those series. Spectra and cross-spectra are estimated using 128 data points and 40 co-variances. The horizontal arrow depicts the bandwidth of the Parzen window used. The vertical arrow shows the asymptotical 90% confidence bands of the estimation of the log spectrum. The abscissa scale is frequency divided by 2π. The broken vertical lines indicate frequencies attributed to periodicities of three and four years.

Fig. 4. Spectra and Coherences

correlations, an important indicator property is satisfied for all Ifo series. Whereas the series of manufacturers' inventory stock can be seen as a coincident indicator, the assessments of retail and wholesale traders turn out to lead the reference series. Albeit quite close to each other, the highest cross-correlation is found with the series of retail traders' inventories. At first glance, this result is puzzling because visual inspection would indicate that, just between these series, the extent of co-cycling is lowest. However, by fading out the enormous peak located around the unification, in the series of retail traders' inventory assessment, we observe a slightly negative trend which seems to inhere in the reference series as well. In other words, the estimated cross-correlation between the series of retail traders' assessment and the reference might be a result of comovement at very low frequencies.

In Fig. 4, the log spectra and coherences of the series are plotted. Inventory investment turns out to possess Granger's (1966) "typical spectral shape of an economic variable" rather than a clear peak at frequencies attributed to "Kitchin cycles". During the last three decades, firms have been able to reduce stockholdings owing to just-in-time production and improvements in information and communication technologies. This long-run effect does not seem to be of less importance than classical inventory cycle movements. Moreover, the convention of the seasonal and calendar adjustment procedure to assign residual seasonal and calendar factors to changes in inventories may be responsible for considerable fluctuations in the very short run.[18] Taking these effects together, we end up with an explanation for the flat decline of the log spectrum of inventory investment.

The Ifo series of retail and wholesale traders' assessments of inventory stocks virtually mimics the reference series in terms of spectral shape. If at all, significant differences turn out to exist between the reference and the Ifo series of manufacturers' assessment at high frequencies.[19] However, the plots of the coherences between the Ifo series and the reference show more substantial results. For manufacturers' and wholesale traders' inventory assessments, the degree of linear association, as measured by its coherence, is largest at inventory cycle frequencies whereas it is negligible for retail traders' assessment.

---

want to measure to what extent the Ifo series are correlated with the "true" inventory fluctuations, which means that only revised data should be used. Second, as already mentioned in footnote 14, the Statistisches Bundesamt uses information from the Ifo business survey in order to cross-check the preliminary figures of inventory investment. Hence, these figures may be (at least) partially affected by Ifo survey information. If we included preliminary figures of inventory investment, we would risk measuring artificial correlations.

[18] See also footnote 7.

[19] Since spectra and coherences are intended to show details in the range of business cycle frequencies, a short bandwidth has been chosen. As a consequence, the uncertainty surrounding the estimation of the spectra is rather high. It is worth mentioning that the general characteristics of the spectral shapes remain unaffected if fewer covariances are used for the estimations.

In the latter case, the absolute peak of the coherence is observed around the zero frequency.

In sum, the Ifo series under consideration may generally serve as indicators of inventory planning of German firms. Whereas the Ifo data of retailers' inventory assessment seem to replicate the general tendency to reduce stockholdings in the past decades, manufacturers' and wholesale traders' assessments show a large extent of co-cycling with the reference at frequencies which are typically attributed to inventory cycle movements. Hence, it is worth considering all indicators at hand because each of them provides specific information.

3 Composite Indices of Inventory Fluctuations

On a monthly basis, the Ifo business survey publishes three series which can generally serve as indicators of inventory fluctuations in Germany. Since several individual indicators may send different signals, one has to decide either to trust only one of them, say, manufacturers' assessment of inventories of finished goods or to construct a composite index amalgamating the information provided by all indicators. In principle, the latter approach aims at extracting comovement of the indicator series at hand.[20] In factor models which have recently become popular, comovement is represented by a (small) number of common factors. An alternative strategy is to identify so-called codependent cycles in a vector autoregressive model. This can be done by using canonical correlation analysis.

The composite indices which will be constructed on the basis of these two methodologies share the simple design. Namely, they can be explicitly or implicitly expressed as a weighted average of the Ifo series.

3.1 Codependent Cycle Analysis

The concept of codependent cycles was introduced by Vahid and Engle (1997) building on an earlier paper written by Gouriéroux and Peaucelle (1992). Two stationary series bearing considerable serial correlation are said to possess a codependent cycle if there is a linear combination between the two which can be represented by a moving average of a very short order, say q [MA(q)]. From that definition, it is clear that codependence relations are unpredictable at horizons larger than q.

It is worth mentioning that the idea of codependent cycles generalizes Engle and Kozicki's (1993) concept of common cycles, which requires that the linear combination be white noise (or unpredictable at all horizons). Whereas

[20] In the present analysis, we only use the three Ifo series. The decision not to use a production-sales index is due to a conceptual change in the statistic of monthly industrial turnover which disturbed the stable relation between production, turnover and producer prices documented in Knetsch (2004).

Table 2. Tests for Codependent Cycles

# Codep. Vectors	Degrees of Freedom	Order of moving average			
		0	1	2	3
1	10	85.11**	24.41**	17.29(*)	6.85
2	22	229.95**	74.80**	47.26**	27.73
3	36	1083.36**	179.91**	103.23**	64.93**

The null hypothesis is that the number of codependent vectors is equal to (or greater than) indicated. Test statistics are asymptotically χ^2-distributed with the reported number of degrees of freedom. **,* ,(*) mean rejection at the 1%, 5% and 10% level, respectively.

co-cycling between the original series needs to be exactly synchronized in the case of common cycles, the more general concept allows for possible phase shifts. In recalling the results of the previous section, if at all, we should only succeed in identifying codependent cycles.

In a system of K variables, there may exist up to $K-1$ independent codependence relations. Given an autoregressive model of order p for the K-dimensional vector x_t, one can test for the number of codependence vectors using a statistic proposed by Tiao and Tsay (1989), which builds on a canonical correlation analysis between x_t and $(x_{t-q-1}, ..., x_{t-q-1-p})$. In fact, the number of zero canonical correlations determines the number of MA(q) codependence vectors. The test statistic for the null hypothesis that there are (at least) s MA(q) codependent vectors is given as follows:

$$\mathrm{C}(s;q) = -(T-p-q)\sum_{i=1}^{s} \ln(1-\lambda_i(q)) \tag{1}$$

where T is the number of observations and $\lambda_i(q)$ the ith smallest squared canonical correlation corrected for the sample autocorrelation of the canonical variates.[21] Tiao and Tsay prove that $\mathrm{C}(s;q)$ is asymptotically χ^2-distributed with $s[K(p-1)+s]$ degrees of freedom.

In a three-dimensional vector autoregressive model comprising the Ifo series at hand, we need to find two independent linear combinations which are moving averages of order q in order to conclude that there is a single codependent cycle which might be interpreted as the composite index of inventory fluctuations.

In the sample between January 1980 and June 2003, we carry out such a canonical correlation analysis in order to test for the number of codependent vectors between the Ifo series. As a prerequisite, we have to determine the lag

[21] See Tiao and Tsay (1989) or Vahid and Engle (1997) for detailed information on the test statistic.

order of the vector autoregressive model. We select $p = 4$, which is indicated as the best choice according to Akaike's information criterion (AIC).[22]

Table 2 reports the results of the codependence tests. As expected, the existence of any common cycle is clearly rejected. Even codependence relations leading to moving averages of orders 1 or 2 are not found in the system. However, if we accept that the codependence relations are predictable up to three months, we will end up with a single codependent cycle.

Using Vahid and Engle's generalized method of moments technique, we estimate the following two codependence relations, which are moving averages of order 3 (standard errors in parentheses):

$$WI_t - \underset{(0.10)}{0.61}\, MI_t \qquad \text{and} \qquad RI_t - \underset{(0.13)}{0.61}\, MI_t \tag{2}$$

where MI_t, RI_t, and WI_t represent the Ifo series of manufacturers', retail and wholesale traders' assessment of inventory stocks, respectively.

For our purposes, however, it is important to know the codependent cycle (or the common factor) of the three Ifo series which is annihilated by the codependence relations. Let us define the three-dimensional vector $x_t \equiv (WI_t, RI_t, MI_t)'$ and collect the two codependence vectors in the (3×2) matrix γ such that $u_t \equiv \gamma' x_t$ are the codependence relations. Following the projection theorem, x_t can be uniquely decomposed as the direct sum of its orthogonal projections onto γ and $\gamma_\perp$, where the three-dimensional vector $\gamma_\perp$ is the orthogonal complement of γ satisfying $\gamma'_\perp \gamma = 0$:

$$x_t = \gamma(\gamma'\gamma)^{-1}\gamma' x_t + \gamma_\perp(\gamma'_\perp\gamma_\perp)^{-1}\gamma'_\perp x_t. \tag{3}$$

Let us define $C \equiv \gamma(\gamma'\gamma)^{-1}$, $D \equiv \gamma_\perp(\gamma'_\perp\gamma_\perp)^{-1}$. Then, (3) can be written as $x_t = Cu_t + D\eta_t$, where $\eta_t \equiv \gamma'_\perp x_t$ is a scalar process which comprises the whole forecasting content of x_t at horizons larger than three months.[23] Owing to this property, the scalar process η_t is taken as an estimate of the common factor driving the three Ifo series.[24] Note that η_t is unique up to a scaling factor. Therefore, in order to fix the common factor estimate, it is natural to define it as a weighted average of the observable series.

Given the codependence relations in (2), we end up with the following estimate of the common factor serving as a composite index of inventory fluctuations based on the codependent cycle analysis:

---

[22] In order to allow for rich dynamics in general, we opt for the AIC which leads to a less parsimonious parametrization compared to other information criteria; see Lütkepohl (1993), Chap. 4, for instance.

[23] Because of codependence, u_t is not predictable at horizons larger than 3, i.e. $E(u_t \mid \Omega_{t-i-1}) = 0$ with $i \geq 3$, where the information set contains the complete history of the process x_t, i.e. $\Omega_t \equiv \{x_t, x_{t-1}, x_{t-2}, ...\}$. Consequently, $E(x_t \mid \Omega_{t-i-1}) = D\,E(\eta_t \mid \Omega_{t-i-1})$ with $i \geq 3$.

[24] Note that, in a canonical transformation, the common factor is mixed up with noise; see Peña and Box (1987).

$$CI_t^c = 0.28WI_t + 0.27RI_t + 0.45MI_t. \tag{4}$$

Manufacturers' assessment of inventory stocks is given the highest weight in the composite index although it is less than one-half. The trade sector as a whole accounts for 55 per cent of the composite index, with the information from retail and wholesale traders being given equal weights.

3.2 Factor Model Approaches

In order to reveal comovement in multivariate time series, factor models are widely applied. Each time series is partitioned into a common and an idiosyncratic component. Whereas the latter is specific to each series, the common component is a linear combination of a (small) number of common factors.

Static factor analysis imposes the following structure on the set of K (mean-adjusted) variables stacked in the vector x_t:

$$x_t = Bf_t + \varepsilon_t \tag{5}$$

where f_t is the r-dimensional vector of (unobserved) factors with $r < K$, B the $(K \times r)$ matrix of factor loadings and ε_t a K-dimensional error term which is assumed to be a multivariate white-noise process with zero mean and the diagonal covariance matrix Ψ. Furthermore, "classical" static factor models assume factors to be white noise with zero means and unit variances and to be uncorrelated with each other and with the error terms, i.e. $E(f_t f_t') = I_r$ and $E(f_t \varepsilon_t') = 0$.

Of course, the assumptions that both the factors and the error terms are not allowed to be serially correlated are too restrictive in the present context. By Doz and Lenglart (1999), however, it is shown that a maximum likelihood estimation of equation (5) leads to consistent parameter estimates as long as f_t and ε_t are (weakly) stationary.

In this setup, it is also possible to test for the number of factors. A likelihood ratio (LR) test of the form $\mathrm{LR}(r) = -2[\hat{L} - \hat{L}_0(r)]$ is asymptotically χ^2-distributed with $\frac{1}{2}[(K-r)^2 - K - r]$ degrees of freedom, where $\hat{L}$ and $\hat{L}_0(r)$ are the values of the log likelihood function under the unrestricted and the restricted model, respectively.

Note that the number of degrees of freedom indicates the number of overidentifying restrictions in the factor structure. In the system of interest where the three Ifo series are driven by a single common factor, the model is exactly identified.[25] Hence we are not able to test for the adequacy of the structure imposed in the present setup. However, since the codependent cycle analysis has shown evidence of a single common factor in the data, we estimate (5) for the three Ifo series under $r = 1$ by maximum likelihood.

---

[25] With $K = 3$ and $r = 1$, the expression which determines the number of degrees of freedom is zero.

With x_t defined as in the previous section, we obtain the following estimates of the factor loadings and the residual covariance matrix:

$$\hat{B} = (0.71, 0.57, 0.86)' \quad \text{and} \quad \hat{\Psi} = \text{diag}(0.50, 0.68, 0.25). \tag{6}$$

An estimate of the unobservable factor f_t is given by the least squares projection $E(f_t \mid x_t) = \Sigma^{-1} B' x_t$, where Σ is the covariance matrix of x_t. In the present case, $\Sigma^{-1} B'$ is a three-dimensional (transposed) vector which, if appropriately normalized, can be interpreted as a weighting scheme.

A composite index of inventory fluctuations based on the maximum likelihood estimation of a static factor model is represented by the following equation:

$$CI_t^f = 0.25 WI_t + 0.15 RI_t + 0.60 MI_t. \tag{7}$$

Here, manufacturers' assessment of inventory investment accounts for 60 per cent of the composite index. Compared to the weighting scheme derived from the codependent cycle analysis, the manufacturing sector is therefore much more important. With 25 per cent, the weight of wholesale traders' inventory assessment is only reduced a little. The contribution of retail trade, however, is clearly lower than in (4).

It is worth noting that, albeit consistent, the maximum likelihood estimation of (5) is not efficient when f_t and ε_t are serially correlated. Hence Doz and Lenglart (1999) propose taking those results only as a first guess. According to their approach, in a second step one should set up a model which explicitly takes into account the dynamics of common and idiosyncratic components.

Whereas, as a standard, the idiosyncratic components are allowed to follow an autoregressive process of order 1, more effort is put on the search of a suitable approximation to the dynamic structure of the common factor. Since cycles are to be modelled, the characteristic roots of the autoregressive polynomial describing the dynamics of the common factor should be complex. Hence the lag order needs to be at least 2. In testing this property, however, we find that only an autoregressive process of order 5 provides the desired result.

Altogether, we set up the following system of equations:

$$x_t = B^* f_t^* + \begin{bmatrix} \varepsilon_{1t}^* \\ \varepsilon_{2t}^* \\ \varepsilon_{3t}^* \end{bmatrix}, \qquad \begin{bmatrix} \varepsilon_{1t}^* \\ \varepsilon_{2t}^* \\ \varepsilon_{3t}^* \end{bmatrix} = \begin{bmatrix} \rho_1 & 0 & 0 \\ 0 & \rho_2 & 0 \\ 0 & 0 & \rho_3 \end{bmatrix} \begin{bmatrix} \varepsilon_{1t-1}^* \\ \varepsilon_{2t-1}^* \\ \varepsilon_{3t-1}^* \end{bmatrix} + \begin{bmatrix} u_{1t} \\ u_{2t} \\ u_{3t} \end{bmatrix} \tag{8}$$

where the common factor is given by

$$f_t^* = a_1 f_{t-1}^* + a_2 f_{t-2}^* + a_3 f_{t-3}^* + a_4 f_{t-4}^* + a_5 f_{t-5}^* + v_t \tag{9}$$

and u_{1t}, u_{2t}, u_{3t}, and v_t are white noise processes which are independent of one another.

Written in state-space form, this model can be estimated by the Kalman filter. Note that the model is identified up to a scaling factor. By analogy to

Doz and Lenglart, we decide to fix the variance of v_t. In fact, we (arbitrarily) set it equal to 0.01. Moreover, we impose zero restrictions on the parameters whenever possible.

The estimates show the following results. First, the vector of factor loadings is given by $B^* = (0.85, 0.69, 1.26)'$ and the dynamic structure of the common factor is described as follows (standard errors in parentheses):

$$f_t^* = \underset{(0.02)}{1.14}\, f_{t-1}^* - \underset{(0.02)}{0.18}\, f_{t-5}^* + v_t. \tag{10}$$

Albeit close to a unit root process, the common factor turns out to be stable inducing oscillations with a duration of roughly four years.[26] Hence shocks to the common factor are highly persistent.

Second, whereas ε_{1t}^* and ε_{2t}^* (i.e. the idiosyncratic components of wholesale and retail traders' inventory assessment) possess significant autocorrelation, ε_{3t}^* turns out to be white noise. The variances of the idiosyncratic components, however, are estimated as $\text{var}(\varepsilon_{1t}^*) = 0.60$, $\text{var}(\varepsilon_{2t}^*) = 0.82$ and $\text{var}(\varepsilon_{3t}^*) = 0.01$, which indicates a trivial factor structure: Apart from a small difference in the degree of smoothness, the series of manufacturers' inventory assessment determines the common factor f_t^*,[27] whereas the two inventory series of the trade sector are dominated by their idiosyncratic components.

Consequently, if the dynamic factor structure of equations (8) and (9) is imposed, the "composite" index of inventory fluctuations can be approximated by manufacturers' assessment of inventory stocks.

4 Evaluation of the Methods

The composite indices of inventory fluctuations proposed in the previous section will be evaluated with respect to two properties which, from our point of view, need to be fulfilled by a good composite index. First, its weighting scheme should be sufficiently stable when estimations are updated using newly entered data. Second, the composite index should possess forecasting power for the reference series. Note that the reference is not the first inventory investment figure reported by the Statistisches Bundesamt. Instead, it is the set of "final" releases as published in the national accounts. In other words, we are in search of an indicator which is able to diagnose the "true" inventory fluctuations in Germany better than the preliminary releases of the official statistics.

[26] It is difficult to test for the presence of a unit root in the common factor. Hence we follow an indirect argumentation: As documented in Appendix A.1, unit root tests indicate that the original series are stationary. Consequently, if the idiosyncratic components are stationary which is given by assumption, the common factor cannot possess a unit root.

[27] In fact, the correlation between the series of manufacturers' inventory assessment and the smoothed estimate of the state f_t^* is virtually perfect.

In addition to the variants resulting from the statistical methodologies used, we also include the unweighted average of the Ifo series in the investigation of forecasting performance. Of course, the unweighted average is the simplest composite index. By comparing its forecasting performance with that of the method-based variants, we are able to check whether the application of the statistical procedures creates any benefit.

The total number of observations used for the subsequent analysis is identical to that of the previous section, i.e. from January 1980 through June 2003. We will evaluate the composite indices which are recursively estimated starting with the first quarter of 1992.[28] It is worth mentioning that the test and estimation procedures are carried out for March, June, September and December of the respective years because we need real-time estimates of the composite indices only on a quarterly basis.

In the first part, we will investigate the stability of the weighting schemes which are obtained applying codependent cycle and static factor analysis. In the second part, we will test whether or not the composite indices are able to predict the revisions of inventory investment. Furthermore, we attempt to find indicator-based forecasting models which outperform the first release published in the national accounts.

4.1 Stability of the Weighting Schemes

Equations (4) and (7) show the weighting schemes of the composite indices which are based on the codependent cycle and the static factor analysis, respectively. In contrast, the Kalman filter technique does not provide an explicit weighting scheme. However, from an inspection of the properties of the resulting common and the idiosyncratic components, it is clear that the total weight is put on manufacturers' assessment of inventories. When the endpoint of the sample is varied, it turns out that this pattern does not change. For the "composite" index based on the Kalman filter technique, the property of stability is therefore fulfilled in a trivial manner.

Whereas the maximum likelihood estimation of the static factor model is carried out in a single step, the codependent cycle analysis is a sequence of specification tests and estimation procedures. Hence, it is not a priori clear whether the lag order of the underlying vector autoregression and the moving-average order of the codependence relations are the same for all samples under investigation.

Starting with the first quarter of 1992, the codependent cycle analysis is carried out quarter for quarter until the end of sample.[29] Figure 5(a) shows the lag orders chosen by the AIC, the Hannan-Quinn (HQ) and the Schwarz

[28]This date is chosen for reasons which are linked to the availability of real-time data of inventory investment and GDP.

[29]In each recursion, the begin of the sample is fixed to January 1980, whereas the end of the sample moves from March 1992 to June 2003.

(a) Lag order selection (b) Tests for codependence

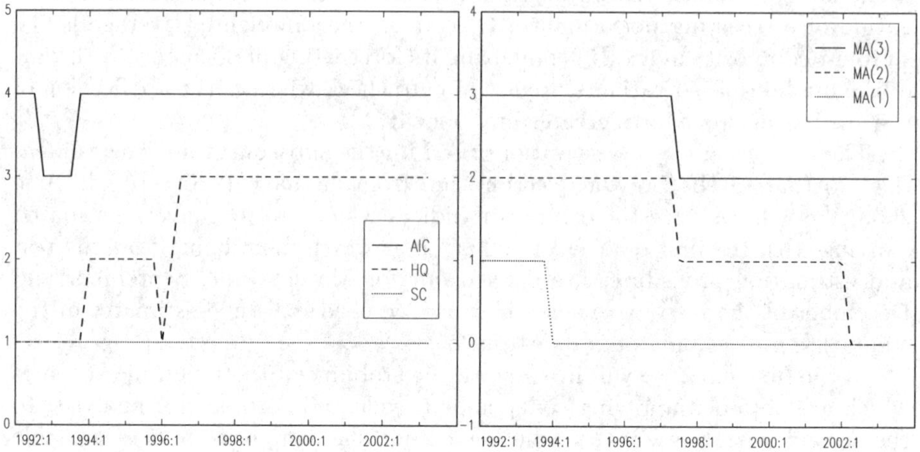

Fig. 5. Recursive Multivariate Analysis of Indicator Series

criterion (SC).[30] Except for a short period in 1992/93, the AIC criterion always selects lag order 4. For simplicity, we therefore decide to set up vector autoregressions of order 4.

Figure 5(b) depicts the test results for the number of codependence relations. Until the second quarter of 1997, we only need to allow for predictability up to order 2 in order to find the desired number of two codependence relations. For the remaining periods, however, two codependence relations which are moving averages of order 3 are identified. Since parameter estimation should be as efficient as possible, this structural change is taken into account.

Figure 6 shows the recursive estimates of the free parameters in the codependence relations. Perhaps with the exception of the first two or three years, the estimates are quite stable; both seem to be around −0.6. Furthermore, the estimates are significantly different from zero. Whereas the structural change in mid-1997 turns out to have a negligible impact on the parameter estimates, the confidence bands are a little bit wider in the scenarios where the codependence relations are moving averages of higher order.

Figure 7(a) shows the weights in the composite index which result from the recursive codependent cycle analysis. The weights are stable which is, of course, a consequence of the stable estimates of the codependence vectors. Over the whole period of interest, manufacturers' assessment of inventories contributes to little more than 40 per cent of the composite index, whereas the remaining share is divided into more or less equal contributions of retail and wholesale traders' assessments.

[30] See, for instance, Lütkepohl (1993), Chap. 4, for an overview of lag order selection in vector autoregressions by means of information criteria.

(a) First codependence vector (b) Second codependence vector

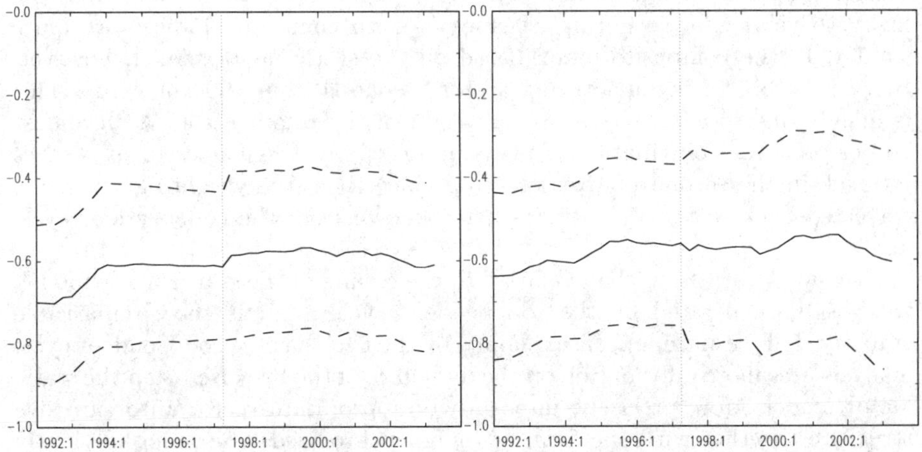

The graph on the left-hand side shows the recursive estimate of the coefficient attached to manufacturers' inventory assessment in its codependence relation with wholesale traders' inventory assessment. The graph on the right-hand side shows the respective estimates with respect to retail traders' inventory assessment. Note that the identification scheme is the same as in (2). Confidence bands of plus/minus two standard errors are given by the dashed lines. The vertical line indicates the structural change with respect to the moving average structure.

Fig. 6. Recursive Estimation of Codependence Vectors

(a) Codependent cycle model (b) Static factor model

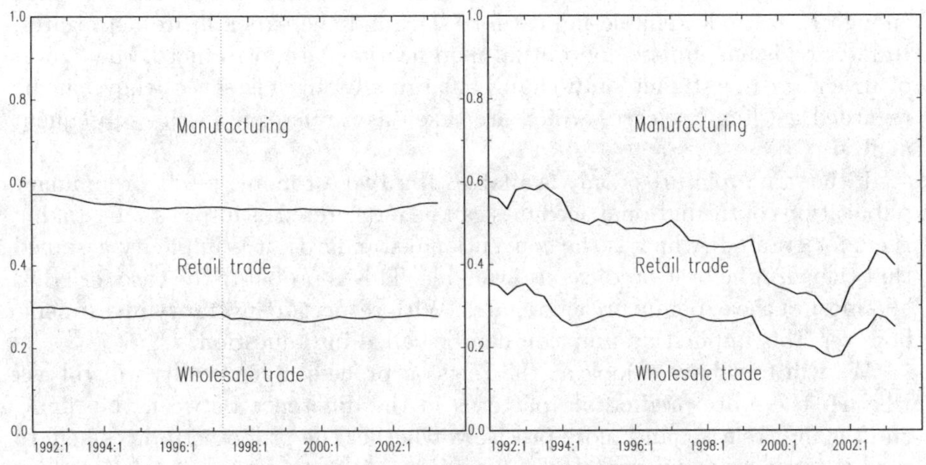

Fig. 7. Recursive Weights of Ifo Series in the Composite Index

As a comparison, Fig. 7(b) plots the weights which are obtained from recursive maximum likelihood estimation of the static factor model. In the first two years, the weighting schemes of both composite indices are quite similar. In the composite index based on the static factor model, however, the weight of the manufacturing sector increases from 1994 onwards. This is mainly due to a reduction of the weight of the retail sector. With almost 70 per cent, the contribution of manufacturers' inventory assessment reaches its peak in the second quarter of 2001. Since then, the weighting scheme is corrected back to the weighting scheme known from the codependent cycle analysis.

It is worth stressing that, relative to the results of the static factor model, the weights generated by the codependent cycle analysis show remarkable stability. This result might be explained by the fact that the codependent cycle analysis uses more information on the dynamics of the Ifo series than the static factor model. More precisely, imposing an appropriate vector autoregressive structure together with the form of (non-synchronized) co-cycling obviously helps to find a common factor which turns out to be rather insensitive to changes in the samples used for estimation. In terms of stability, we therefore conclude that the composite index based on the codependent cycle analysis is preferable to the alternative obtained from static factor analysis.

4.2 Predictive Content for Inventory Investment

In Sect. 2.1, we argued that the series of inventory investment as published in the national accounts will be a good proxy for aggregate inventory fluctuations if, after at least two years, the statistical basis is comprehensive and detailed enough to compile reliable figures for GDP and the expenditure aggregates. In later revisions, unless conceptual modifications are introduced, the figures of inventory investment only change marginally. In this sense, they can be regarded as "final" releases which are taken as a reference in the subsequent analysis.

If the "true" picture is only available after two (or more) years, preliminary publications of the national accounts can be interpreted as forecasts. By taking them for granted (which is the conventional standard), it is implicity assumed that they are the best predictions available. This is probably the case for GDP and most of the expenditure aggregates. With respect to inventory investment, however, this implicit assumption can be called into question.

We will first have a look at the revision process. Specifically, we will ask whether there are predictable patterns in the difference between the "final" and the first release, and more precisely, whether the proposed indices help to predict the revision process. But even if this is the case, it is not yet clear how to use those indices in order to obtain better predictors for the "true" inventory fluctuations than the first release of the national accounts. In the second step, we will therefore set up simple indicator-based forecasting models and ask whether these estimates outperform the first publication of the Statistisches Bundesamt (taken as a predictor of the "final" release).

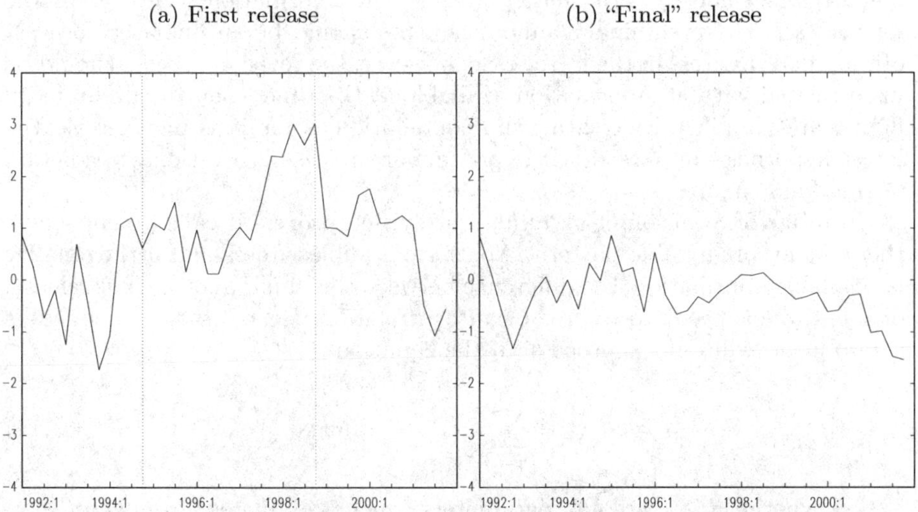

In the graphs, the inventory-investment-to-GDP ratios are plotted. The scale on the vertical axis is in percent. In the left-hand graph, vertical lines indicate the dates of statistical breaks.

Fig. 8. Different Releases of the Inventory-Investment-to-GDP Ratio

During the 1990s, German national accounts data undergo several important statistical breaks. The first is due to unification, the second due to the adoption of the ESA 95 accounting principles. In Appendix A.2, more information on this issue is presented. As a result, we base the subsequent analysis on inventory investment as a percentage of GDP in order to ensure the comparability between the first and the "final" releases. The sample used starts in the first quarter of 1992 and ends in the fourth quarter of 2001.[31]

For our purposes, it is not necessary to examine the full revision process which takes into account all vintages. We only look at the first (or preliminary) release p_t vis-à-vis the "final" release y_t which is taken as the "true" picture of inventory investment as a percentage of GDP. In Fig. 8, the first and the "final" release of the inventory-investment-to-GDP ratio are plotted. From visual inspection, it is obvious that, during the revision process, the variability is reduced significantly.[32] In general, this is an indication that the

[31] As before, the last observations available are dropped from the analysis because they cannot be regarded as "final" releases.

[32] In the sample from the first quarter of 1992 to the fourth quarter of 2001, the standard deviation of the time series of first releases of the inventory-investment-to-GDP ratio is 1.13 percentage points whereas it is 0.56 percentage points in the case of the final releases.

first announcements are measured with a considerable amount of error.

According to Mankiw et al. (1984) as well as Mankiw and Shapiro (1986), at the extremes, the revision process can be regarded as reducing measurement errors ("noise") or as incorporating new information ("news"). In the former case, the preliminary announcements should be an unbiased forecast of the "final" figures. In the latter case, however, the revision process should be uncorrelated with all information available at the time when the preliminary figures are compiled. By treating this compilation as a forecasting exercise, the latter hypothesis implies that the preliminary release is a rational prediction of the "final" figure.

In terms of Swanson et al. (1999), a revision process is called inefficient if there is any predictable pattern. Apart from unbiasedness and orthogonality to available information, the difference between the "final" and the first release, denoted by e_t, needs to be free of autocorrelation. Hence, with ϵ_t defined as a zero-mean white-noise process, in the equation

$$e_t = \text{const.} + \sum_{i=1}^{m} \theta_i e_{t-i} + \omega \, \text{index}_t + \epsilon_t, \tag{11}$$

we ask whether there are any parameters which are different from zero.

Table 3 reports the regression results of different specifications of equation (11). Variant (A) simply tests whether the preliminary release is an unbiased predictor of the "final" release. Hence the first conclusion is that even the minimum requirement of unbiasedness is not fulfilled in this context. However, the Durbin–Watson and the Breusch–Godfrey statistics indicate that the residual process is not free of autocorrelation. In variant (B), we therefore use lags of e_t as additional regressors. Apart from the first lag, we also need to include the fourth lag in order to obtain a white-noise residual sequence.

As argued in Sect. 2.1, preliminary data on inventory investment are to a large extent the result of a matching process between the production and expenditure accounts of GDP. Thereby, the aggregates are compiled by extrapolation based on the respective values of the year before. Additionally, these results are checked in terms of whether the seasonally adjusted figures implied also create a "sensible" picture. In some sense, both the first and the fourth lag are reference points in the process of compilation of national accounts. These procedural peculiarities may be responsible for the above-mentioned empirical result.

The variants (C) contain the full set of regressors as described in (11). Apart from the method-based composite indices, we also present the regression result where index_t is given by the unweighted average of the Ifo series, denoted by AV_t. For either choice, we find that the composite index of inventory fluctuations helps to predict the revision process of the series of interest.

From a forecaster's perspective, however, this result is not fully satisfying because we do not yet have an indicator-based forecasting model which outperforms the first reported national accounts figure. In other words, we need

Table 3. Modeling the Revision Process

Dep. Var.	e_t					
Sample	1993:1–2001:4 (36 obs.)					
Variant	(A)	(B)	(C)			
Index			CI_t^c	CI_t^f	MI_t	AV_t
const.	1.13 (0.17)	0.24 (0.21)	0.48 (0.19)	0.44 (0.19)	0.45 (0.18)	0.47 (0.19)
e_{t-1}		0.50 (0.14)	0.27 (0.13)	0.29 (0.13)	0.27 (0.13)	0.29 (0.13)
e_{t-4}		0.30 (0.13)	0.44 (0.12)	0.41 (0.12)	0.38 (0.11)	0.45 (0.12)
index_t			1.09 (0.29)	0.99 (0.28)	0.73 (0.19)	1.11 (0.33)
R^2	0.00	0.47	0.63	0.62	0.64	0.61
AIC	2.89	2.35	2.05	2.08	2.02	2.10
SC	2.93	2.49	2.23	2.26	2.20	2.28
DW	0.67	1.75	1.93	1.91	1.94	1.93
LM(4)	6.09** [0.001]	0.26 [0.899]	1.17 [0.347]	1.02 [0.416]	0.92 [0.464]	1.19 [0.337]

The difference between the "final" and the preliminary release of inventory investment is denoted by e_t. Standard errors of the parameter estimates are given in parentheses. R^2 is the determination coefficient, AIC is Akaike's and SC Schwarz's information criterion, DW is the Durbin–Watson statistic, and LM(4) is the F-statistic of the Breusch–Godfrey LM test for serial autocorrelation of order 4; p-values are given in brackets. $^{**}, ^{*}, ^{(*)}$ mean rejection of the null hypothesis at the 1%, 5% and 10% level respectively.

to find a function $\xi_t = f(\text{index}_t)$ where ξ_t is a predictor of y_t based on the composite index. For simplicity, we choose the linear form

$$\xi_t = \delta_0 + \delta_1 \,\text{index}_t \tag{12}$$

where the coefficients δ_0 and δ_1 are the least squares estimates of an auxiliary regression of y_t on the composite index and a constant.

In the subsequent evaluation, the predictions ξ_t are recursive out-of-sample forecasts. For the auxiliary regressions, we actually need to have the complete set of data vintages of inventory investment and GDP for all forecasting dates, i.e. the first quarter of 1992 through the fourth quarter of 2001, and each vintage has to start in the first quarter of 1980. Such a data set is not available. However, since solely data which are regarded as "final" should be included in the auxiliary regressions, we are able to mimic the real-time forecasting exercise as follows. The August 2003 release of the inventory-investment-to-GDP ratio is used as the "final" release for all forecasting dates. However, the auxiliary regression is run over a sample which always starts in the first quarter of 1980 but which ends two years before the respective forecasting date.[33]

[33] By doing so, we implicitly assume that the figures which are regarded as "fi-

Table 4. Forecast Evaluation

	Predictor				
	p_t	$f(CI_t^c)$	$f(CI_t^f)$	$f(MI_t)$	$f(AV_t)$
ME	−1.05	−0.45	−0.45	−0.44	−0.45
MAE	1.22	0.60	0.61	0.65	0.59
RMSE	1.44	0.75	0.76	0.78	0.73
Bias	0.53	0.36	0.36	0.31	0.37
Var.	0.16	0.15	0.16	0.11	0.16
Cov.	0.31	0.49	0.48	0.58	0.47

The preliminary release of the inventory-investment-to-GDP ratio is denoted by p_t, whereas $f(\cdot)$ denotes the forecasting model based on the respective composite index. ME is the mean error, MAE the mean absolute error, and RMSE the root mean squared error of the respective forecast. In the lower part of the table, the decomposition of the mean squared error of a forecast in its bias, variance and covariance contribution is presented.

In Table 4, basic measures of forecasting accuracy are reported for the preliminary release p_t as well as for the outcomes of the indicator-based forecasting models. The results of the first column once again highlight the extremely weak performance of the first publication of the national accounts in predicting the "true" ratio of inventory investment and GDP. In the sample used, the mean error is about one percentage point, which is enormous given that the quarterly inventory-investment-to-GDP ratio in absolute terms, averaged over the last three decades, is 0.7 per cent. In fact, the bias contributes to more than 50 per cent of the mean squared error between first and "final" release.

As Table 4 further shows, in terms of the mean absolute error and the root mean squared error, the indicator-based forecasting models clearly outperform the first official publication. However, with mean errors of 0.45 percentage points (in absolute terms), the bias of these forecasts remains considerable. By comparing the results of the indicator-based forecasting models with one another, we find that the unweighted average performs best in the period under investigation. It is worth stressing that these differences are far from being statistically significant.[34] Hence, while it is totally misleading to derive any ranking between the indicator-based forecasting models, we can conclude

nal" at the respective forecasting dates are identical to the August 2003 release of national accounts. Especially for inventory investment, this assumption is certainly not correct. However, the error appears to be limited.

[34] According to Ashley's (2003) simulation results, in the case of about 40 observations and substantially cross-correlated but only modestly autocorrelated forecast errors (which can be assumed in the present case), a 25% to 35% reduction in mean squared error is necessary to obtain a result which is statistically significant at the 5% level.

Table 5. Forecast Accuracy Tests

	Predictor: $\xi_t =$			
	$f(CI_t^c)$	$f(CI_t^f)$	$f(MI_t)$	$f(AV_t)$
Mod. Diebold–Mariano				
$\text{H}_0 : \xi_t \sim p_t$	3.60^{**} [0.001]	3.55^{**} [0.001]	3.44^{**} [0.001]	3.65^{**} [0.001]
Forecast Encompassing				
$\text{H}_0 : p_t\,\text{CE}(\xi_t)$	3.67^{**} [0.000]	3.65^{**} [0.000]	3.66^{**} [0.000]	3.68^{**} [0.000]
$\text{H}_0 : \xi_t\,\text{CE}(p_t)$	1.23 [0.113]	1.28 [0.104]	$1.61^{(*)}$ [0.057]	1.11 [0.136]
White's Reality Check				
$\text{H}_0 : \xi_t^{opt} \not\succ p_t$				$\times^{*}$ [0.03]

The modified Diebold–Mariano test is a test for equal ("$\sim$") predictive ability where the original Diebold and Mariano (1995) statistic is small-sample corrected according to Harvey et al. (1997). Critical values are taken from a t-distribution with 39 degrees of freedom. The test for forecast encompassing or conditional efficiency (CE) is in the spirit of Chong and Hendry (1986). The test statistic and the asymptotic distribution are taken from Harvey (1998). Finally, White's (2000) method checks whether the best indicator-based model (marked by "$\times$") is not superior ("$\not\succ$") to the benchmark p_t. The stationary bootstrap, see Politis and Romano (1994), is based on 10 000 resamples where the smoothing parameter is given by 0.1. $^{**}, ^{*}, ^{(*)}$ mean rejection of the null hypothesis at the 1%, 5% and 10% level, respectively; p-values are given in brackets.

that the statistical procedures applied do not provide a weighting scheme for the composite index which outperforms a simple unweighted average of the Ifo series.

Table 5 reports formal tests for equal predictive ability and forecast encompassing. Since the difference between the indicator-based forecasting models are very small in terms of root mean squared errors, we do not test these models against one another. The Diebold–Mariano tests show that the reductions of mean squared errors implied by the indicator approach vis-à-vis the first publication of the national accounts are highly significant for all variants. Moreover, it comes as no surprise that, conditional on the information of the Ifo business survey, the first announcement of the Statistisches Bundesamt is not an efficient forecast of the "final" figure.

More interesting, however, are the results as regards the question whether or not the indicator-based forecasts encompass the information which is contained in the first publication of the national accounts. As reported in Table 5, for the truly composite indices, the hypothesis that the indicator-based forecast is conditionally efficient cannot be rejected at the 10 per cent level, whereas it is rejected for the Ifo series of manufacturers' assessment on inventory stocks. Hence, in order to predict inventory fluctuations without any loss of relevant information, it is obviously necessary to incorporate the Ifo series on retail and wholesale traders' inventory assessment.

Apart from the first publication of the Statistisches Bundesamt, the predictors under consideration result from some kind of specification search. Furthermore, the indicator-based forecasting models are estimated. Following the arguments of West (1996), West (2001) and White (2000), both properties tend to distort the applicability of the asymptotic distributions of the test statistics. White's reality check is a simulation-based method of testing the predictive superiority to a benchmark and thereby taking into account the specification search previously undertaken. Whereas the benchmark is easily found with the first release of the national accounts, it is difficult to include the specification search within each class of models. For simplicity, in the set of forecasts, we only include the results of those indicator-based predictors which are the best choice within their specific class.

As reported in the last row of Table 5, White's reality check confirms that forecasting with the unweighted average is best among the set of specifications under comparison. This comes as no surprise because the unweighted average provides the forecast with the lowest (root) mean squared error in the sample under investigation. However, the more important result is that, as the bootstrapped p-value indicates, indicator-based forecasts are (in terms of statistical significance) superior to the first figure reported by the Statistisches Bundesamt.

All in all, the inventory-investment-to-GDP ratio first available in the national accounts is far from being a rational forecast of the "final" figure. Apart from a bias and serial correlation, information taken from the Ifo business survey helps to predict how inventory investment is revised. Furthermore, simple forecasting models based on (even trivial) composite indices amalgamating the Ifo series provide better forecasts of the "true" inventory fluctuations than the first release of the national accounts. At least in the sample under investigation, the statistical methods applied do not end up with a weighting scheme which outperforms a simple unweighted average of the Ifo series.

5 Conclusion

Using data from the Ifo business survey, we have sought to find a composite index of inventory fluctuations in Germany. Such an index seems to be necessary because the preliminary figures of changes in inventories published in the German national accounts are unreliable.

Owing to the process of compilation of quarterly national accounts, the first announcement of inventory investment reported by the Statistisches Bundesamt is more a product of lack of statistical information rather than a measure of firm behavior. However, after two years or so, when more detailed information is available, the time series of inventory investment shows features which are typically attributable to inventory fluctuations. Consequently, the "final" releases of the national accounts serve as a suitable reference for the German inventory cycle.

By applying standard time series methods in the time and frequency domain, we have shown that there is considerable comovement between the reference and the three Ifo series documenting manufacturers', retail traders' and wholesale traders' assessments of stockholdings. On a monthly basis, we have therefore constructed composite indices of inventory fluctuations by means of codependent cycle analysis (i.e. a method based on canonical correlations) and static factor modeling. In a recursive analysis, the variants have been evaluated with respect to the stability of the weighting schemes and the ability to forecast the "true" inventory fluctuations. We have found clear evidence that, regardless of which alternative is considered, the composite indices outperform the preliminary release of the national accounts. With respect to the stability of the weighting schemes, however, the codependent cycle analysis turns out to perform better than the static factor model approach.

The three Ifo series have been chosen because they are published monthly and provide specific information from sectors holding significant proportions of the aggregate inventory stock in Germany. However, this data set has some shortcomings. First, only West German retail and wholesale traders are included in the Ifo business survey. Second, on a monthly basis, manufacturers are asked to assess the inventory stocks of finished goods only. Hence changes in the stocks of purchased material and supplies which also seem to be important sources of inventory fluctuations are not included in the composite indices. It is worth mentioning that the Ifo institute asks manufacturers to assess the stock of raw materials and the extent of potential shortages. However, these data are only collected on a quarterly basis.

A Appendix

A.1 Tests for Unit Roots in the Ifo Series

In the sample from January 1980 to June 2003, we test for the presence of a unit root in the Ifo series under consideration. On the one hand, we apply the augmented Dickey–Fuller (ADF) test and the Phillips–Perron (PP) test.[35] In both test procedures, the null hypothesis is that the time series has a unit root. On the other hand, we carry out the KPSS test proposed by Kwiatkowski et al. (1992), which tests the null of stationarity against nonstationary alternatives. Since no series is trending over time, the respective test equations do not exhibit a linear trend.

In the ADF test, the lag order is chosen such that no significant lagged difference is omitted from the test equation. For the PP and the KPSS test, an

[35] For further details on the test statistics, see Hamilton (1994), Chap. 17, for instance.

Table 6. Unit Root Tests of the Ifo Series

Indicator	ADF	PP	KPSS
Manufacturers' Inventories	(5) -3.31^{*}	(11) $-2.63^{(*)}$	(14) 0.20
Retail Traders' Inventories	(3) -3.49^{**}	(11) -9.39^{**}	(13) 0.32
Wholesale Traders' Inventories	(2) -4.43^{**}	(10) -8.66^{**}	(13) 0.36

The numbers in parentheses indicate the lag length in the ADF procedure and the bandwidth parameter in the PP and KPSS procedures. MacKinnon (1991) critical values for the ADF and the PP tests are −3.45, −2.87 and −2.57 for significance at the 1%, 5% and 10% level, respectively. For the KPSS test, the respective asymptotic values are 0.74, 0.46 and 0.35. **,*,$^{(*)}$ mean rejection of the null hypothesis at the 1%, 5% and 10% level, respectively.

estimation of the so-called long-run variance (i.e. the spectrum at frequency zero) of the residual sequence is needed. We apply an estimator based on a Bartlett kernel whose bandwidth is determined using the automatic data-based method proposed by Newey and West (1994).

Table 6 reports the results of the unit root tests. At the 1% level, both the ADF and the PP test reject the presence of a unit root in the Ifo series of retail and wholesale traders' assessments of inventories. For the series of manufacturers' assessment, the PP test only rejects at the 10% level whereas the ADF test rejects at the 5% level. Using the KPSS procedure, the null of stationarity is rejected in neither case. We can therefore conclude that all Ifo series under consideration are stationary.

A.2 Structural Data Revisions

During the 1990s, German national accounts data are subject to several important statistical breaks which might limit the comparability of different data vintages: In May 1999, the Statistisches Bundesamt published for the first time the national accounts statistics according to the principles agreed upon in the European System of Accounts 1995 (ESA 95).[36] Until September 1995, no seasonally adjusted data for Germany as a whole had been released.[37] As a consequence, whereas the final release is defined by the series of inventory investment as published in August 2003, i.e. for Germany as a whole and according to the ESA 95 principles, the first releases before May 1999 are measured according to the previous accounting standards (ESA 79), and additionally, the first releases before September 1995 refer to West Germany.

[36] Details concerning the nature and the extent of revisions in the German national accounts are presented in Statistisches Bundesamt (1999a), Statistisches Bundesamt (1999b).

[37] The impact of the change of the territorial basis on the national accounts figures, especially the problems this induced for seasonal adjustment, is documented in Deutsche Bundesbank (1995).

(a) Unification (b) Change in the accounting standards

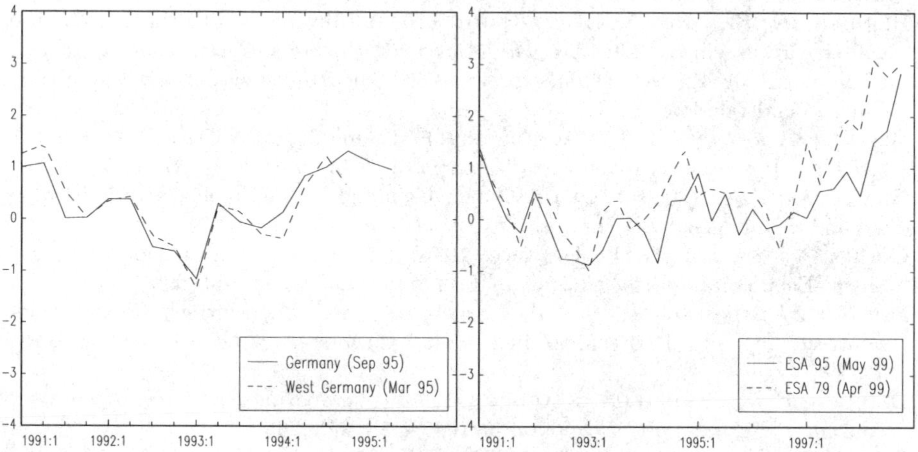

In the graphs, the inventory-investment-to-GDP ratios are plotted. The scale on the vertical axis is in per cent.

Fig. 9. Structural Data Revisions

We are able to circumvent the problem of different territorial bases by using inventory investment as a percentage of GDP. As shown in Fig. 9(a), regardless of which territorial basis is considered, the ratios do not differ significantly from one another. In contrast, Fig. 9(b) shows that the switch to the new accounting standards obviously caused major changes in the shape of the time series. For the construction of a series of preliminary releases, however, only the final figure of each vintage is used. The first releases according to the different accounting standards can be compared only once, namely in the fourth quarter of 1998 which is the last data point in Fig. 9(b). We do not find any big difference between the two. Let us assume that this would also hold for the other realizations where comparisons are not possible. Under these circumstances, we are able to use the first ESA 79 publications as if they were releases which are compiled according to the ESA 95 principles.

References

ABRAMOVITZ, M. (1950): *Inventories and Business Cycles.* National Bureau of Economic Research, New York.

ASHLEY, R. (2003): "Statistically Significant Forecasting Improvements: How Much Out-of-Sample Data Is Likely Necessary?," *International Journal of Forecasting*, 19, 229–239.

BAXTER, M., AND R. G. KING (1999): "Measuring Business Cycles: Approximate Band-Pass Filters for Economic Time Series," *Review of Economics and Statistics*, 81, 575–593.

BLINDER, A. S. (1981): "Retail Inventory Behavior and Business Fluctuations," *Brookings Papers on Economic Activity*, 2, 443–520.

BLINDER, A. S., AND D. HOLTZ-EAKIN (1986): "Inventory Fluctuations in the United States since 1929," in *The American Business Cycle: Continuity and Change*, ed. by R. J. Gordon, pp. 183–236. The University of Chicago Press, Chicago and London.

BLINDER, A. S., AND L. J. MACCINI (1991): "Taking Stock: A Critical Assessment of Recent Research on Inventories," *Journal of Economic Perspectives*, 5, 73–96.

BRAAKMANN, A. (2003): "Qualität und Genauigkeit der Volkswirtschaftlichen Gesamtrechnungen," *Allgemeines Statistisches Archiv*, 87, 183–199.

CHONG, Y. Y., AND D. F. HENDRY (1986): "Econometric Evaluation of Linear Macro-Economic Models," *Review of Economic Studies*, 53, 671–690.

DEUTSCHE BUNDESBANK (1995): "Ergebnisse der Volkswirtschaftlichen Gesamtrechnungen für Deutschland insgesamt," *Monatsbericht Oktober 1995*, pp. 47–60.

DIEBOLD, F. X., AND R. S. MARIANO (1995): "Comparing Predictive Accuracy," *Journal of Business and Economic Statistics*, 13, 253–263.

DÖPKE, J., AND E. LANGFELDT (1997): "Die Vorratsveränderungen im Rahmen von Konjunkturprognosen," *Konjunkturpolitik*, 43, 344–377.

DOZ, C., AND F. LENGLART (1999): "Analyse Factorielle Dynamique: Test du Nombre de Facteurs, Estimation et Application à l'Enquête de Conjoncture dans l'Industrie," *Annales d'Economie et de Statistique*, 54, 91–127.

ENGLE, R. F., AND S. KOZICKI (1993): "Testing for Common Features," *Journal of Business and Economic Statistics*, 11, 369–395.

GOURIÉROUX, C., AND I. PEAUCELLE (1992): "Séries Codépendantes: Application à l'Hypothèse de Parité du Pouvoir d'Achat," *Revue d'Analyse Economique*, 68, 283–304.

GRANGER, C. W. (1966): "The Typical Spectral Shape of an Economic Variable," *Econometrica*, 34, 150–161.

HAMILTON, J. D. (1994): *Time Series Analysis.* Princeton University Press, Princeton and New Jersey.

HARVEY, D., S. LEYBOURNE, AND P. NEWBOLD (1997): "Testing the Equality of Prediction Mean Squared Errors," *International Journal of Forecasting*, 13, 281–291.

——— (1998): "Tests for Forecast Encompassing," *Journal of Business and Economic Statistics*, 16(2), 254–259.

HOWREY, E. P. (1984): "Data Revision, Reconstruction, and Prediction: An Application to Inventory Investment," *Review of Economics and Statistics*, 66, 384–393.

KNETSCH, T. A. (2004): "The Inventory Cycle of the German Economy," Discussion Paper 09/2004, Economic Research Centre of the Deutsche Bundesbank.

KWIATKOWSKI, D., P. PHILLIPS, P. SCHMIDT, AND Y. SHIN (1992): "Testing the Null Hypothesis of Stationarity Against the Alternative of a Unit Root: How Sure Are We That Economic Time Series Have a Unit Root?," *Journal of Econometrics*, 54, 154–178.

LÜTKEPOHL, H. (1993): *Introduction to Multiple Time Series Analysis.* Springer, Berlin et al., second edn.

MACKINNON, J. G. (1991): "Critical Values for Cointegration Tests," in *Long-Run Economic Relationships: Readings in Cointegration*, ed. by R. F. Engle, and C. W. Granger, pp. 267–276. Oxford University Press, Oxford.

MANKIW, N., D. RUNKLE, AND M. SHAPIRO (1984): "Are Preliminary Announcements of the Money Stock Rational Forecasts?," *Journal of Monetary Economics*, 14, 15–27.

MANKIW, N. G., AND M. D. SHAPIRO (1986): "News or Noise: An Analysis of GNP Revisions," *Survey of Current Business*, 66(5), 20–25.

METZLER, L. A. (1941): "The Nature and Stability of Inventory Cycles," *Review of Economics and Statistics*, 3, 113–129.

MOORE, G. H., AND V. ZARNOWITZ (1986): "The Development and Role of the National Bureau of Economic Research's Business Cycle Chronologies," in *The American Business Cycle: Continuity and Change*, ed. by R. J. Gordon, pp. 735–779. The University of Chicago Press, Chicago and London.

NEWEY, W. K., AND K. D. WEST (1987): "A Simple Positive Semi-Definite, Heteroscedasticity and Autocorrelation Consistent Covariance Matrix," *Econometrica*, 55, 703–708.

——— (1994): "Automatic Lag Selection in Covariance Matrix Estimation," *Review of Economic Studies*, 61, 631–653.

OPPENLÄNDER, K. H., AND G. POSER (1989): *Handbuch der Ifo-Umfragen*. Duncker und Humblot, Berlin and Munich.

PEÑA, D., AND G. E. BOX (1987): "Identifying a Simplifying Structure in Time Series," *Journal of the American Statistical Association*, 82, 836–843.

POLITIS, D. N., AND J. P. ROMANO (1994): "The Stationary Bootstrap," *Journal of the American Statistical Association*, 89, 1303–1313.

RAMEY, V. A., AND K. D. WEST (1999): "Inventories," in *Handbook of Macroeconomics*, ed. by J. B. Taylor, and M. Woodford, vol. 1, pp. 863–923. Elsevier Science Publishers, Amsterdam.

STATISTISCHES BUNDESAMT (1999a): "Revision der Volkswirtschaftlichen Gesamtrechnungen 1991 bis 1998," *Wirtschaft und Statistik*, pp. 449–478.

——— (1999b): "Revision der Volkswirtschaftlichen Gesamtrechnungen 1999—Anlaß, Konzeptänderungen und neue Begriffe," *Wirtschaft und Statistik*, pp. 257–281.

——— (2003): *Volkswirtschaftliche Gesamtrechnungen: Inlandsprodukt nach ESVG 1995 – Methoden und Grundlagen –*, Fachserie 18/Reihe S.22. Metzler-Poeschel, Stuttgart.

SWANSON, N., E. GHYSELS, AND M. CALLAN (1999): "A Multivariate Time Series Analysis of the Data Revision Process for Industrial Production and the Composite Leading Indicator," in *Cointegration, Causality, and Forecasting—A Festschrift in Honour of Clive W.J. Granger*, ed. by R. F. Engle, and H. White. Oxford University Press, Oxford and New York.

TIAO, G. C., AND R. S. TSAY (1989): "Model Selection in Multivariate Time Series," *Journal of the Royal Statistical Society*, B(51), 153–213.

VAHID, F., AND R. F. ENGLE (1997): "Codependent Cycles," *Journal of Econometrics*, 80, 199–221.

WEST, K. D. (1996): "Asymptotic Inference about Predictive Ability," *Econometrica*, 64, 1067–1084.

——— (2001): "Tests for Forecast Encompassing When Forecasts Depend on Estimated Regression Parameters," *Journal of Business and Economic Statistics*, 19, 29–33.

WHITE, H. (2000): "A Reality Check for Data Snooping," *Econometrica*, 68, 1097–1126.

Zarnowitz, V. (1985): "Recent Work on Business Cycles in Historical Perspective: A Review of Theories and Evidence," *Journal of Economic Literature*, 23, 523–580.

Do Ifo Indicators Help Explain Revisions in German Industrial Production?*

Jan Jacobs[1] and Jan-Egbert Sturm[2]

[1] University of Groningen, The Netherlands j.p.a.m.jacobs@eco.rug.nl
[2] University of Konstanz and CESifo, Germany, Thurgau Institute of Economics, Switzerland jan-egbert.sturm@uni-konstanz.de

1 Introduction

The Ifo Institute for Economic Research was founded in 1949. Ifo – short for ***I**nformation und **Fo**rschung*, information and research – is particularly known for its Ifo Business Climate Index, based on monthly surveys of German firms; see Theil (1955) for an early appraisal and, e.g., Strigel (1990) or Oppenländer (1997). A business climate indicator provides qualitative information on the business cycle and is therefore frequently included in composite leading indicators, see, e.g., Zarnowitz (1992).

Rather than focusing on the forecasting ability of Ifo Business Survey indicators, as is done for instance by Langmantel (1999), Fritsche and Stephan (2002) and Hüfner and Schröder (2002), our paper deals with the strength of some of these indicators in explaining revisions of growth rates of German industrial production. We carry out a real-time analysis and examine vintages of data series on industrial production. A typical vintage of data consists of preliminary, first reported or unrevised data, partially revised, and fully revised or final data. Recently, problems associated with real-time data sets attracted a lot of attention. Three broad areas are distinguished: data revision, forecasting and policy analysis.[1] Real-time macroeconomic data sets exist for the US (Croushore and Stark 1999, 2001), the UK (Egginton, Pick and Vahey,

*Corresponding author: Jan-Egbert Sturm, University of Konstanz, Department of Economics, P.O. Box D 131, 78457 Konstanz, Germany. We thank Wolfgang Meister for sharing his knowledge regarding data revisions in Germany and his excellent research assistance, and Theo Eicher for his comments. This research project was started while Jan-Egbert Sturm was associated with and Jan Jacobs was visiting the Ifo Institute for Economic Research, Munich, Germany. The present version of the paper has benefited from comments following presentations at the Victor Zarnowitz Seminar, RWI, Essen, Germany, June 2003, and the Academic Use of Ifo Survey Data Conference, Munich, Germany, December 2003.

[1]See http://www.phil.frb.org/econ/forecast/reabib.html for literature on real-time data analysis.

2001) and Australia (Stone and Wardrop, 2002). However, to our knowledge a real-time data set for Germany is not available.

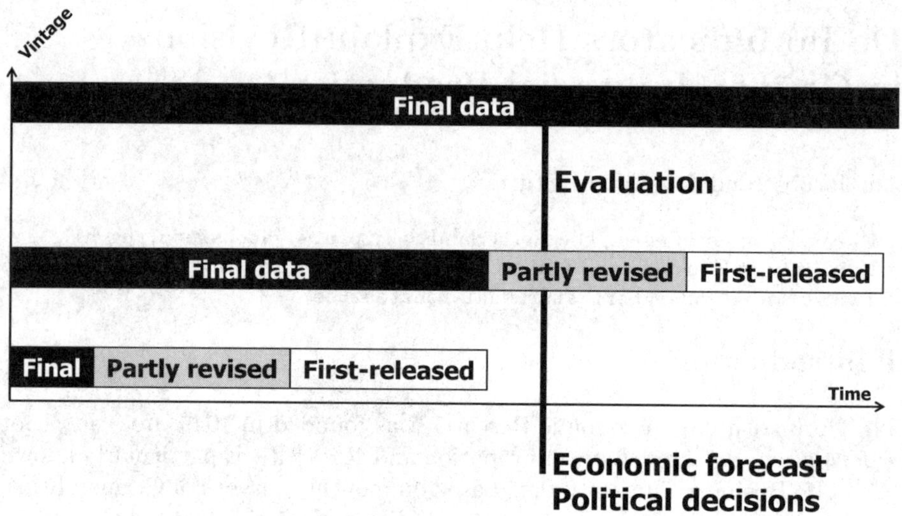

Fig. 1. Real-Time Data

Figure 1 illustrates some of the difficulties associated with real-time data. Especially for economic forecasting a closer look at questions pertaining to the quality of preliminary data releases is needed. Economic forecasters routinely use "currently available" data, which are almost by definition formed of final, partly-revised and first-released data. Their predictions are initially appraised against preliminary releases. Ex post or in sample benchmarking of forecasting performance, however, is usually based on final figures, i.e. a recently released vintage. Along the same lines, policymakers most often use preliminary data, while ex post, their actions are scrutinized on the basis of revised or even final data. Assuming that we are interested in the true but unobserved situation and data revisions improve the quality of our observable indicator, then a natural question to ask is whether it is possible to improve preliminary data by predicting future revisions using past revisions or other available indicators.

Our paper is inspired by Swanson, Ghysels and Callan (1999), who examine a real-time dataset for the US consisting of vintages of seasonally adjusted and unadjusted industrial production, and the composite leading indicator. We carry out a similar exercise for Germany. Our dataset consists of industrial production and two Ifo Business Survey indicators, one on the current business climate (Ifo business situation), the other on developments in industrial production (Ifo production). A feature of our dataset is that Ifo indicators are not revised in subsequent releases in contrast to US composite leading indicators or inflation, one of the variables used by Bajada (2003) in a similar study for Australia. Since Ifo indicators measure the sentiment of firm managers qualitatively and directly, they might be informative on revisions in industrial production growth rates. We conclude that this is indeed the case: our Ifo indicators help explain revisions in industrial production. However, the Ifo Business Situation Indicator actually has more explanatory power, i.e. contains more complementary information with respect to industrial production, as the Ifo Production indicator.

The paper proceeds as follows. Section 2 describes the Ifo Business Survey and some of the indicators that can be derived from it. Section 3 presents our real-time data set on growth rates of German industrial production and discusses the actual revision practice as conducted by the official statistical agency (Statistisches Bundesamt) in Germany. Section 4 shows our data. In Sect. 5 we carry out a number of regressions to model the revison process of industrial production and investigate the impact of the Ifo indicators on the quality of German industrial production revision forecasts. Section 6 concludes.

2 The Ifo Business Survey and Its Indicators

Each month, Ifo sends a survey ('Konjunkturtest Gewerbliche Wirtschaft') to close to 7,000 firms in the sectors industry, construction and (retail and wholesale) trade all over Germany (Nerb, 2004). In general, this so-called Ifo Business Survey intends to capture the firm's appraisals of the business situation and their short-term planning and expectations. For instance, it asks firms to judge their current business situation, tendencies in production volume against the previous month and business expectations for the next six months. These and other questions are posed on a monthly basis. Special questions are included, which return at a quarterly (or annual) frequency. For example, the March, June, September and December surveys enquire whether firms work overtime or are faced with a reduction in working hours. Occasionally, the survey is completed with a question that is only included once to serve, for instance, scientific purposes.[2]

Firms are invited to answer most of the questions on a three-category scale: "good/better", "satisfactorily/same" or "bad/worse". The replies are weighted according to the importance of each firm and its industry, and aggregated. The percentage shares of the positive and negative responses to each question are balanced (ignoring the answer "satisfactorily"). In this way each qualitative question is converted into a single Ifo indicator.[3]

The well-known Ifo Business Climate Index combines the assessment of the current business situation and business expectations for the next six months.

---

[2] For more detailed information, we refer to Oppenländer (1997).

[3] The series of balances thus derived are linked to a base year (currently 1991) and seasonally adjusted.

To be precise, it is the geometric mean of the indicators derived from the balances to question 1) "We judge our current business situation for product group XY to be good, satisfactorily, or bad"; and question 12) "With respect to the business cycle, our business situation for product group XY is expected to be somewhat better, more or less the same, or somewhat worse in the next six months."

Instead of using the Ifo business climate index, we prefer to analyse the information content of two Ifo indicators that do not have an expectation component: the Ifo business situation indicator and the Ifo production indicator. The former is constructed from the answers to the above-mentioned question 1) of the survey. The latter explicitly asks for the development of production as compared to the previous month: question 6) "Our domestic production for XY has increased, has stayed more or less the same, or has become less" as compared to the previous month (complemented with a fourth option of no notable domestic production at all).[4]

Apart from publishing Ifo Business Survey indicators for west and east Germany separately, Ifo has recently started to release figures for the whole of Germany as well.[5] We will use these relatively new figures as they allow for better comparison with our other series of interest, the official index of German industrial production. Furthermore, for obvious reasons we concentrate on that part of the survey which captures the industrial sector (*Verarbeitendes Gewerbe*) and therefore exclude construction firms and enterprises focusing on retail and wholesale trade.

One important feature of Ifo Business Survey indicators is the fact that they are not revised in the course of time.[6] As we will see, this quality of Ifo Business Survey indicators can be helpful when investigating series, like industrial production, in which revisions frequently take place.

3 Industrial Production

The official index of German industrial production is collected by the Statistical Government Agency (Statistisches Bundesamt).[7] Each month t new

[4]Starting January 2002 this question is asked in retrospect, i.e. comparing the production in the previous month with that of the month before.

[5]Due to differences in the division of sectors, the weighting schemes in the aggregation procedure vary. This makes direct comparison of the indicators for west, east and whole Germany difficult.

[6]Only when using seasonally-adjusted Ifo data some very minor realignments might occur. To be nevertheless on the safe side, we use unadjusted series in our analysis.

[7]See Jung (2003) for a detailed analysis of the revision process of German industrial production.

official data are published, giving a preliminary, first estimate for month $t-2$ and partially revised figures for earlier months.[8]

We have vintages released in March 1990 up to December 2003, which include data from 1990:1 up to and including 2003:10. As we are using growth rates and need at least one revision for each month, our dataset in principle covers 1990:1–2003:8. However, we confine our analyses to 1995:12–2003:8, starting from the first vintage (March 1996) that contains more than two observations and utilises data for the whole of Germany. We adopt the convention that our first release for period t is the figure published two months later, our second release the figure published three months later, etc.

Our dataset has some peculiarities. First, the statistical agency did not publish figures on industrial production in March and April 1999. To correct this, two issues were published during May and June that same year.[9] This gave the statistical agency the opportunity to incorporate additional information in these releases, which normally would have taken place in March and April. To capture this, we experimented by including dummy variables for releases during this period. The qualitative results do not change and are not reported for sake of brevity. Secondly, whereas data on thirteen months are published between March 1996 and February 1999, only six monthly figures are supplied from the May 1999 publication onwards with the exception of five months between December 2001 and April 2002, with two, five, three, thirteen and fourteen observations, respectively.

In this paper we analyse the revision process for the monthly growth rates of industrial production (seasonally unadjusted). The data is not rebased, thus avoiding problems associated with level shifts. Let $y_i(t)$ be the ith release of the growth rate of industrial production in period t. Two types of revisions are distinguished, fixed width revisions and increasing width revisions. Fixed Width Revisions are defined as $\Delta y_i \equiv y_{i+1}(t) - y_i(t)$. Increasing Width Revisions are defined as $\nabla y_i(t) \equiv y_{i+1}(t) - y_1(t)$. By construction, the first fixed width revision equals the first increasing width revision (and is therefore omitted from all tables that follow). The increasing width revisions represent the accumulated fixed width revisions.

The increasing width revision for $i = \infty$ is the difference between the "final" release (FR), and the first release. It is quite possible that true final data will never be available for the economic time series we use. This is because benchmark and definitional changes are ongoing and may continue into the indefinite future, for instance. Ideally, no revisions should be made after the final release. We assume that a period of two years is sufficient to reach this

[8] In fact, twice each month data are released: normally a first estimate is given in the second week, whereas at the end of the month its first revision takes place. However, as we have to rely on written publications, i.e. Statistisches Bundesamt (several issues), we only have access to the first publication each month (in which the first revision as released at the end of the previous month is reported as well).

[9] This delay was caused by changes in the way in which survey results for east and west Germany were aggregated.

goal, and hence when comparing the final release for industrial production $y_\infty(t)$ with the first release $y_1(t)$, we take the sample 1995:1–2001:10 and use the official data as available in February 2004 (in which data up to 2003:12 are incorporated).

4 Data

Our data set consists of two Ifo indicators and fixed and increasing width revisions of German industrial production. Figure 2 shows the two Ifo indicators for the period under consideration 1995:12–2003:8. Although the pattern in the Ifo production indicator is quite erratic, the correlation between the indicators is fairly high (0.62). In Sect. 5 we will use the *change* in the Ifo business situation indicator to explain actual revisions. The correlation between this and the Ifo production indicator is 0.52 in our sample.

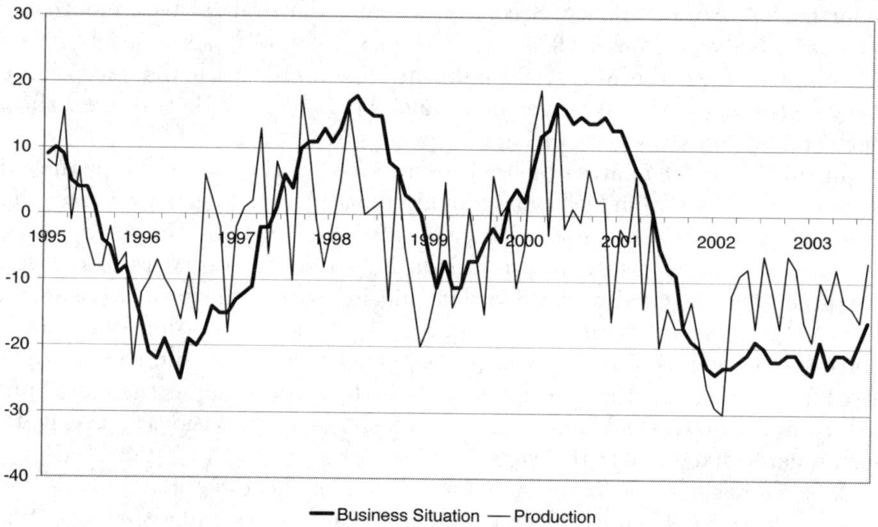

Fig. 2. Ifo Business Survey Indicators

The top panel of Table 1 lists summary statistics of the Ifo indicators. We report the mean, standard deviation, skewness and kurtosis, together with the number of observations. We observe that there is a downward trend in both indicators. The level and annual difference of the Ifo production indicator shows evidence of relatively large (but symmetric) tails. The other indicators seem to follow a normal distribution with some clear differences in variance. For the interpretation of the estimates in Sect. 5, it is important to note that the standard error of the change in the Ifo business situation indicator is small compared to the other series.

Table 1. Summary Statistics for Ifo Indicators and German Industrial Production (available observations in 1995:12–2003:8)

Panel A. Ifo Indicators

	Obs.	Mean	St.Dev.	Skewness	Kurtosis
	Production				
Level	93	−6.0000	10.5191	0.253	−0.245
First Difference	93	−0.0108	10.8583	0.167	−0.297
Annual Difference	93	−1.5699	12.6735	−0.012	−0.699
	Business Situation				
Level	93	−5.3763	14.1958	0.190	−1.495**
First Difference	93	0.0860	3.1335	0.161	0.204
Annual Difference	93	−2.9570	19.3160	0.008	−1.190*

Panel B. Monthly Growth of Industrial Production

	Obs.	Mean	St.Dev.	Skewness	Kurtosis
First Release	93	0.1736	8.4182	0.337	−0.051
Final Release	71	0.6514	9.5927	0.486	−0.237

Panel C. Fixed Width Revisions

	Obs.	Mean[a]	St.Dev.	Skewness	Kurtosis
$i = 1$	93	0.1389	0.9527	−0.031	0.972
$i = 2$	92	−0.0368	0.1821	−5.068**	30.762**
$i = 3$	91	0.0105	0.2327	6.618**	58.943**
$i = 4$	90	0.0093	0.3075	0.969**	22.507**

Panel D. Increasing Width Revisions

	Obs.	Mean[a]	St.Dev.	Skewness	Kurtosis
$i = 1$	93	0.1389	0.9527	−0.031	0.972
$i = 2$	92	0.1036	0.9885	−0.033	0.873
$i = 3$	91	0.1140	0.9647	0.111	0.823
$i = 4$	90	0.1236	0.9724	0.063	0.804
$i = FR$	71	0.2130	1.1413	0.026	0.462

Notes: The superscripts * and ** denote significance at the 5% and 1% level, respectively. For the final release we take the official figures as published in February 2004 and use the sample 1995:12–2001:10.

[a] The null hypothesis that the mean is equal to zero is not rejected for all revisions.

Figure 3 shows first and final revisions for German industrial production for the period 1995:12–2001:10. It suggests that the first revision ($i = 1$) is the dominant one, with revisions between -2.5 and $+2.5$ per cent.[10] Among the first four revisions on which we focus, first revisions have by far the largest number of non-zero observations (86 out of 93 observations). The next three fixed width revisions ($i = 2, 3, 4$), which are associated with quarterly revisions, occur less frequently but are sizeable too.[11] After the fourth revision the industrial production revision process is far from over; in more than 95 per cent of the cases (i.e., 68 out of 71 observations) we observe subsequent revisions in our database.

As follows from the number of black bars compared to the number of white bars in Fig. 3, most subsequent revisions go in the same direction as the first revision. Nevertheless, in nearly 40 per cent (i.e. 26 out of 71 observations) of the cases the first revision is partly undone by subsequent revisions.

The last two panels of Table 1 present summary statistics for fixed width and increasing width revisions, respectively. The horizon is $i = 1, \ldots, 4$, for both types, while the final release as defined above is included for increasing width revisions. For the US, Swanson, Ghysels and Callan (1999) find a systematic (downward) bias in early revisions of industrial production. Using this information would allow an increase in the accuracy of preliminary releases in the US. For Germany the null hypothesis of a mean equal to zero is never rejected independent of whether we look at fixed or increasing width revisions. In other words, there is no systematic bias in the revisions for Germany. The skewness and kurtosis statistics indicate deviations from normality in the second, third and fourth fixed width revisions, which is probably due to a large number of zeros in these revisions.

Before we present the outcomes of our empirical analyses, we show 3D-bar graphs of autocorrelation functions for revisions in German industrial production growth in Fig. 4. One axis displays the autocorrelation order j, the other the revision index i. So, each row i shows the autocorrelations of one revision, $\rho\,[\Delta y_i(t), \Delta(y_i(t-j)]$ for fixed width revisions, and $\rho\,[\nabla y_i(t), \nabla(y_i(t-j)]$ for increasing width revisions, where ρ denotes autocorrelation, i is the revision index, and j is the autocorrelation order or lag. The figure only shows correlation outcomes that differ from zero at the 10 per cent level.[12]

For the fixed width revisions in the top panel of the figure, almost all significant autocorrelations are first revisions. Autocorrelations for first revisions

[10] Note that the monthly growth rates of industrial production during our sample fluctuate between roughly -17 and $+25$ per cent.

[11] Approximately 25 per cent of the fixed width observations for $i = 2, 3, 4$ are non-zero.

[12] We approximate the variance of the autocorrelation estimators by $\mathrm{var}\,(\hat{\rho}(j)) \approx \frac{1}{T}\left(1 + 2\sum_{k<j}\hat{\rho}^2(k)\right)$, where T is the number of observations. This is an increasing function of j, the autocorrelation order. We use the t-distribution to determine the significance level.

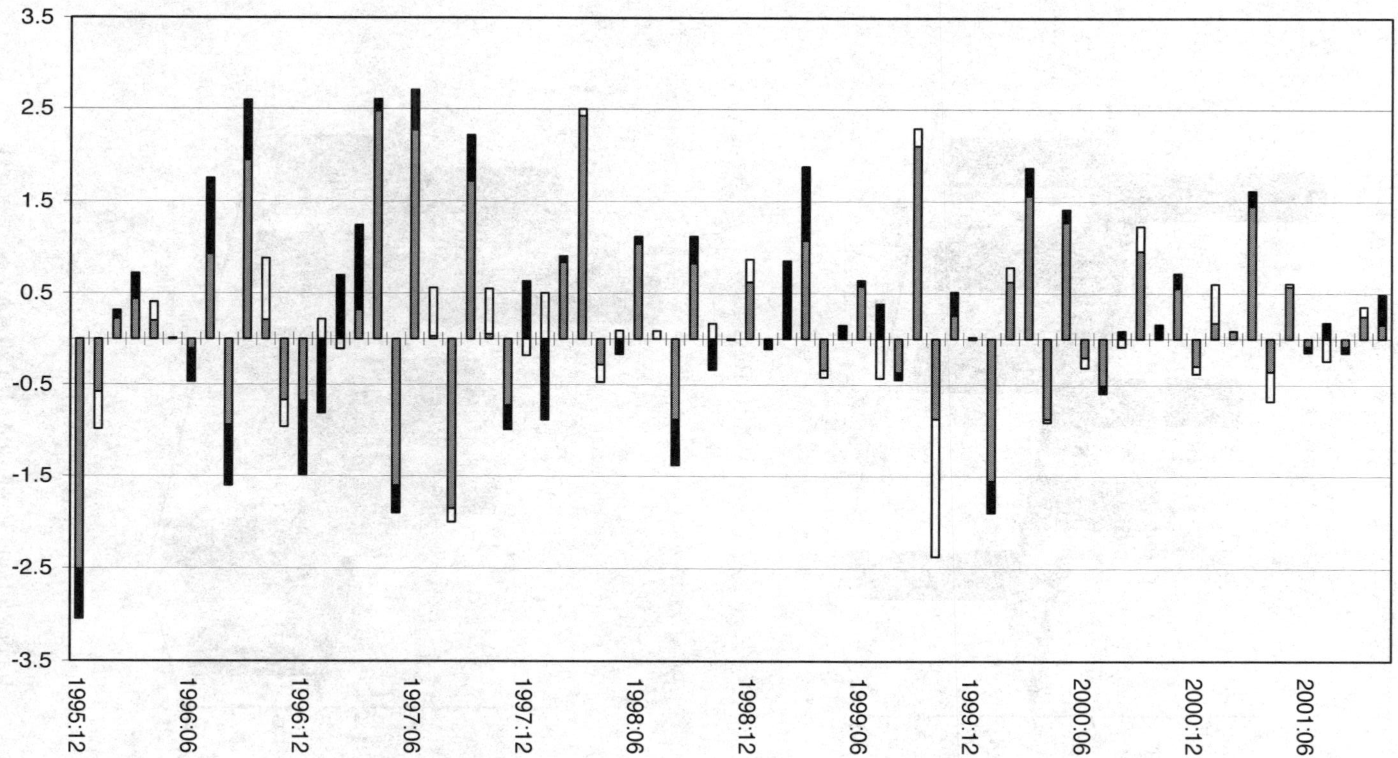

The sum of the grey and white bars depict the first revision of industrial production growth in Germany, i.e. Δy_1. The sum of all revisions (i.e. the increasing width final revision, ∇y_{FR}) is shown by the sum of the grey and black bars. Therefore, black bars indicate that the sum of all subsequent revisions went in the same direction as the first revision, whereas white bars point out that subsequent revisions undo part of the first revision.

Fig. 3. First and Final Revisions of German Industrial Production (1995:12–2001:10)

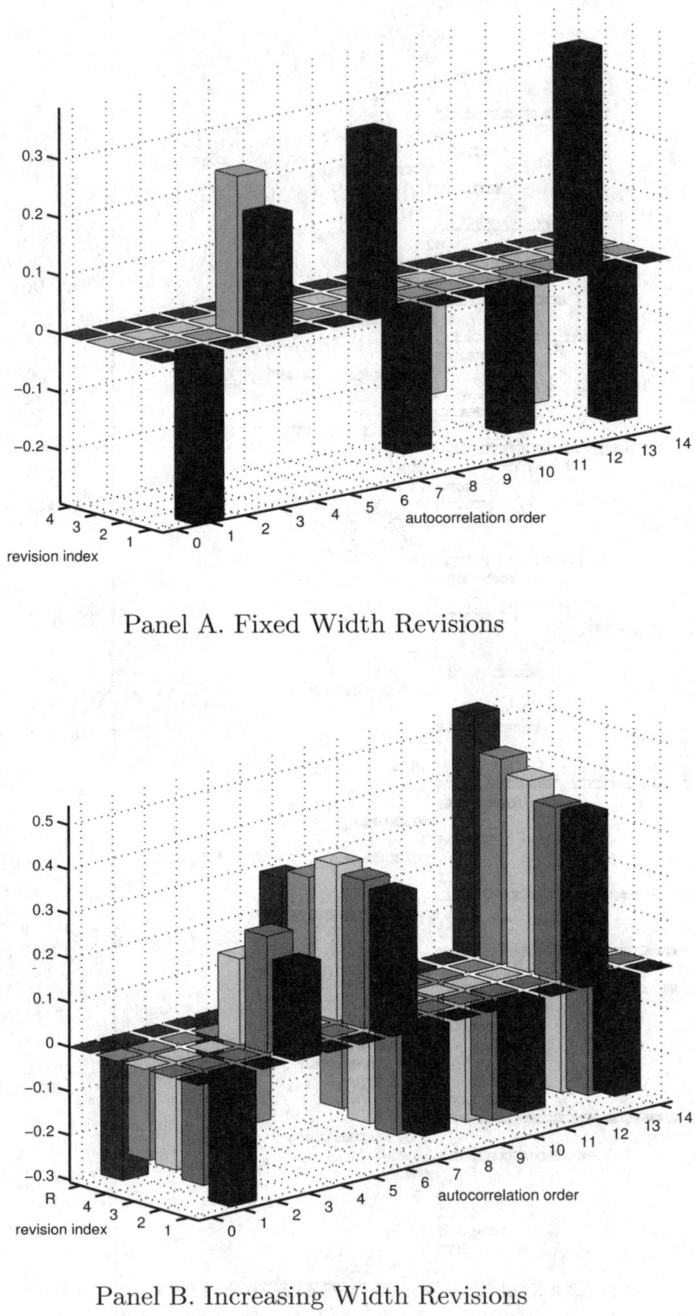

Note: Only autocorrelations significant at a 10% level are shown.

Fig. 4. Autocorrelation Functions for German Industrial Production

appear at lags of approximately one month, one quarter, two quarters, three quarters and a year. The second revision ($i = 2$) only shows one positive and significant autocorrelation at three months lag. At three quarters and a year's lag the third revision ($i = 3$) turns out to have significant negative autocorrelation coefficients. All this is in line with the revision patterns as discussed in Sect. 3.

The bottom panel illustrates the cumulative property of increasing width revisions. Autocorrelations are more persistent and are significant at lags of one month, two quarters, 10 months and a year for all revisions.

5 Modelling Revisions

In this section, we investigate whether there are predictable patterns in the revision process, in particular we seek to establish a role for our Ifo indicators in the revision process. Jung (2003) and Nierhaus and Sturm (2003) observe the following pattern in the revision process. The first estimate of industrial production is a very preliminary one. For firms that did not yet provide their most recent figures the statistical agency imputes production figures as observed in the previous month. The first revision takes place within three weeks in which the imputed figures of last month are updated. We label this the *partial carry-over* effect. The statistical agency releases both monthly and quarterly figures on industrial production. The latter is based on a substantially larger survey. For this reason, a second revision of the monthly figures occurs as soon as the quarterly survey results are utilised. New annual information may necessitate a further revision.

Apart from the partial carry-over effect (i) we assume that revisions depend on: (ii) autoregressions, (iii) earlier revisions and (iv) deviations of release i from one of our Ifo Business Survey indicators (*ifo*). For fixed width revisions this amounts to

$$\Delta y_i(t) = \underbrace{\vartheta_i y_i(t)}_{\text{(i)}} + \underbrace{\sum_j \theta_j \Delta y_i(t-j)}_{\text{(ii)}} + \underbrace{\sum_{k=1}^{i-1} \phi_k \Delta y_k(t)}_{\text{(iii)}} \underbrace{-\gamma_i(y_i(t) - \delta_i ifo(t)}_{\text{(iv)}} + \varepsilon_i(t),$$

where constants and dummies are omitted. For increasing width revisions the difference operator Δ is replaced by ∇, and the partial carry-over channel becomes $\vartheta_i y_1(t)$.

We analyse the last three channels first individually and then jointly. In the first two models we also test for the partial carry-over effect (as described in Sect. 3) by including a level term, i.e. we add $+\vartheta y_i(t)$) in fixed width models and $+\vartheta y_1(t)$ in increasing width models. Here we sequentially add variables and lags to the model and employ Akaike's (1969, 1970) Final Prediction

Error (FPE) criterion to select significant regressors.[13] In the tables below the regressors are listed in the order in which they are selected by the FPE criterion, i.e. the lag which results in the lowest FPE criterion when compared to all other possible explanatory variables is listed first. The third model, in which only the deviation of industrial production from an Ifo indicator is included, is handled slightly differently, as will be explained later. In the final model, we allow for all four channels to play a role and use the FPE criterion to select the regressors. Besides the estimated coefficients, we report the number of observations, the adjusted R^2 and a Lagrange Multiplier test statistic for autocorrelation of order 1 for each of the models in the subsequent tables. In general, we do not find serious autocorrelation problems.

Autoregressions

Table 2 presents the outcomes of the autoregressions for both types of regressions; fixed width revisions in the top panel, increasing width revisions in the bottom panel. In the upper half of each panel only lagged dependent variables are included using Akaike's FPE as selection criterion. To capture the partial carry-over effect, each lower half contains the first-released growth rate as additional explanatory variable.

In the fixed width revision regressions lags enter at one, three, five, six, nine, ten and twelve months, in line with the revision schedule sketched above. Previous revisions are especially important for first revisions. In subsequent revisions autocorrelations do not play a role. The level term y_i significantly enters the autoregression for the first revision and very clearly improves the fit (The adjusted R^2 jumps to 0.66 coming from 0.31). As expected, we do not find a level effect for the other revisions.

Since the level is important in the first revision, this effect feeds through in all increasing width revisions, as can be seen from the bottom panel. We further observe that more lags enter the equations here, which is in line with the 3D-bar autocorrelation graphs in Fig. 4.

Effects of Earlier Revisions

The top panel of Table 3 illustrates that earlier revisions as selected by the FPE criterion occasionally contribute to the explanation of fixed width revisions. The impact for especially the fourth revision is substantial in terms of increase in fit. Apparently, autocorrelations (i.e. revisions of earlier data points) seem to be able to explain early revisions, whereas later revisions in turn depend more on these earlier revisions (of the same data point).

[13] As with all information criteria which have been proposed for allowing the data to determine the model, it involves using a function of the residual sum of squares RSS combined with a penalty for large numbers of parameters (K): $T \log(RSS) + 2K$, where T is the number of observations.

Table 2. Revisions of German Industrial Production: Autoregressions

Panel A. Fixed Width Revisions

$\Delta y_i(t)\,(\equiv y_{i+1}(t) - y_i(t)) = c + \vartheta y_i(t) + \sum_j^J \theta_j \Delta y_i(t-j) + \varepsilon_i(t)$

	Constant	y_i	Significant Regressors as Selected by the FPE Criterion					Obs.	$\bar{R}^2$	LM(1)
$i=1$	0.164^{+}		$0.320^{**}\Delta y_1(-12)$	$-0.306^{**}\Delta y_1(-1)$	$-0.165\ \Delta y_1(-10)$	$0.156\ \Delta y_1(-6)$		81	0.31	0.23
$i=2$	-0.028		$0.271^{*}\ \Delta y_2(-3)$					89	0.04	0.21
$i=3$	0.017							91	0.05	1.77
$i=4$	0.008							90	-0.02	0.00
$i=1$	0.112^{+}	$0.093^{**}y_1$	$0.086\ \Delta y_1(-3)$	$0.220^{**}\Delta y_1(-9)$	$-0.166^{*}\ \Delta y_1(-12)$	$-0.095\ \Delta y_1(-5)$		81	0.66	0.56
$i=2$	-0.030	$0.002\ y_2$	$0.260^{*}\ \Delta y_2(-3)$					89	0.04	0.30
$i=3$	0.018	$-0.000\ y_3$						91	0.04	1.85
$i=4$	0.008	$-0.002\ y_4$						90	-0.03	0.00

Panel B. Increasing Width Revisions

$\nabla y_i(t)\,(\equiv y_{i+1}(t) - y_1(t)) = c + \vartheta y_1(t) + \sum_j^J \theta_j \nabla y_i(t-j) + \varepsilon_i(t)$

	Constant	y_1	Significant Regressors as Selected by the FPE Criterion					Obs.	$\bar{R}^2$	LM(1)
$i=2$	0.117		$0.311^{**}\nabla y_2(-12)$	$-0.256^{*}\ \nabla y_2(-1)$	$-0.185^{+}\nabla y_2(-10)$	$0.176^{+}\nabla y_2(-6)$		80	0.30	0.07
$i=3$	0.139		$0.332^{**}\nabla y_3(-12)$	$-0.244^{*}\ \nabla y_3(-1)$	$-0.189^{+}\nabla y_3(-10)$	$0.186^{+}\nabla y_3(-6)$		79	0.33	0.01
$i=4$	0.194^{*}		$0.439^{**}\nabla y_4(-12)$	$-0.239^{*}\ \nabla y_4(-1)$	$-0.167^{+}\nabla y_4(-4)$	$-0.164\ \nabla y_4(-10)$		78	0.34	1.29
$i=FR$	0.401^{**}		$0.462^{**}\nabla y_{FR}(-12)$	$-0.287^{**}\nabla y_{FR}(-1)$	$-0.260^{*}\ \nabla y_{FR}(-4)$	$-0.161^{+}\nabla y_{FR}(-10)$	$-0.156\nabla y_{FR}(-5)$	59	0.52	7.41^{**}
$i=2$	0.063	$0.088^{**}y_1$	$0.195^{**}\nabla y_2(-3)$					89	0.64	0.15
$i=3$	0.067	$0.099^{**}y_1$	$0.271^{**}\nabla y_3(-9)$	$-0.189^{*}\ \nabla y_3(-12)$	$0.143^{*}\ \nabla y_3(-6)$	$0.097\ \nabla y_3(-1)$		79	0.73	0.07
$i=4$	0.098	$0.102^{**}y_1$	$0.208^{**}\nabla y_4(-9)$	$-0.135\ \nabla y_4(-12)$	$0.128^{+}\nabla y_4(-6)$	$0.121\ \nabla y_4(-1)$	$-0.092\nabla y_4(-4)$	78	0.71	3.27^{+}
$i=FR$	0.188^{*}	$0.093^{**}y_1$	$0.211^{**}\nabla y_{FR}(-9)$	$-0.204^{**}\nabla y_{FR}(-4)$	$0.086\ \nabla y_{FR}(-10)$			61	0.72	0.79

Notes: The superscripts $^{+}$, * and ** denote significance at the 10%, 5% and 1% level, respectively. The maximum number of lags for the autocorrelation part (J) is set at 12. LM(p) denotes the Lagrange Multiplier test statistic for autocorrelation of order p. Dummies for the irregular publications of March and April 1999 are not reported. For the final release we take the official figures as published in February 2004 and use the sample 1995:12–2001:10.

Interestingly, a level effect appears in some of these models. Despite including the first revision in which the partial carry-over effect is clearly incorporated (see Table 2 and the above discussion), subsequent revisions are still affected by it. For third revisions the level term (y_i or y_1) is even significant at the 1 per cent level in both fixed and increasing width specifications.

The parameter estimates for earlier increasing width revisions add approximately up to one, see the bottom panel, as is to be expected because of the cumulative character of this type of revision.

Effects of Ifo Indicators

The regression model to test for the effect of deviations of industrial production from our Ifo Business Survey indicators is derived from an error-correction mechanism

$$\text{Fixed Width: } \Delta y_i(t) = -\gamma\left(y_i(t) - \delta \text{ifo}(t)\right), \tag{1}$$

$$\text{Increasing Width: } \nabla y_i(t) = -\gamma\left(y_1(t) - \delta \text{ifo}(t)\right). \tag{2}$$

Note that due to the carry-over effect, the level term (y_i or y_1) may play a separate role in the explanation of the revisions as well through ($+\vartheta y_i(t)$ or $+\vartheta y_1(t)$). So, the parameters γ (and ϑ) are not identified. Therefore, we simplify the framework to an equation with separate parameters for the level effect ($\alpha = \vartheta - \gamma$) and the Ifo indicator ($\beta = \gamma \times \delta$). We employ the two Ifo indicators described in Sect. 2: *Ifo Business Situation* denoted by ifo^{BS} and *Ifo Production* indicated by ifo^{P}. The first enters the regression models in first-differenced form, whereas the latter already is a flow variable by construction and therefore enters in levels.[14]

We observe a significant Ifo effect on only the first fixed width revision, both for the Ifo business situation indicator and the Ifo production indicator (Tabel 4, top panel). The latter effect is, however, more than four times as large. This cannot completely be explained by the difference in volatility of the two Ifo indicators (see Table 1). Also the explanatory power of the Ifo business situation indicator is slightly higher than that of the Ifo production indicator. For the first fixed width revision, the positive and significant α-coefficient indicates that the partial carry-over effect dominates the error-correction mechanism. Confirming the results in Tables 2 and 3 and the estimated β-coefficients, the partial carry-over and error correction effects do not show up in subsequent revisions.

The bottom panel shows that in general our Ifo indicators contribute to the explanation of increasing width revisions. The Ifo production indicator is always significant at the 5 per cent level, except when using final release data. The Ifo business situation indicator is even significant at the 1 per cent

[14] The inclusion of the level of the Ifo business situation indicator produces qualitatively similar outcomes, albeit less significant.

Table 3. Revisions of German Industrial Production: Effects of Earlier Revisions

Panel A. Fixed Width Revisions

$\Delta y_i(t)\,(\equiv y_{i+1}(t) - y_i(t)) = c + \vartheta y_i(t) + \sum_k^{i-1} \phi_k \Delta y_k(t) + \varepsilon_i(t)$

	Constant	y_i	Significant Regressors as Selected by the FPE Criterion			Obs.	$\bar{R}^2$	LM(1)
$i = 2$	-0.038^{+}					92	−0.02	0.14
$i = 3$	0.026		$-0.060^{*}\ \Delta y_1$			91	0.11	2.40
$i = 4$	−0.022		$-0.873^{**}\ \Delta y_2$	$-0.279^{*}\ \Delta y_3$		90	0.29	0.01
$i = 2$	-0.039^{+}	$0.003\ y_2$				92	−0.01	0.19
$i = 3$	0.035	$0.013^{**} y_3$	$-0.160^{**}\ \Delta y_1$			91	0.20	1.79
$i = 4$	−0.023	$0.001\ y_4$	$-0.883^{**}\ \Delta y_2$	$-0.280^{*}\ \Delta y_3$		90	0.28	0.03

Panel B. Increasing Width Revisions

$\nabla y_i(t)\,(\equiv y_{i+1}(t) - y_1(t)) = c + \vartheta y_1(t) + \sum_k^{i-1} \phi_k \nabla y_k(t) + \varepsilon_i(t)$

	Constant	y_i	Significant Regressors as Selected by the FPE Criterion			Obs.	$\bar{R}^2$	LM(1)
$i = 2$	-0.039^{+}		$1.014^{**} \nabla y_1$			92	0.97	0.23
$i = 3$	0.023		$0.944^{**} \nabla y_2$			91	0.95	2.47
$i = 4$	−0.021		$0.863^{**} \nabla y_1$	$0.712^{**} \nabla y_3$	$-0.583^{**} \nabla y_2$	90	0.93	0.00
$i = FR$	0.043		$1.047^{**} \nabla y_4$			71	0.89	1.61
$i = 2$	-0.038^{+}	$0.005\ y_1$	$0.983^{**} \nabla y_1$			92	0.97	0.12
$i = 3$	0.028	$0.013^{**} y_1$	$0.862^{**} \nabla y_2$			91	0.95	2.06
$i = 4$	−0.015	$0.006\ y_1$	$0.839^{**} \nabla y_1$	$0.660^{**} \nabla y_3$	$-0.551^{*}\ \nabla y_2$	90	0.93	0.04
$i = FR$	0.053	$0.016^{+}\ y_1$	$0.943^{**} \nabla y_4$			71	0.89	1.91

Notes: The superscripts $^{+}$, * and ** denote significance at the 10%, 5% and 1% level, respectively. LM(p) denotes the Lagrange Multiplier test statistic for autocorrelation of order p. Dummies for the irregular publications of March and April 1999 are not reported. For the final release we take the official figures as published in February 2004 and use the sample 1995:12–2001:10.

level for all revisions. The adjusted R^2's in models using the second indicator slightly outperform those using the first. We therefore conclude that the (change in the) Ifo business situation indicator does a better job in explaining revisions than the Ifo production indicator.[15] A possible explanation for this result is that – because we have the level of industrial production already included – the Ifo Production indicator, which more or less measures the same, does not contain as much additional complementary information as the Business Situation indicator. Indeed, when the partial carry-over term is removed from the regressions, the adjusted R^2's for models with Ifo Production clearly outperform those with the Ifo Business Situation included.[16]

Full Model

The final table brings it all together and presents the outcomes of the full model in which the statistical relevance of the channels is judged by Akaike's FPE criterion. All previously distinguished channels seem to play a role in the fixed width revisions as well as in the increasing width revisions when combining them. We observe an autoregression effect at a lag of one quarter in the top panel for first and second revisions, at a lag of three quarters (and at one year and five months in the model with the Ifo production indicator) for the first revision and at one month for the third revision. An earlier revisions effect is present in the third and fourth revisions, and a carry-over effect in the first and third revisions. Most important from our perspective is the outcome that both the Ifo production indicator (ifo^P) and the Ifo business situation indicator (ifo^{BS}) have explanatory power in the system for the first revisions. For third revisions the Ifo Production idicator also explains a small part. The fit of the equation for the first revisions is by far the best. In those specifications a one standard deviation shock in either Ifo indicator results in a revision of roughly 0.2 per cent.

As expected, the regressions using increasing width revisions show that once earlier revisions are included as explanatory variables not much is left to explain by the other channels. Only for $i = 3$ and $i = FR$ the autocorrelation parts and the partial carry-over effect play a role. For the final revision this is at least partly caused by data limitations; we do not have the most recent earlier revision included in that model (i.e. $\nabla y_{FR-1}(t)$). For the same reason, the goodness of fit – as measured by the adjusted R^2 – is lower than for the other increasing width revision models. The Ifo business situation indicator

[15] We also have estimated models in which both Ifo indicators are included. In such regressions only the Ifo business situation indicator appears significant, which confirms our conjecture that this indicator has more explanatory power when analysing revisions in industrial production growth than the Ifo production indicator.

[16] Another possible explanation might be structural breaks in the first indicator: the Ifo Production question has been slightly reformulated a couple of times during the sample under consideration (see e.g. footnote 4). This has not been the case for the question from which the Ifo Business Situation is derived.

Table 4. Revisions of German Industrial Production: Effects of Ifo Indicators

Panel A. Fixed Width Revisions

$y_{i+1}(t) - y_i(t) = c + \alpha y_i(t) + \beta ifo(t) + \varepsilon_i(t)$

	Constant	y_i	Production	Bus.Situation	Obs.	$\bar{R}^2$	LM(1)
$i = 1$	0.184*	0.075**	0.014*		93	0.65	1.75
$i = 2$	−0.020	0.001	0.003		92	−0.00	0.41
$i = 3$	0.035	−0.002	0.003		91	0.05	1.78
$i = 4$	−0.003	−0.000	−0.002		90	−0.04	0.01
$i = 1$	0.103+	0.076**		0.062**	93	0.67	1.42
$i = 2$	−0.039+	0.003		0.001	92	−0.02	0.15
$i = 3$	0.018	−0.000		0.001	91	0.03	1.95
$i = 4$	0.009	−0.003		0.010	90	−0.03	0.03

Panel B. Increasing Width Revisions

$y_{i+1}(t) - y_1(t) = c + \alpha y_1(t) + \beta ifo(t) + \varepsilon_i(t)$

	Constant	y_1	Production	Bus.Situation	Obs.	$\bar{R}^2$	LM(1)
$i = 2$	0.170*	0.080**	0.020*		92	0.62	0.86
$i = 3$	0.211**	0.078**	0.019**		91	0.64	0.57
$i = 4$	0.218**	0.082**	0.017*		90	0.63	0.67
$i = FR$	0.224*	0.091**	0.015		71	0.61	1.68
$i = 2$	0.061	0.084**		0.066**	92	0.63	0.27
$i = 3$	0.103+	0.082**		0.069**	91	0.65	0.44
$i = 4$	0.122+	0.084**		0.072**	90	0.65	0.38
$i = FR$	0.186*	0.091**		0.081**	71	0.65	0.81

Notes: The superscripts +, * and ** denote significance at the 10%, 5% and 1% level, respectively. LM(p) denotes the Lagrange Multiplier test statistic for autocorrelation of order p. Dummies for the irregular publications of March and April 1999 are not reported. For the final release we take the official figures as published in February 2004 and use the sample 1995:12–2001:10.

is included in the fourth fixed width revisions; the Ifo production indicator enters the second increasing width revision model.

Table 5. Revisions of German Industrial Production: Full Model

Panel A. Fixed Width Revisions

$\Delta y_i (\equiv y_{i+1}(t) - y_i(t)) = c + \sum_j^J \theta_j \Delta y_i(t-j) + \sum_{k=1}^{i-1} \phi_k \Delta y_k(t) + \alpha y_1(t) + \beta ifo(t) + \varepsilon_i(t)$

	Constant	Significant Regressors as Selected by the FPE Criterion						Obs.	$\bar{R}^2$	LM(1)
	Production									
$i=1$	0.197*	$0.084^{**} y_1$	$0.089\ \Delta y_1(-3)$	$0.016^{*}\ ifo^P$	$0.220^{**} \Delta y_1(-9)$	$-0.183^{*} \Delta y_1(-12)$	$-0.090 \Delta y_1(-5)$	81	0.68	1.10
$i=2$	−0.008	$0.272^{*}\ \Delta y_2(-3)$	$0.004^{+}\ ifo^P$					89	0.08	0.43
$i=3$	0.063*	$-0.184^{**} \Delta y_1$	$0.012^{**} y_3$	$0.004\ \ ifo^P$	$0.115\ \ \Delta y_3(-1)$			90	0.24	0.27
$i=4$	−0.022	$-0.873^{**} \Delta y_2$	$-0.279^{*}\ \Delta y_3$					90	0.29	0.01
	Business Situation									
$i=1$	0.111+	$0.076^{**} y_1$	$0.118^{+}\ \Delta y_1(-3)$	$0.064^{**} ifo^{BS}$				90	0.64	1.80
$i=2$	−0.028	$0.271^{*}\ \Delta y_2(-3)$						89	0.04	0.21
$i=3$	0.038+	$-0.176^{**} \Delta y_1$	$0.014^{**} y_3$	$0.129\ \ \Delta y_3(-1)$				90	0.22	0.12
$i=4$	−0.022	$-0.873^{**} \Delta y_2$	$-0.279^{*}\ \Delta y_3$					90	0.29	0.01

Panel B. Increasing Width Revisions

$\nabla y_i (\equiv y_{i+1}(t) - y_1(t)) = c + \sum_j^J \theta_j \nabla_i y_i(t-j) + \sum_{k=1}^{i-1} \phi_k \nabla y_k(t) + \alpha y_1(t) + \beta ifo(t) + \varepsilon_i(t)$

	Constant	Significant Regressors as Selected by the FPE Criterion				Obs.	$\bar{R}^2$	LM(1)
	Production							
$i=2$	−0.014	$0.991^{**} \Delta y_1$	$0.004^{+}\ ifo^P$			92	0.97	0.36
$i=3$	0.025	$0.846^{**} \nabla y_2$	$0.017^{**} y_1$	$0.058^{*}\ \nabla y_3(-1)$		90	0.95	0.67
$i=4$	−0.021	$0.863^{**} \Delta y_1$	$0.712^{**} \nabla y_3$	$-0.583^{**} \nabla y_2$		90	0.93	0.00
$i=FR$	0.100+	$0.824^{**} \nabla y_4$	$0.056\ \ \nabla y_{FR}(-12)$	$-0.084^{+}\ \nabla y_{FR}(-4)$	$0.017^{+}\ y_1$	59	0.90	0.35
	Business Situation							
$i=2$	−0.039+	$1.014^{**} \Delta y_1$				92	0.97	0.23
$i=3$	0.025	$0.846^{**} \nabla y_2$	$0.017^{**} y_1$	$0.058^{*}\ \nabla y_3(-1)$		90	0.95	0.67
$i=4$	−0.016	$0.849^{**} \Delta y_1$	$0.685^{**} \nabla y_3$	$-0.565^{**} \nabla y_2$	$0.015\ \ ifo^{BS}$	90	0.93	0.18
$i=FR$	0.100+	$0.824^{**} \nabla y_4$	$0.056\ \ \nabla y_{FR}(-12)$	$-0.084^{+}\ \nabla y_{FR}(-4)$	$0.017^{+}\ y_1$	59	0.90	0.35

Notes: The superscripts $^{+}$, * and ** denote significance at the 10%, 5% and 1% level, respectively. The maximum number of lags for the autocorrelation part (J) is set at 12. LM(p) denotes the Lagrange Multiplier test statistic for autocorrelation of order p. Dummies for the irregular publications of March and April 1999 are not reported. For the final release we take the official figures as published in February 2004 and use the sample 1995:12–2001:10.

Forecast Experiments

So far, we have concentrated on describing past revisions without explicitly looking at the forecast ability of these models for future revisions. Now, we turn to the role of the Ifo indicators in predicting revisions. As a first step, we explore how often the Ifo indicators have been right in predicting the direction of the future first revisions in our sample. Table 6 summarizes the outcomes of this signalling test. Both the Ifo Production and the Ifo business situation indicator gave a correct signal for the direction of the first revision of German industrial production growth in over 62 percent of the time. Bootstrap techniques show that this significantly outperforms "throwing a coin", which would correctly predict the sign in only 49 percent of the cases due to the long-run trend in industrial production growth. The production indicator seems to slightly outperform the business situation indicator when it comes to signalling the direction of the first revision.

Table 6. Signalling Quality of Ifo Indicators

	Sample	Observations	Correct Signal	Percentage	t-Statistic
	Predicting Direction of First Revision (Δy_1)				
ifo^P	1995:12–2003:8	93	61	0.656	3.268**
ifo^{BS}	1995:12–2003:8	93	58	0.624	2.647**
ifo^P	1995:12–2001:10	71	49	0.690	3.392**
ifo^{BS}	1995:12–2001:10	71	45	0.634	2.437*
	Predicting Direction of Final Increasing Width Revision (∇y_{FR})				
ifo^P	1995:12–2001:10	71	43	0.606	1.960*
ifo^{BS}	1995:12–2001:10	71	49	0.690	3.392**

Notes: In case of the sample 1995:12–2003:8 (1995:12–2001:10) with 93 (71) observations the bootstrapped distribution – based upon 10,000 draws – has a mean of 0.486 (0.489) and a standard deviation of 0.052 (0.059) if we use the Ifo production indicator. If we use the Ifo business situation indicator the mean changes somewhat to 0.489 (0.500), whereas the standard deviation is not affected. The superscripts * and ** denote significance at the 10%, 5% and 1% level, respectively, of the null hypothesis that the Ifo indicators do not outperform pure chance.

Of course, we are not only interested in predicting the first revision, but also in getting as close as possible to the final release data. The lower part of Table 6 reports that the Ifo business situation indicator does a good job in signalling the direction of the final increasing width revision. Whereas the performance of the Ifo production indicator deteriorates (from 49 to 43 correct signals), the Ifo business situation indicator becomes more successfull (from 45 to 49 correct signals).

Finally, we assess the forecasting performance of the Ifo business situation indicator in the preferred specification of Table 5 for the first revision. We begin with using only data up to and including 2001:10 and forecast the first revision for 2001:11. This procedure is repeated 22 times in which the sample is successively expanded by one month to forecast next month's revision.[17] These forecasts are then compared with the realisations of the first revisions. We use Theil's U statistic to assess the forecast quality. This statistic is the ratio of the root mean square error for the model of interest to the root mean square error for a "zero-forecast" model, i.e. a model which sets each revision forecast equal to zero. This is a convenient measure because it is independent of the scale of the variable. If the Theil's U statistic is below one, then the model in question outperforms the naive zero-forecast model, i.e. has a smaller root mean squared error.

This exercise is carried out with and without the business climate indicator. In the first case, Theil's U statistic turns out to be 0.778, whereas in the latter it results in 0.774. Hence, both models clearly outperform the zero-forecast model and show that there is ample room for improving the first release data. Furthermore, the Ifo indicator does improve the forecast ability of our partly carry-over/autoregression model, but this effect is quite moderate.

6 Conclusion

Ifo Business Survey indicators, with the Ifo business climate index as most prominent member, have an outstanding position in the world, both domestically and overseas. Recent figures are published in the popular press each month and scrutinized by financial specialists and policy analysts alike. This paper has studied one aspect of the information content of Ifo Business Survey indicators: do some of these indicators help explain subsequent data revisions of German industrial production? To that purpose we constructed a real-time data set of industrial production and exploited the property that Ifo indicators are not revised in subsequent releases.

We can indeed establish a relationship between the Ifo indicators we analyse – one on current production developments, the other on the current business situation – and especially the first and by far most dominant revision of industrial production growth. Furthermore, we find evidence that past revisions of industrial production have predictive content for current and future

[17] When using the same procedure as underlying Table 5 for this smaller sample results in exactly the same model specification with only slightly changed coefficient estimates: $\Delta y_i = 0.117 + 0.078 y_1 + 0.148 \Delta y_1(-3) + 0.067 ifo^{BS}$. These variables are held fixed, whereas the coefficients are re-estimated using the expanded data set.

revisions. All this suggests that it is possible to improve upon our estimates (or preliminary releases) of final data for industrial production.

The Ifo Business Survey asks firm managers about their ideas on the current situation and plans and expectations for the near future. An untested assumption of ours is that Business Survey indicators are more reliable in assessing the current business situation than other sentiment indicators based on for instance consumer surveys or expert opinions, since firm managers are asked to judge their own production and order position. Future real-time data analyses should reveal whether the Ifo Business Survey indicators indeed give "better" signals than other sentiment indicators. For obvious reasons, such an exercise should not only be restricted to industrial production. Other aspects of the information content of the indicators, their strength in forecasting and policy analysis, should then be addressed as well. For all this, a first important step would be the construction of a comprehensive real-time data set for Germany.

References

AKAIKE, H. (1969): "Fitting autoregressive models for prediction," *Annals of the Institute of Statistical Mathematics*, 21, 243–247.

——— (1970): "Statistical predictor identification," *Annals of the Institute of Statistical Mathematics*, 22, 203–217.

BAJADA, C. (2003): "The effects of inflation and the business cycle on revisions of macroeconomic data," *The Australian Economic Review*, 25, 276–286.

CROUSHORE, D., AND T. STARK (1999): "A real-time data set for macreconomists," *Working Paper No.* 99-4, Federal Reserve Bank of Philadelphia.

——— (2001): "A real-time data set for macroeconomists," *Journal of Econometrics*, 105, 111–130.

EGGINTON, D., A. PICK, AND S. P. VAHEY (2001): ""Keep it real!": a real-time UK data set," mimeo, University of Cambridge.

FRITSCHE, U., AND S. STEPHAN (2002): "Leading indicators of German business cycles: An assessment of properties," *Journal of Economics and Statistics*, 222(3), 289–315.

HÜFNER, F., AND M. SCHRÖDER (2002): "Forecasting economic activity in Germany—How useful are sentiment indicators?," *Discussion Paper* 02-56, ZEW.

JUNG, S. (2003): "Revisionsanalyse des deutschen Produktionsindex (The revision history of the production index in Germany)," *Wirtschaft und Statistik*, 2003(9), 819–826.

LANGMANTEL, E. (1999): "Das Ifo Geschäftsklima als Indikator für die Prognose des Bruttoinlandsprodukts," *ifo Schnelldienst*, 52(16-17), 16–21.

NERB, G. (2004): "Survey activity of the Ifo institute," in *Ifo Survey Data in Business Cycle and Monetary Policy Analysis*, ed. by J.-E. Sturm, and T. Wollmershäuser. Physica Verlag.

NIERHAUS, W., AND J. STURM (2003): "Methoden der Konjunkturprognose," *ifo Schnelldienst*, 56(4), 7–23.

OPPENLÄNDER, K. (ed.) (1997): *Business cycle indicators*. Avebury, Aldershot etc.

Statistisches Bundesamt (various issues): "Indizes der Produktion und der Arbeitsproduktivität im Produzierenden Gewerbe," Fachserie 4, Reihe 2.1, Statistisches Bundesamt.

Stone, A., and S. Wardrop (2002): "Real-time national accounts data," *Research Discussion Paper* 2002-15, Economic Research Department, Reserve Bank of Australia.

Strigel, W. (1990): "Business cycle surveys: a new quality in economic statistics," in *Analyzing modern business cycles. Essays honoring G.H. Moore*, ed. by P. Klein, chap. 5, pp. 69–84. M.E. Sharpe, Inc., Arnouk (NY) and London.

Swanson, N., E. Ghysels, and M. Callan (1999): "A multivariate time series analysis of the data revision process for industrial production and the Composite Leading Indicator," in *Cointegration, Causality, and Forecasting. A Festschrift in Honour of Clive W.J. Granger*, ed. by R. Engle, and H. White. Oxford University Press, Oxford.

Theil, H. (1955): "Recent experiences with the Munich business test: an expository article," *Econometrica*, 23, 184–192.

Zarnowitz, V. (1992): *Business cycles: theory, history, indicators and forecasting*, vol. 27 of *NBER Studies in Business Cycles*. The University of Chicago Press, Chicago and London.

A Leading Indicator for the Dutch Economy:
A Methodological and Empirical Revision of the CPB System

Henk Kranendonk[1], Jan Bonenkamp[2], and Johan Verbruggen[3]

[1] CPB Netherlands Bureau for Economic Policy Analysis, P.O. Box 80510, 2508 GM The Hague, The Netherlands h.c.kranendonk@cpb.nl *
[2] University of Groningen, The Netherlands janbonenkamp@hotmail.com †
[3] CPB Netherlands Bureau for Economic Policy Analysis, The Hague, The Netherlands j.p.verbruggen@cpb.nl ‡

1 Introduction

The large-scale econometric quarterly model SAFE plays a key role in the short-term projections for the Dutch economy prepared by the Netherlands Bureau for Economic Policy Analysis (CPB).[1] Since 1990 the CPB had also used a leading indicator for the Dutch economy, the so-called CPB leading indicator.[2] Since that time the quarterly reports on the projections for the economy also refer to the signal given by this indicator. The CPB leading indicator consists of two elements. The "realisation" is meant to describe the actual development of the growth of gross domestic product (GDP) in the Netherlands. The "indicator" summarizes all the available information of lead-

*Senior Economist at the Cyclical Analysis Unit. His main task is monitoring short-term developments of the Dutch economy. Research activities concern leading indicators, model-building and output gaps, forecasting short-term developments Dutch economy.

†He participates in the Honours Program of the Economics Department of the University of Groningen. This program is especially designed for students who are looking for an intellectual challenge and are interested in research. During his studies he has conducted research at the CPB Netherlands Bureau for Economic Policy Analysis in the field of leading indicators. He is presently writing a masters thesis about Real Business Cycle theory as applied to the Netherlands.

‡Head of Cyclical Analysis Unit of CPB. Worked previously at the Ministry of Economic Affairs, preparing economic policy on entrepeneurship, SME's and innovation. Received Ph.D. on a thesis "From Macro to meso, A trend in Dutch economic modelling" in 1992. His fields of activities are model-building and forecasting short-term developments for the Netherlands.

[1]See CPB (2003) for a description of the SAFE model.

[2]See Kranendonk (1990).

ing time series and is designed to give an indication of GDP in the near future and to signal turning points in advance.[3]

The structure of the CPB leading indicator is tailored to its use as a supplement to model-based projections and has a unique character in several respects. Thus (GDP) is used as the reference series, and the system of the CPB leading indicator is composed of ten separate composite indicators, seven for expenditure categories ("demand") and three for the main production sectors ("supply"). A detailed study was conducted recently into the methods and techniques used. Particular attention was paid to the way in which time series are adjusted for their trend-based development and to the way in which the cyclical dynamics of a series can best be calculated.[4] Public spending was also included in the system as a separate expenditure category. And finally, all existing and potential new basic series were again tested for their predictive abilities. This has led to a situation where the CPB leading indicator now uses 25 different basic series, including two series from Ifo Institute. This CPB leading indicator has a lead of three or four months. From the 25 series we selected 7 series which have a lead of at least nine months. These are aggregated to the "long-leading" indicator, which has therefore a lead of three quarters to the reference series.

This article is structured as follows. Section 2 examines the methodological innovations and the current structure of the CPB leading indicator. Section 3 considers the empirical results of the construction and pays particular attention to the role and significance of Ifo data. The performance of the CPB leading indicator and its components is discussed in Sect. 4. Finally Sect. 5 explains how the indicator is used in the preparation of the CPB's short-term projections.

2 Methodology and Structure

2.1 Choice of Reference Series

The CPB's methodology, which is based on the widely applied NBER methodology, uses so-called "deviation cycles".[5] Deviation cycles regard cyclical movements as fluctuations around a permanent trend component. The first step is choosing a reference series which offers an appropriate reflection of economic activity. Manufacturing output is often used for this. The CPB leading indicator is the only Dutch economic indicator which uses GDP as the reference series.[6]

---

[3] In this article the terms CPB leading indicator and composite indicator are used as synonyms.

[4] See Bonenkamp (2003).

[5] See e.g. Burns and Mitchell (1946) and OECD (1987).

[6] There are two other leading indicators for the Netherlands. The Dutch Central Bank uses manufacturing production as reference series and has selected five series

On the assumption that the purpose of an economic indicator is to give an impression of overall economic developments in the future, GDP is in principle a more suitable reference series than manufacturing output. After all, manufacturing output accounts for only 15% of Dutch GDP, while the services sector accounts for 50% of GDP. Although it must be said that the small share of manufacturing output need not as such be a reason for disqualification in this regard. For if the industrial sector is broadly as dynamic as the services sector, then the small share of manufacturing in the total economy is not a problem. Moreover, GDP has a practical disadvantage in that the actual figures only become available on a quarterly basis, whereas manufacturing output figures are published every month.

Figure 1 shows the economic cycles of manufacturing output and GDP for the years between 1975 and 2001. It also shows the performance of the services sector.

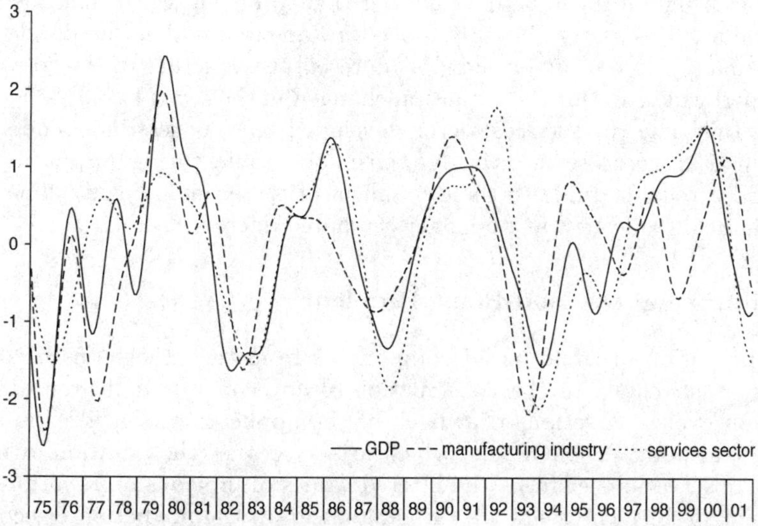

The series have been filtered with the band pass filter of Christiano and Fitzgerald (2003). The selected bandwidth is 18–120 months.

Fig. 1. Economic Cycles of GDP and the Production of Manufacturing Industry and the Services Sector in the Netherlands

(see Reijer (2002)). The Rabobank uses a composite index of five series for the description of the business cycle. Their leading indicator consists of five other series (see Assenbergh (2000)).

At a value of 0.70, the correlation coefficient between the manufacturing output and GDP series is quite high. During the period under consideration, manufacturing output had an additional peak and through during the second half of the 1990s. It is also worth noting that the turning points in manufacturing output occurred earlier than those for GDP, with the exception of the second half of the 1990s. Finally, the pattern of both series has varied sharply in recent years, as evident from a correlation coefficient of 0.17 between 1994 and 2001. Since 1994 GDP was determined to a large extent by the development of the services sector, which from that year deviated sharply from the performance of the industrial sector. Until 1994 the cyclical pattern of the manufacturing industry and the services sector were quite comparable. At most turning points, manufacturing industry is leading some months. After 1994 the resemblance is much lower, because manufacturing industry shows three cycles and the services sector only one.

In short, up to and including the first half of the 1990s the small share of manufacturing output in GDP is not a serious problem. Until then the industrial and services sectors broadly moved in tandem, so that the development of manufacturing output provided a representative picture of the total economy's performance. But this situation changed in the second half of the 1990s. During this time the services sector developed more or less independently of the industrial sector, so that the dynamism of manufacturing output no longer provided a reliable guide to the dynamism of the economy as a whole. Thus manufacturing output was no longer a reliable reference series.

2.2 Filters and the End-Point Problem

The elimination of trend-based components from the time series used is an important next step in the construction of an economic indicator based on deviation cycles. A serious drawback of the application of a filter is known as the "end-point problem", i.e. which arises because the addition of new or revised observations changes the filtered values of previous observations. The end-point problem presents a serious handicap in the prediction of economic developments on the basis of leading series. In terms of the functionality of an indicator of economic activity, it is therefore very important to have an understanding of the sensitivity to new observations. This section examines, on the basis of empirical data, to what extent the sensitivity to new observations differs between filters. Three filters are compared, namely the Christiano and Fitzgerald (CF) filter, the Baxter and King (BK) filter and the Hodrick and Prescott (HP) filter.

The interpretation of the end-point problem differs from filter to filter. The HP filter calculates the trend component and identifies the cyclical component as the difference between the original series and the trend component. The end-point problem is therefore concentrated on changes in the trend component. This is different for the band pass filters, since these filters, given the standard decomposition of an economic time series in a trend-based, cyclical and disrupting component, calculate at least two components. The interpretation of the end-point problem is thus not restricted to a single component, as in the case of the HP filter.[7]

The fact that filtered observations change when new figures are added can lead on the one hand to changes in the intensity of the cyclical fluctuations at the end of the series, and on the other hand – and this is far more serious – to phase shifts. Depending on the type of filter, the end-point problem has two causes. To prevent observations from dropping off at the end of the series, it is usual to expand the routine of a symmetrical filter with an extrapolation method. However, if the filtered values depend in part on artificial observations, it is hardly surprising that the addition of actual observations can bring about changes. An asymmetrical filter calculates the trend component at the end of the series on the basis of "the past". Consequently the availability of new figures will inevitably also lead to changes.

Filters

The Christiano and Fitzgerald (CF) filter and the Baxter and King (BK) filter are band pass filters. A band pass filter is a linear moving average which leaves cyclical fluctuations in tact while filtering out the high frequencies (month-to-month fluctuations) and low frequencies (underlying trend). The CF filter has an asymmetrical weighting scheme which uses all observations for the calculation of the filtered values.[8]The BK filter, on the other hand, is a symmetrical filter with a constant weighting scheme. In contrast with an asymmetrical filter, a symmetrical filter has a moving average with the same number of leads and lags. The advantage of a symmetrical filter lies in the prevention of phase shifts in the filtered series.[9]In contrast with the band pass filters, the Hodrick and Prescott (HP) filter only eliminates the low frequencies or long-term waves from a time series. The relationship between the variances of the trend component and the cyclical component, represented by the parameter λ, plays a key role in the HP filter.[10]The parameter λ determines the curve of the trend component. In case $\lambda = 0$, there is no difference between the trend component and the original series. As λ approaches infinity, the trend-based component begins to appear as a linear trend.

[7]See Bonenkamp (2003).

[8]See Christiano and Fitzgerald (2003).

[9]See Baxter and King (1999).

[10]See Hodrick and Prescott (1997).

Figures 2 to 4 illustrate the end-point problem on the basis of the cyclical component of Dutch exports. In each chart, one year (i.e. 12 monthly figures) is added systematically. The first month is December 1994 and the last month December 2001. In this case the HP filter has $\lambda = 129600$, and the band pass filters have a bandwidth with 18 months as the lower limit and 120 months as the upper limit. These two input values are comparable, so that differences in the sensitivity to the end values cannot be traced back to differences in the *extent* of filtering.

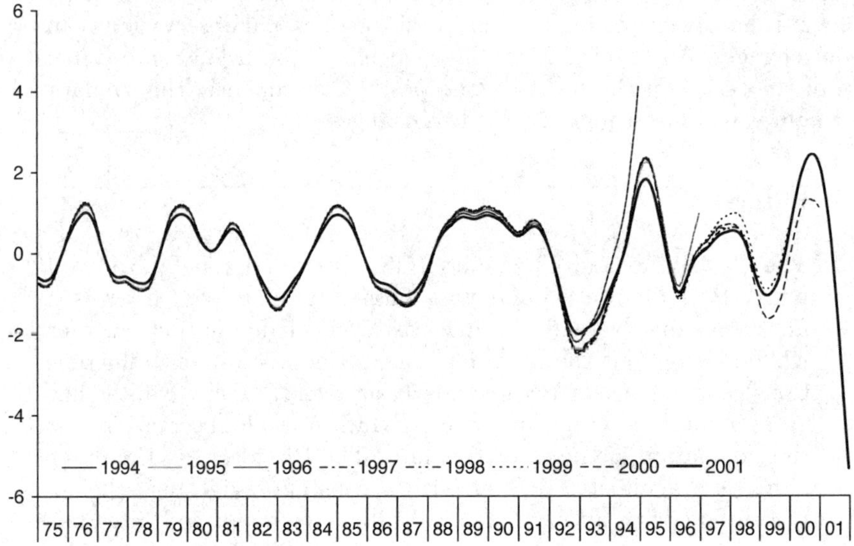

Fig. 2. Cyclical Component of Exports – HP Filter ($\lambda = 129600$)

A comparison of Figs. 2 to 4 shows that, leaving aside the revisions arising from the addition of new observations, the three series move closely in line. This tallies with the general picture which emerges from the literature: no matter how different the filters in a technical and/or theoretical sense, the generated filtered series usually barely differ from each other.[11] But there are some differences, caused by the addition of new observations. The HP-filtered series shows a spike when 1994 is the final year, which is not evident to the same extent in the other two series and which eventually, following the addition of new observations, proves to be a false signal. Bearing this in mind, the downward spike in 2001 may reveal more about the inadequacies of the HP filter than about the actual economic situation. The two other series also show downward phases in 2001, but these are significantly gentler than in the HP

[11] See e.g. Zarnowitz and Ozyildirim (2002), Chadha and Nolan (2000) and Agresti and Mojon (2001).

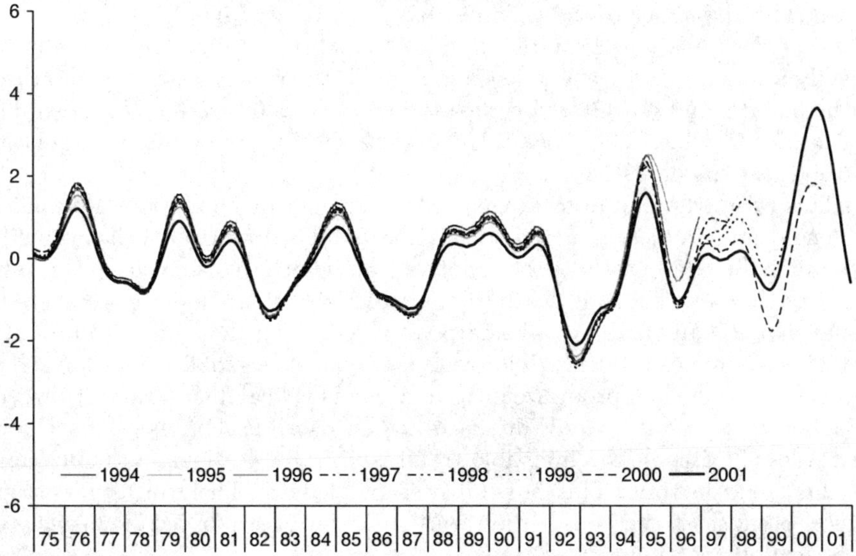

Fig. 3. Cyclical Component of Exports – BK Filter (Bandwidth 18–120)

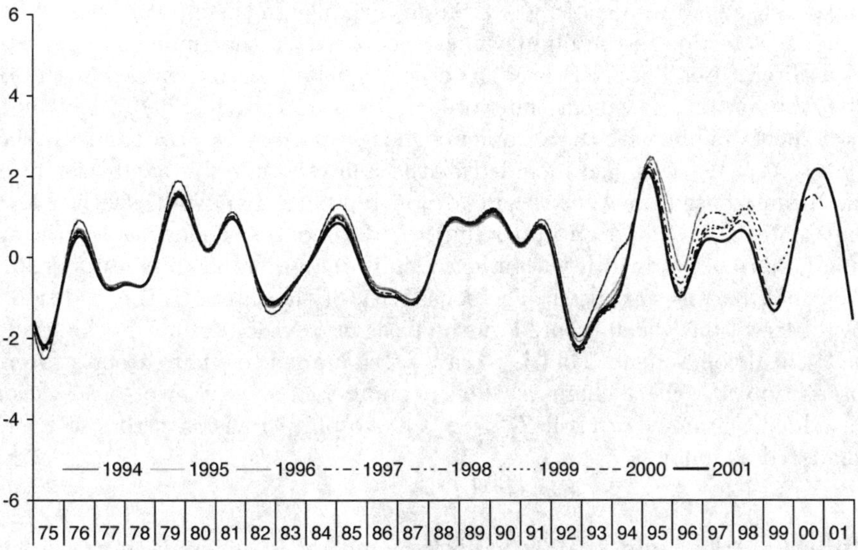

Fig. 4. Cyclical Component of Exports – CF Filter (Bandwidth 18–120)

series. This drawback of the HP filter has already been highlighted by Giorno et al. (1995). It seems that the trend which this HP filter generates is too heavily influenced by cyclical developments in the recent past. In comparison with the HP- and CF-filtered series, the spike in 2000 in the BK series does not seem plausible. This may be related to the nature of the extrapolation method used in the BK filter.

This raises the question to what extent changes in the input values affect the end-point problem. For the HP filter this boils down to another value for λ, and for the band pass filters to another bandwidth. An increase in the value of λ has the same effect as a wider bandwidth. De Haan and Vijselaar (1998) argue that a high value for λ has a positive effect on the end-point problem. A higher λ implies a less flexible trend component, so that this becomes less susceptible to the inappropriate introduction of cyclical fluctuations. However, a higher λ or a wider bandwidth also has a downside. For there is a chance that a less flexible or too inflexible trend is not able to signal actual changes in that trend in time. This possibility is particularly likely in asymmetrical filters, because at the end of the series these filters are based exclusively on historical observations.

To gain a better understanding of the sensitivity of the three filters to the end-point problem, we carried out a formal sensitivity test, following Reijer (2002). We also examined to what extent a change in the input values plays a role. The selection of the input values was based on the guidelines suggested in the literature. The CPB leading indicator uses monthly data. For the HP filter this meant, based on the work of Ravn and Uhlig (2002), a value of $\lambda = 129600$. In line with the arguments and selection by De Haan and Vijselaar (1998), $\lambda = 10^6$ was also included in the analysis. For the band pass filters this meant, based on Agresti and Mojon (2001), a bandwidth with a lower limit of 18 months and an upper limit of 120 months. Following Baxter and King (1999), a bandwidth with a lower limit of 18 months and an upper limit of 96 months was also used. The sensitivity of the filters to the addition of new observations was measured on the basis of "revision errors" in the level of the cyclical component. That is to say, we examined to what extent a filtered observation at time t changes when a number of n year(s) of observations are added successively until T ($T > t$). Absolute revision errors (RE) are calculated as follows:

$$RE_n = |LI_{t|t+n} - LI_{t|T}| \tag{1}$$

where "LI" stands for "leading indicator" and the symbols in this case have the following values: $t = 1994:12, T = 2001:12$ and $n = 0, 1, \ldots, 7$. Equation (1) determines to what extent a filtered value at time t (given data until $t + n$) deviates from its "real" value (given data until T). We assumed that a filtered value after seven years (which in the case of monthly figures means no fewer than 84 observations) will not change. Sixteen different time series were included in the analysis, such as GDP, the expenditure categories, manufacturing output, output in the services sector, the money supply, long-term interest rates and the Ifo indicator. Table 1 shows the average outcomes for these series.[12]

Table 1. Revision Errors in the Level of the Cyclical Component [a]

Filter	**n=0**	**n=1**	**n=2**	**n=3**	**n=4**	**n=5**	**n=6**	**n=7**
HP_129600	1.12	0.50	0.24	0.12	0.11	0.10	0.09	0.00
HP_10^6	0.93	0.49	0.44	0.22	0.10	0.05	0.04	0.00
BK_18–96	0.58	0.45	0.20	0.11	0.10	0.10	0.05	0.00
BK_18–120	0.59	0.52	0.21	0.10	0.10	0.09	0.07	0.00
CF_18–96	0.44	0.30	0.12	0.08	0.06	0.06	0.05	0.00
CF_18–120	0.44	0.30	0.19	0.09	0.05	0.03	0.03	0.00

[a] The revision errors are averages calculated over the standardised cyclical components of 16 time series. The analysis was conducted with December 1994 (1994:12) as the first month and December 2001 (2001:12) as the last month.

The results from Table 1 confirm the observations in Figs. 2 to 4. With regard to differences within the filters, or the effect of a change in the input values, the differences in the revision errors of both bandwidths in the CF and BK filters are too small to draw clear conclusions. The situation is different for the HP filter. The HP_10^6 filter performs better for $n = 0$, while HP_129600 performs better for $n = 1, 2$ and 3. From $n = 4$ both the revisions themselves and the differences between them are too small to draw any meaningful conclusions. The results for $n = 0$ correspond to the conclusion by De Haan and Vijselaar (1998) that an inflexible trend yields less significant revisions when new figures become available. But from $n = 1$ the downside of a high λ becomes evident. Compared to $\lambda = 129600$, the value $\lambda = 10^6$ is less able to signal *actual* fluctuations in the trend in time. These trend changes are picked up after an average of one year of observations ($n = 1$), which leads to revision errors exceeding those of HP_129600.

With regard to the differences between the filters, the most striking is doubtless the revision of the HP filter for $n = 0$. Regardless of the value of λ, the HP-filtered series deviate far more from their "real" values than series which have been filtered with a band pass filter. Of the two band pass filters, the CF filter performs better than the BK filter; the revision errors in the CF filter are smaller, especially for $n = 0$ and $n = 1$. The suspicion already evident from Figs. 2 to 4 is confirmed when more than one series are included in the analysis. The symmetrical BK filter, which uses an extrapolation method

[12] For the outcomes of the 16 different series, see annex 1 in Bonenkamp (2003).

to extend the series artificially, is more sensitive to the end values than the asymmetrical CF filter.

In short, both the graphical exercise and the quantitative analysis show that the HP filter is more sensitive to the end values than the band pass filters. Of the two band pass filters, the CF filter performs better than the BK filter. This sensitivity analysis is based on a single time moment. A repetition of this experiment for several time moments is an option for future research.[13] It does not seem very likely, however, that a dynamic analysis will change these findings significantly. After all, our experiment was based on several time series which, around the time moment at which the analysis was conducted, differed sharply in terms of their movements. On the basis of the above findings, the series in the revised CPB leading indicator are filtered with the CF filter. The bandwidth of 18–120 months has been retained, because a wider bandwidth makes it easier to distinguish between relevant cycles and irrelevant cycles.

2.3 Structure of the CPB Leading Indicator

The CPB is interested not only in "economic activity" in general, as summarized in the GDP figure, but also in the development of key components of the economy. If growth accelerates, it is relevant to know whether the growth impulse originates from abroad or at home. It is also interesting to know in which sector or sectors growth accelerates first. That is why the CPB leading indicator consists of subindicators for both expenditure categories ("demand") and production sectors ("supply"). Public spending has also been included in the system as a separate expenditure category. This structure of the CPB indicator is quite unique, also by international standards.[14] Figure 5 shows the ten components which are distinguished in the CPB-system of leading indicators.

The CPB's approach has three advantages over the usual structure, in which the basic series are directly linked to a single specific reference series. Firstly, the indicator provides more information, because it is possible to discover which expenditure categories or production sectors will underpin GDP growth in the future. It is thus easier to understand and tell the story behind the movements of the indicator. Secondly, because of its structure the CPB leading indicator can be used as an instrument of verification. The indicator can be compared with projections resulting from the macro-economic model used, not only with regard to output, but also consumption or investment for instance (see also Sect. 5). Thirdly, a detailed structure also offers more options to select series. Both series relating to demand components and to

[13] Reijer (2002) conducted a dynamic sensitivity analysis for the HP filter (with $\lambda = 1.000.000$) and the CF filter (with a bandwidth of 18–120). He concludes that the differences between the two filters are small. It should be noted that this analysis was based on only a single time series.

[14] Several years ago a comparable version of the CPB system was applied to the Belgian economy. See Lebrun (1999).

Fig. 5. Composition of CPB Leading Indicator

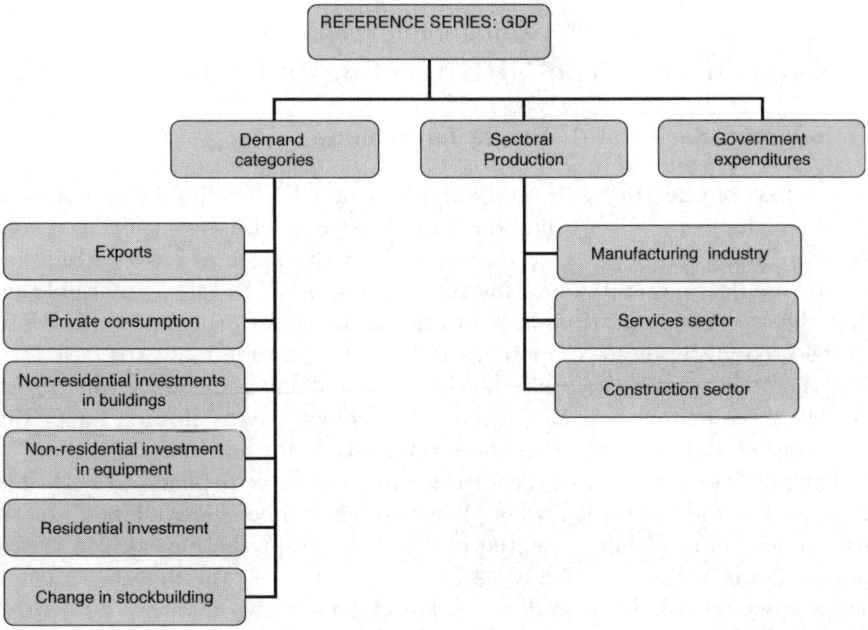

specific sectors can be examined. This gives a greater assurance that a theoretical correlation can be established between a reference series and a basic series.

GDP is determined not only by expenditure and production in the market sector, but also by expenditure and production by the public sector. The original CPB leading indicator took no account of the latter. This is a drawback, certainly for those years when public spending makes a substantial contribution to GDP growth, as was the case in the Netherlands between 1997–2002 for instance. For that reason the revised CPB leading indicator has been supplemented with a subindicator for the public sector. Government expenditure and production in a particular year (i.e. calendar year) are laid down in the Budget Memorandum, which is published in September of the previous year. The government budget outlined in the Budget Memorandum can be regarded as the best available leading indicator for public spending and output. It remains an indicator, because not all the plans unveiled by the government in the Budget Memorandum will be realized. Hence new information is incorporated into this projection in the course of the year.

In the CPB system the reference series is thus divided into 10 components: six expenditure demand categories, three sectoral production variables and government expenditures (see Fig. 5). For each of these components an indicator is constructed. The aggregate of these indicators is called the CPB leading indicator.

3 Composition of the CPB Leading Indicator

3.1 Selected Series and Weighting Scheme

The process of selecting series to be used in the CPB leading indicator corresponds to the usual NBER methodology. After determining the cyclical component of each series, we then determined on the basis of cross-correlations and the predictive quality of dating turning points which series are usable and what the optimum lead time is. From the many series considered we eventually selected 25 series as components of the CPB leading indicator (see Table 2).[15] In some areas it was possible to include many indicators, but in others only three or four proved suitable. The choice is very limited for private consumption and production of the services sector in particular.

The prediction horizon of the CPB leading indicator depends on lead times of the series and on the speed with which series become available. On the basis of the composition presented in Table 2, the prediction horizon is very limited. Somc variables have a lead of only three of four months. Most of the variables also have a publication lag of one or two months. As a result for some variables there is almost no effective lead. Dropping these variables would reduce the quality of the leading indicator. That is why we opted to "extrapolate" a limited number of series in order to shift the prediction horizon several months. This is done by estimating a time series model (ARIMA) per series, and then predicting several months on that basis.[16] Table 2 shows which series are extrapolated. By application of this method we have a lead of least three months for each component, compared with the last realisations of GDP.

There are several methods available for weighting the selected basic series in a composite indicator of economic activity:

- the method of principal components;
- weighting with regression analysis
- weighting scheme on the basis of correlations;
- weighting scheme with equal weights

The first method, principal components analysis, is often applied in the context of indicators of economic activity. The indicators for the Dutch economy of the Nederlandsche Bank (DNB) and the CCSO Centre for Economic Research, for instance, use this method.[17] This is an advanced multivariate

[15] The choice of the selected series is based on Bonenkamp (2003).
[16] See McGuckin and Zarnowitz (2003).
[17] See Berk and Bikker (1995) and Jacobs, Salomons, and Sterken (1997).

technique which boils down to the optimum distillation of common fluctuations in a set of variables.[18] A drawback of principal components analysis is that this method does not take explicit account of the relationship between the basic series and the reference series, and this has to be "predicted".

The weights can also be determined with the help of regression analysis. This method has the disadvantage that in theory it can only be applied when the variables are not linked to each other. But this condition can almost never be met in the case of an indicator of economic activity.[19] An alternative method uses correlation coefficients between a basic series and a reference series as weights. The advantage of this method is that series with a higher statistical correlation with the reference series also receive a heavier weighting. In the previous version of the CPB leading indicator the coefficients were calibrated in this way.[20]

The simplest method, and this is used by the OECD for instance, uses equal weights.[21]

Bonenkamp (2003) has shown that the results between the three methods do not differ that much. That is why, for the sake of simplicity, we have used equal weights in the weighting of indicators for the various components.

3.2 Aggregate

After the indicators have been constructed, with the help of the basic series, for the 10 different components, an aggregate is compiled which serves as the indicator for GDP. To that end the subindicators have to be weighted. This is done in two stages. First the subindicators for the expenditure categories are weighted into an "expenditure indicator" (left column in Fig. 5), and those for production sectors into a "production indicator" (column in the mid of Fig. 5). These two indicators together constitute the two main components of the CPB leading indicator. These two components are merged with public spending into the aggregate.

How is the weighting scheme determined? Until recently the expenditure categories were weighted at their nominal share in total expenditure, with an adjustment for the different variances of the components. In this way investments were given a slightly heavier weighting, because their cyclical fluctuations are relatively large. Conversely, the weighting of consumption was reduced somewhat. The production sectors were weighted in the same way, that is, at their nominal shares in total output.

---

[18]For a brief technical exposition of the method of principal components, see Jacobs (1998), pp. 57–58.

[19]Correlation of the regressors leads to multicollinearity. Consequently the estimated coefficients are unbiased, but they have a high standard error. Thus the information value of the coefficients is low.

[20]See Kranendonk (1990), p. 30.

[21]See OECD (1987).

Table 2. Composition and Lead of CPB Leading Indicator's Components

Expenditures		Lead	**Sectors**		Lead
Consumption	Retail trade confidence indicator	12	Manufacturing Industry	Production trend observed	5
	Economic climate	15		Money supply (M1, real)	13
	Bankruptcies[a]	3[b]		Ifo business climate (expectations)	6
	Willingness to buy	12		OECD Leading indicator Europe	5
				Total inflow orders	7
Exports	Exchange rate dollar euro	6[c]		Production expectations	6
	Money supply (M1, real)	13			
	Ifo business climate (expectations)	6	Construction sector	Production tendency non-residential buildings	12
	Long-term interest rate[a]	20		Production tendency residential buildings	14
	OECD Leading indicator Europe	4		Buildings permits granted, private non-residential	6[b]
	Inflow foreign orders	6		Buildings permits granted, residential	6[b]
Non-residential investment (buildings)	Production tendency non-residential buildings	4		Long-term interest rate[a]	22
	Buildings permits granted, private non-residential	3[b]		OECD Leading indicator Europe	12
	Bankruptcies[a]	7[b]		OECD Leading indicator US	16
Non-residential investment (equipment)	Production tendency non-residential buildings	6	Services sector	Buildings permits granted, non-residential	4[b]
	Capacity utilisation manufacturing sector	8		Retail trade confidence indicator	9
	Consumer confidence	4		Bankruptcies[a]	4[b]
	Inflow domestic orders	14			
	Orderposition	8			
Residential investment	Production tendency residential buildings	6	**Government**	Government expenditure (CPB forecast based on Budget memorandum)	0
	Buildings permits granted, residential	5[b]			
	Long-term interest rate[a]	14			
Change in stockbuildings	Ifo business climate	7			
	Inflow domestic orders	7			
	Producer confidence manufacturing industry	9			

[a] Inverted.
[b] Series extrapolated with ARIMA-forecast.
[c] Exchange rate compared with twelve months ago.

In the course of the project on the revision of the CPB leading indicator we found that this method yielded disappointing results. For more recent years in particular the aggregated indicator did not adequately reflect the actual economic situation. The reason why the old method did not function properly may well be related to the changed filter method. After all, there is no guarantee that weighting components which have been filtered separately will yield the same result as filtering the trend component directly from the aggregate of those components.[22]

The current approach for weighting into the CPB leading indicator is based on regression analysis. By regressing the actual series for the GDP components (both expenditure categories and production sectors) on the actual GDP series, we have tried to estimate the optimum weighting. We only used the cyclical components of the series. Unfortunately unrestricted regression leads to negative shares for the smaller components of GDP, such as public spending, residential investment and other private non-residential investment. Setting the weights of these smaller components at 5% yielded plausible weights, which have been included in Table 3.

Table 3. Structure of CPB Leading Indicator (in %)

Reference Series	Expenditures	Sectoral Production	Total
Exports	25,0		10,6
Private consumption	40,0		17,0
Non-residential investment in buildings	10,0		4,3
Non-residential investment in equipment	5,0		2,1
Residential investment	5,0		2,1
Change in stockbuilding	15,0		6,4
Total expenditures			42,5
Manufacturing industry		30,0	15,8
Services sector		55,0	28,9
Construction sector		15,0	7,9
Total sectoral production			52,5
Government expenditures			5,0
Total (GDP)	100	100	100

By combining the information in Tables 2 and 3 it is possible to infer the weighting of the basic series in the composition of the CPB leading indicator. In Table 4 the series are clustered in a number of different sources from which the indicators can be obtained, namely international indicators,

[22]Incidentally, this was not guaranteed either under the phase-average-trend (PAT) filter method applied until recently.

monetary variables, business surveys among manufacturers, business surveys in the construction industry, business surveys in the services sector, consumer surveys and other indicators. The table shows that three of the 25 series have a relatively heavy weighting of more than 10%, namely business confidence in the retail sector, the number of bankruptcies and the number of permits for industrial and commercial buildings. This is because only three series have been selected for "production in the services sector" and "private consumption", and these two categories have a considerable share in the total. Partial comparisons of the basic series confirm, however, that these series are more closely correlated with GDP than the other series. That is why we have decided not to reduce the weighting of these three series.

The clustering of the series shows that the various sources each contribute between 10–15%. This indicates that the CPB leading indicator is based on a broad range of information with a relatively balanced composition.

3.3 Long-Leading Indicator

Table 2 shows that many of the series have a lead time of four to seven months. Bearing in mind the delayed availability of information and the extension of some series, this makes it possible to detect a turnaround at most one or two quarters ahead. However, there are also a number of variables with lead times of nine months or longer. These variables make it possible to look three quarters ahead. But because only a limited number of series are involved, these series are only combined for the aggregate (GDP) and not for the individual components. To that end we determined the optimum lead time in relation to GDP, and we did not take the lead time from Table 2. Table 4 includes the composition of this long-leading indicator in the right-hand column, with the lead time shown in brackets. A summary of the whole system of indicators in model form is provided in the Appendix A.

3.4 Role and Significance of Ifo Data

Of the 25 selected indicators, four are based on economic developments in other countries.[23] For an open economy like the Dutch, international economic conditions are very important. Both upturns and slowdowns in economic growth often receive an initial impulse from abroad. After a certain time lag this has a ripple effect in consumer spending and/or private non-residential investment. When the economy is in recession, as in 2003, it therefore makes sense to analyze indicators from other countries to see whether they show any signs of recovery. Since Germany is the destination of around 25% of Dutch goods exports, an indicator for the Dutch economy should pay special attention to German leading indicators.

[23] These are the OECD's leading indicators for Europe and the United States and Ifo's business climate indicator and its component on expectations for the near future (see Table 2).

Table 4. Weight of the Indicator Series in the CPB Leading Indicator and Long-Leading Indicator

Series	CPB leading indicator	Long-leading (lead in months)
International indicators	13.0	
Ifo business climate	2.1	
Ifo business climate (expectations)	4.4	14.3 (9)
Leading indicator Europe (OECD)	5.4	
Leading indicator US (OECD)	1.0	
Monetary variables	11.0	
Exchange rate dollar euro	1.8	
Money supply (M1, real)	5.4	14.3 (13)
Long-term interest rate (inverse)	3.5	14.3 (20)
Business surveys manufacturing industry	15.0	
Capacity utilisation rate manufacturing industry	0.4	
Production trend observed	2.6	
Inflow domestic orders	2.6	
Inflow foreign orders	1.8	
Total inflow orders	2.6	
Orderposition	0.4	
Producer confidence manufacturing industry	2.1	
Production expectations	2.6	
Business surveys construction	5.0	
Production tendency non-residential buildings	2.8	
Production tendency residential buildings	1.7	
Business surveys services sector	14.0	
Producer confidence retail sector	13.9	14.3 (10)
Questionnaire amongst consumers	9.0	
Consumer confidence	0.4	
Economic climate	4.3	14.3 (15)
Willingness to buy	4.3	14.3 (12)
Other indicators		
Bankruptcies (inverse)	15.3	
Buildings permits granted, non-residential	12.0	14.3 (10)
Buildings permits granted, residential	1.7	
CPB-forecast government expenditure	5	
Total	100	100

Ever since its introduction in 1990, the CPB leading indicator has relied on two major international sources of indicators, the OECD and the Ifo Institute. The CPB indicator uses the OECD's leading indicators for Europe and the United States. These serve as proxies for the general international climate. The CPB indicator has also used the Ifo's business climate indicator for German manufacturing industry. As part of the revision of the CPB indicator, we analyzed the contribution of the Ifo indicator in detail. The findings are discussed in this section.

The business climate for the German economy was included in 1990 as an indicator for non-energy exports and manufacturing output, in both cases with lead times of five months. In the course of the recent study it emerged that the optimum lead time was now only a few months, which may be related to shorter production and delivery times. The current method diverges in three ways from the approach adopted in 1990, with the first point having a particularly significant bearing on the outcomes:

The trend-based development is now eliminated with a different filter technique. In the past the phase-average-trend (PAT) method was used; since the revision the Christiano–Fitzgerald filter has been used (see Sect. 2.2).

In the past the business climate indicator was not adjusted for the trend; now it is.

The time series for exports and manufacturing output have been changed twice since 1990 as a result of international revisions of the national accounts.

With the current series and filters the lead time is only two to three months. This is not long enough to be of any use. That is why we analyzed separately the two questions of which the business climate indicator is composed, namely an assessment of the current situation and the expectations for the near future. Table 5 shows that the question relating to expectations for the near future has a lead time of six months or longer. Partly on the basis of an analysis of turning points, the expectations variable has been included in the revised CPB leading indicator with a lead time of six months (see Table 2). The question relating to the current situation has no lead time and therefore cannot be used. It is also apparent from the table that in recent years the expectations question has been much more closely linked to the reference series, since the correlation coefficient rose from 0.3–0.4 in the first period to around 0.75 in the second period.

Table 5. Correlation Ifo-Series with Exports and Manufacturing Industry

	Correlation		Lead (months)	
	1975–1988	1989–2002	1975–1988	1989–2002
Exports				
Ifo business climate	0.61	0.80	2	2
* current situation	0.71	0.80	0	-1
*expectations	0.25	0.76	7	6
Manufacturing industry				
Ifo business climate	0.74	0.85	4	3
* current situation	0.84	0.86	3	0
* expectations	0.38	0.74	9	7

Figure 6 shows that the correlation was weaker during the first half of the 1980s in particular, but that it was much stronger between 1986–2000. This applies both for the dating of the turning points and for the intensity of the fluctuations. A striking aspect in recent years is that the upswing for 2002 indicated in the expectations question of the business climate survey did not materialize, probably partly due to geopolitical uncertainties.

Incidentally, the influence of the Ifo business climate indicator on the overall CPB leading indicator is greater than the effects through exports and manufacturing output discussed here. The CPB indicator uses the *average* Ifo business climate indicator for stock building, because in this case the lead

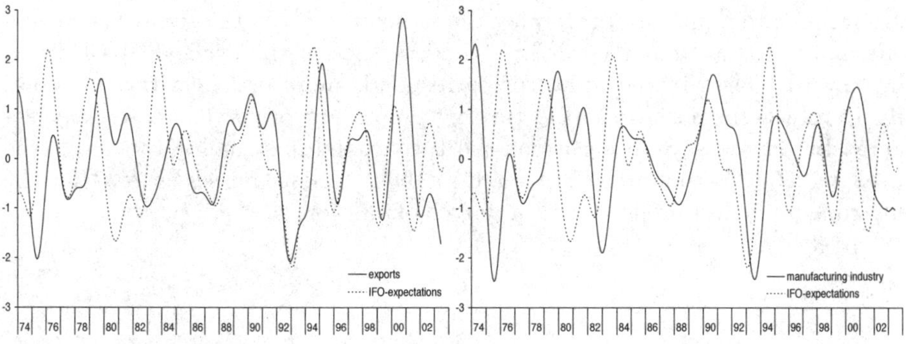

Note: Ifo expectations not moved with optimal lead.

Fig. 6. Cyclical Pattern of Exports, Manufacturing Industry and Ifo Expectations

time of seven months is sufficient (see Table 2). Together the Ifo series contribute 6.5% to the CPB leading indicator. This contribution is the same as that of the OECD's two leading indicators. Compared to the contribution of variables from surveys among Dutch manufacturers (15%), the contribution of the international indicators is limited.

International indicators play a relatively larger role in the long-leading indicator, which looks slightly further ahead into the future. As explained in Sect. 3.3, the long-leading indicator is not calculated for the individual components, but directly for GDP. Among the international indicators, only Ifo's expectations question among German manufacturers has a sufficient lead time (nine months) for inclusion. Its contribution to the long-leading indicator is 14.3%. The variables from the survey among Dutch manufacturers have too short a lead time to be included in the long-leading indicator. Thus the German expectations variable is the most important source of information for the longer horizon (i.e. two to three quarters ahead) for Dutch exports and manufacturing output. This is because the other variables in the long-leading indicator relate to household spending (consumer confidence), production in the services sector (business confidence among retailers) and construction (building permits), or they are of a general nature (money supply and interest rates).

4 Performance of CPB Leading Indicator

Section 3 explains the composition of the CPB leading indicator. In this section we will briefly discuss the result. In Fig. 7 the "realisation" line represents the economic cycle of GDP. The indicator, based on the 25 selected series, can track this line quite accurately. The correlation coefficient between the indicator and the reference series is high, 0.82. The main upturns and downturns are represented quite accurately by the indicators. Only the subcycles during the mid 1970s are not recorded.[24] The intensity of the cyclical upward and downward phases in the indicator corresponds more or less with the actual fluctuations. In most cases the turning points are predicted reasonably accurately, but on several occasions the turnaround is signalled too soon (the peak in 2000) or too late (the trough in 1989). These "misses" show that the instrument should be used with a degree of caution.

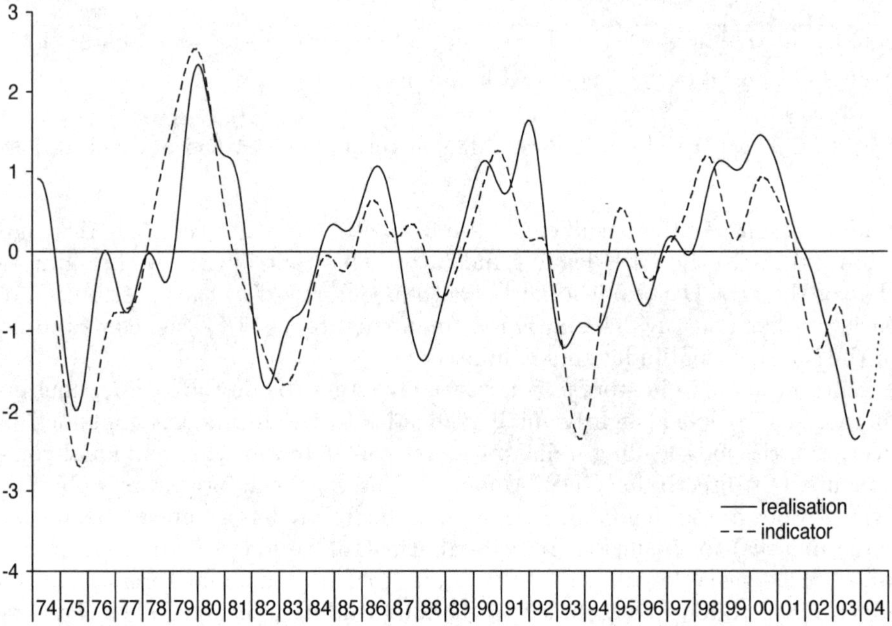

Note: Date of calculation is February 2004

Fig. 7. CPB-Leading Indicator, 1974–2003

Figure 7 also includes the long-leading indicator. To prevent the three lines – realisation, indicator and long-leading indicator – intertwining too much, we have opted for a presentation in which the dynamic of the long-leading indicator is added to the most recent observation of the normal indicator. In the figure the dashes are based on the CPB leading indicator, and the dots for the most recent months are derived from the long-leading indicator. We have deliberately opted for a change from dashes to dots, because the seven series constituting the long-leading indicator account for only half of the total information. The "prediction" for the longer time horizon (more than three

[24] Incidentally, in the selection process the early years were weighted less heavily.

months ahead, say) is thus based on less information and should therefore be interpreted with particular caution.

Figure 8 shows the actual outcomes and the leading indicators for the 10 components of the CPB leading indicator. They illustrate that the cyclical patterns differ significantly between categories. Private consumption, for example, has only four cycles during the period 1974–2003, while export shows seven cycles. The indicators for most components perform quite well measured by the number of cycles and the dating of turning points. The performance of the change in stockbuilding is relatively poor, probably caused by statistical measurement problems. The horizon of the indicators of the components differ, depending on the lead of the selected basic series. The indicator for private consumption in February 2004 includes information up to September 2004, but most of the other indicators are only available up to April or May 2004.

5 Application in Practice

Each quarter the CPB publishes a projection of economic growth for the current and the following year. The quarterly model SAFE plays a key role in the preparation of the forecasts.[25] This model is fed with data covering the past and with exogenous assumptions on international developments and the government's economic policies. Other information sources, such as the views of experts, are also used in estimating the economy's performance. Figure 9 shows the process in schematic form. A key feature is that the preparation of the projections is an iterative process, in which the model assures consistency.[26] The projections are adjusted via the autonomous terms in the model. This means that the outcomes for specific behavioral equations, such as private consumption, investment or exports, can be adjusted if necessary. The advantage of this procedure is that the model calculates the consequences for all variables if an adjustment is made for a specific variable.

Information from the CPB leading indicator sometimes prompts an adjustment of the model's projection. The model makes projections on a quarterly basis and takes as much account as possible of the actual outcomes published by Statistics Netherlands (CBS) at regular intervals. Often the indicators provide some information on those quarters for which CBS has not yet published any figures. That is why the signal of a possible turning point in the CPB leading indicator is compared with the profile based on the model's projection. For the current quarter and the following two quarters the analysis attaches considerable weight to an acceleration or deceleration of growth as indicated by the barometer.

This can be illustrated with two examples. A relatively positive development of disposable household incomes leads to an optimistic projection for

[25] See CPB (2003).

[26] For more information, see Kranendonk and Jansen (1997).

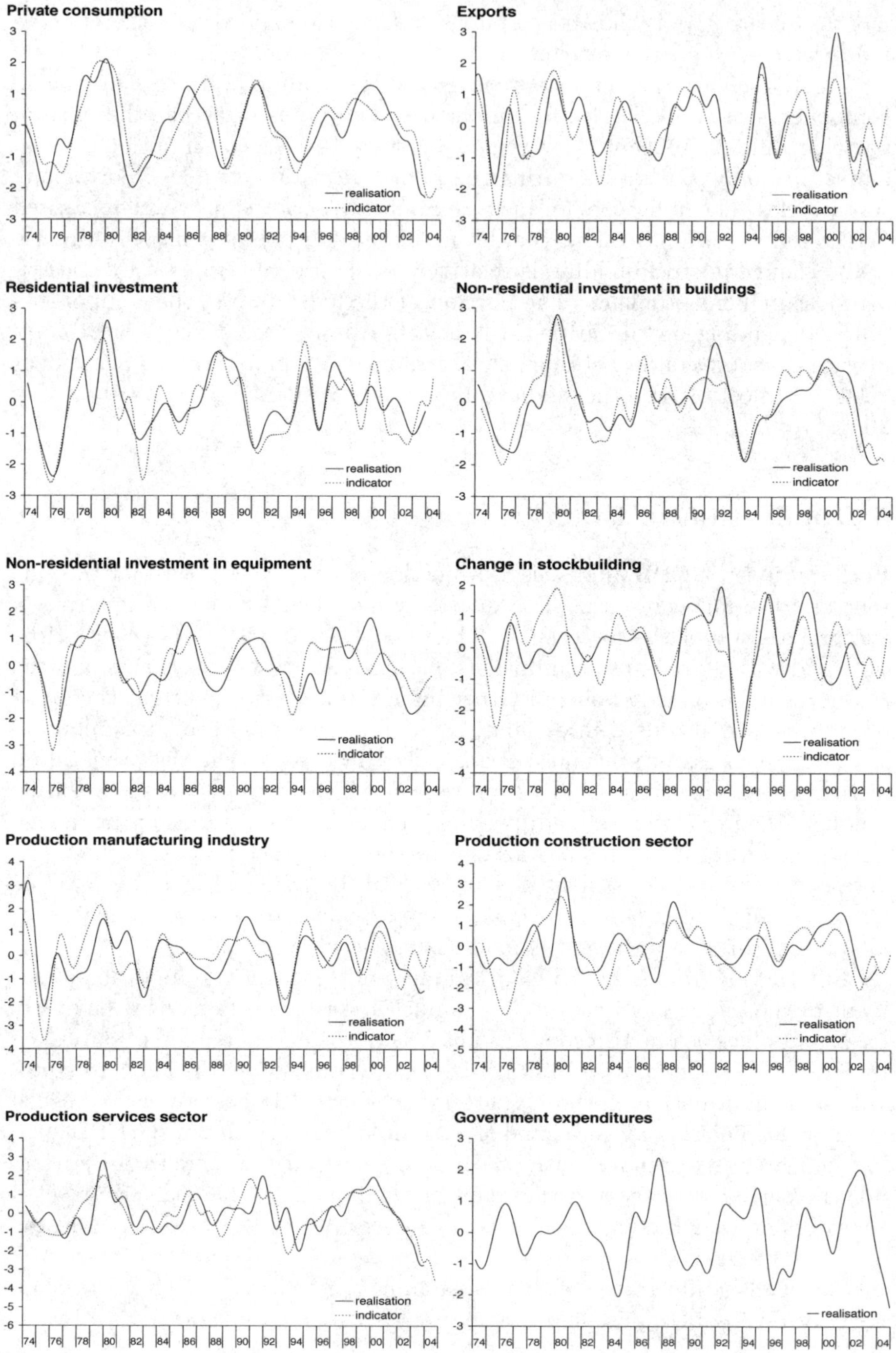

Fig. 8. Components of CPB Leading Indicator

household consumption. But if households report in the monthly survey that they do not have much confidence in the economic outlook or if they are pessimistic about their own financial situation, this signal could lead to a more cautious projection of consumer spending than would have happened purely on the basis of the relevant economic variables.

Similarly it may be necessary to temper the projection for exports if Dutch businesses are still pessimistic about orders received from abroad. In Sect. 3.4 we highlighted the usefulness of analyzing international indicators in addition to Dutch indicators and of seeing what signals they give off. Because of the importance of developments in Germany, strong or weak confidence among German manufacturers, as reflected in the expectation component of the Ifo business climate indicator, may thus be sufficient reason to reconsider the model's export projection and perhaps to adjust it.

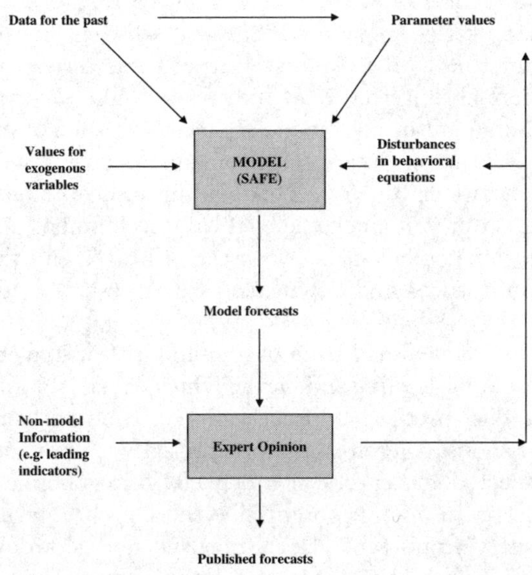

Fig. 9. Process of Making Short-Term Forecasts at CPB

6 Summary

Since 1990 CPB uses a leading indicator for the Dutch economy. The structure of the CPB leading indicator is tailored to its use as a supplement to model-based projections, and thus has a unique character in several respects. Gross domestic product (GDP) is used as the reference series. CPB is interested not only in "economic activity" in general, as summarized in GDP, but also in the development of key components of the economy. That is why the CPB leading indicator consists of subindicators for both expenditure categories ("demand") and production sectors ("supply"). Public spending has also been included in the system as a separate expenditure category.

CPB's methodology, which is based on the widely applied NBER methodology, uses so-called "deviation cycles". The elimination of trend-based components from the time series used in this approach is an important aspect of this approach. A serious drawback of the application of a filter is known as the "end-point problem", which arises because the addition of new or revised observations changes the filtered values of previous observations. Both a graphical exercise and a quantitative analysis show that the Hodrick Presscott (HP) filter is more sensitive to the end values than band pass filters. Of the two analyzed band pass filters, the Christiano Fitzgerald (CF) filter performs better than the Baxter and King (BK) filter and is now used in the revised CPB leading indicator

From the many series considered, 25 were selected for the 10 components of the CPB leading indicator. A clustering of these series shows that the different sources, namely international indicators, monetary variables, business surveys among manufacturers, business surveys in the construction industry, business surveys in the services sector, consumer surveys and other indicators contribute each between 10–15%. This leading indicator has a lead of 3 to 4 months. The indicator can track the cyclical development of real GDP rather well. The correlation coefficient between the indicator and the reference series is 0.82. The main upturns and downturns are represented quite accurately by the indicators.

Seven variables have a lead time of nine months or longer. These variables are combined in a long-leading indicator, which make it possible to look three quarters ahead. The "prediction" for the longer time horizon is based on less information and should therefore be interpreted with particular caution.

Of the 25 selected indicators, 4 are based on economic developments in other countries. For an open economy like the Dutch, international economic conditions are very important. Both upturns and slowdowns in economic growth often receive an initial impulse from abroad. Just like the two selected OECD's leading indicators for Europe and the US, the two selected Ifo series contribute 6.5% to the CPB leading indicator of the Dutch economy. Compared to the contribution of variables from surveys among Dutch manufacturers (15%), the contribution of the international indicators is limited. Ifo data about the expectations among German manufacturers play a larger role (14.3%) in the CPB long-leading indicator.

CPB leading indicator signals are compared with the projections based on the large-scale macro-econometric model used. This can lead to an adjustment of the model's projection by applying add-factors in specific behavioral equations, such as private consumption, investment or exports.

A Appendix

A.1 System of Equations CPB Leading Indicator

Consumption:

$$\mathrm{e} = [\ \mathrm{dol}(-6) + \mathrm{ifoe}(-6) + \mathrm{lieur}(-4) - \mathrm{rl}(-20) + \mathrm{m1}(-13) + \mathrm{oif}(-6)\ ] / 6$$

$$\mathrm{cp} = [\ \mathrm{cret}(-12) + \mathrm{ecc}(-15) - \mathrm{br}(-3) + \mathrm{wtob}(-12)\ ] / 4$$

$$\mathrm{ib} = [\ \mathrm{bpn}(-3) + \mathrm{ptn}(-4) - \mathrm{br}(-7)\ ] / 3$$

$$\mathrm{ie} = [\ \mathrm{cap}(-8) + \mathrm{ptn}(-8) + \mathrm{ccon}(-4) + \mathrm{oid}(-14) + \mathrm{orp}(-8)\ ] / 5$$

$$\mathrm{ir} = [\ \mathrm{bpr}(-5) + \mathrm{ptr}(-6) - \mathrm{rl}(-14)\ ] / 3$$

$$\mathrm{st} = [\ \mathrm{ifo}(-7) + \mathrm{oid}(-7) + \mathrm{mcon}(-9)\ ] / 3$$

Sectors:

$$\mathrm{ymi} = [\ \mathrm{prto}(-5) + \mathrm{ifoe}(-6) + \mathrm{lieur}(-5) + \mathrm{m1}(-13) + \mathrm{oit}(-7) + \mathrm{ptm}(-6)\ ] / 6$$

$$\mathrm{yci} = [\ \mathrm{ptn}(-12) + \mathrm{bpn}(-6) + \mathrm{stfp}(-10) + \mathrm{bpr}(-6) + \mathrm{ptr}(-14) + \mathrm{lieur}(-12) + \mathrm{lius}(-16) - \mathrm{rl}(-22) + \mathrm{m1}(-13) + \mathrm{orp}(-7)\ ] / 10$$

$$\mathrm{yserv} = [\ \mathrm{bpn}(-4) + \mathrm{cret}(-9) - \mathrm{br}(-4)\ ] / 3$$

$$\mathrm{yexp} = 0{,}25 * \mathrm{e} + 0{,}40 * \mathrm{cp} + 0{,}10 * \mathrm{ib} + 0{,}05 * \mathrm{ie} + 0{,}05 * \mathrm{ir} + 0{,}15 * \mathrm{st}$$

$$\mathrm{ysec} = 0{,}30 * \mathrm{ymi} + 0{,}55 * \mathrm{yserv} + 0{,}15 * \mathrm{yci}$$

$$\mathrm{conjind} = 0{,}425 * \mathrm{yexp} + 0{,}525 * \mathrm{ysec} + 0{,}05 * \mathrm{gov}$$

$$\mathrm{ll} = [\mathrm{cret}(-10) + \mathrm{ecc}(-15) + \mathrm{ifoe}(-9) + \mathrm{wtob}(-12)\ \mathrm{t}\ \mathrm{rl}(-20) + \mathrm{m1}(-13) + \mathrm{bpn}(-10)] / 7$$

Abbreviations:

conjind	CPB leading indicator
cp	private consumption
e	exports of goods excluding energy
gov	government expenditures
ib	non-residential investment in buildings
ie	non-residential investment in equipment
ir	residential investment
ll	long-leading indicator
st	change in stockbuildings
yci	production construction industry
yexp	production, expenditure approach
ymi	production manufacturing industry
ysec	production, sectoral approach
yserv	production services sector

Indicators:

bpn	buildings permits granted, non-residential
bpr	buildings permits granted, residential
br	bankruptcies
cap	capacity utilization
ccon	consumer confidence
cret	retail trade confidence indicator
dol	exchange rate dollar euro
ecc	economic climate
ifo	Ifo business climate (manufacturing industry)
ifoe	Ifo business climate (expectations, manufacturing industry)
lieur	leading indicator Europe (OECD)
lius	leading indicator United States (OECD)
mcon	producer confidence manufacturing industry
m1	money supply (M1, real)
oid	inflow domestic orders
oif	inflow foreign orders
oit	total inflow orders
orp	orderposition
prto	production trend observed
ptm	production expectations
ptn	production tendency non-residential buildings
ptr	production tendency residential buildings
rl	long-term interest rate
wtob	willingness to buy

References

AGRESTI, A., AND B. MOJON (2001): "Some stylised facts on the euro area business cycle," Working Paper Series No. 95, ECB, Europese Centrale Bank, Frankfurt.

ASSENBERGH, W. V. (2000): "Vernieuwde conjunctuurindicatoren," Themabericht 2000/04, Rabobank.

BAXTER, M., AND R. KING (1999): "Measuring business cycles: approximate band pass filters for noindent economic time series," *Review of Economics and Statistics*, 81, 575–93.

BERK, J., AND J. BIKKER (1995): "International interdependence of business cycles in the noindent manufacturing industry: the use of 'leading indicators' for forecasting and analysis," *Journal of Forecasting*, 14, 1–23.

BONENKAMP, J. (2003): "Herziening van de CPB-conjunctuurindicator," CPB Memorandum 71, Centraal Planbureau, Den Haag.

BURNS, A., AND W. MITCHELL (1946): "Measuring Business cycles," Studies in Business Cycles Vol. 2, National Bureau of Economic Research, New York.

CHADHA, J., AND C. NOLAN (2000): "A long view of the UK business cycle," *National Institute Economic Review*, 182, 72–89.

CHRISTIANO, L., AND T. FITZGERALD (2003): "The band pass filter," *International Economic Review*, 44, 435–465.

CPB (2003): "SAFE: A quarterly model of the Dutch economy for short-term analysis," CPB Document 42, The Hague.

DE HAAN, L., AND F. VIJSELAAR (1998): "Herziening van de DNB-conjunctuurindicator," MEB-Serie 1998-7, Onderzoeksrappor WO&E Nr. 545.

GIORNO, C., P. RICHARDSON, D. ROSEVEARE, AND P. VAN DEN NOORD (1995): "Estimating potential output, output gaps and structural budget balances," *OECD Economic Studies*, 24, 167– 209.

HODRICK, R., AND E. PRESCOTT (1997): "Post-war U.S. business cycles: an empirical investigation," *Journal of Money Credit and Banking*, 29, 1–16.

JACOBS, J. (1998): *Econometric Business Cycle Research*. Kluwer Academic Publishers, Boston/Dordrecht/London.

JACOBS, J., R. SALOMONS, AND E. STERKEN (1997): "The CCSO composite leading noindent indicator of the Netherlands: construction, forecasts and comparison," CCSO Series No. 31, Center for Cyclical and Structural Research, Groningen.

KRANENDONK, H. (1990): "CPB-conjunctuurindicator," Working Paper No. 36, CPB, Den Haag.

KRANENDONK, H., AND C. JANSEN (1997): "Using leading indicators in a model-based noindent forecast," CPB Report 1997/3, CPB.

LEBRUN, I. (1999): "Le système d'indicateurs avancés du BfP. Un nouvel outil pour l'analyse noindent conjuncturelle," Working Paper 2 / 99, Bureau fédéral du Plan, Brussel.

MCGUCKIN, R., A. O., AND V. ZARNOWITZ (2003): "A More Timely and Useful Index of leading Indicators," Economic program Working Paper 03–01, The Conference Board, New York.

OECD (1987): "OECD Leading indicators and business cycles in member countries 1960–1985," Sources and methods, OECD, Paris.

RAVN, O., AND H. UHLIG (2002): "On adjusting the HP-filter for the frequency of observations," *Review of Economics and Statistics*, 84, 371–376.

Reijer, A.H.J, D. (2002): "International business cycle indicators, measurement and forecasting," Research Memorandum WO No. 689, De Nederlandsche Bank, Amsterdam.

Zarnowitz, V., and A. Ozyildirim (2002): "Time series decomposition and measurement of noindent business cycles, trends and growth cycles," Working Paper 8736, NBER.

Part II

Monetary Policy Analysis

Firm Size and Monetary Policy Transmission – Evidence from German Business Survey Data

Michael Ehrmann*

European Central Bank, DG Research, Kaiserstraße 29, 60311 Frankfurt/Main, Germany michael.ehrmann@ecb.int

1 Introduction

Numerous recent publications have been devoted to a theoretical analysis of the various channels of monetary policy transmission.[1] On the empirical side, the evidence is still far from complete. This paper aims to contribute further evidence on two channels of monetary policy transmission, namely the balance sheet and the bank lending channel.

The balance sheet channel is built on the argument that asymmetric information in the credit markets necessitates the use of collateral for borrowing. As a consequence, the availability of credit for firms is dependent on the value of their assets. If credit market conditions are tightened by rising interest rates, this will affect the balance sheet positions of firms: higher interest payments reduce cash flow and higher interest rates lower the market value of assets. A monetary policy tightening can thus possibly leave firms with a restricted access to credit. The firms which are more likely to be affected by this channel are small firms: due to higher informational asymmetries, the amount of collateral they have to pledge is relatively higher. A balance sheet weakening due to a monetary policy tightening can thus imply that they might become credit-constrained.

The bank lending channel comes into play if the central bank has leverage over the volume of intermediated credit in the economy and at least some firms depend on intermediated credit. If the first condition holds, a tighter monetary policy decreases the volume of credit available to borrowers. If the second

*The survey data used in this paper was provided by CESifo, Munich. This paper is a revised version of ECB Working Paper No. 21. I would like to thank Mike Artis, Frank Browne, Stephen Cecchetti, Martin Ellison, Matteo Iacoviello, Benoît Mojon, Gabriel Perez Quiros, Frank Smets and Philip Vermeulen for helpful discussions, seminar participants at the Deutsche Bundesbank for comments and Anders Warne and Henrik Hansen for sharing their econometrics code. The views expressed are the author's and do not necessarily reflect those of the European Central Bank.

[1]For an overview of those channels see Cecchetti (1995).

condition holds, some borrowers cannot substitute intermediated credit with other forms of financing and will be left with a restricted access to finance their investment projects. It is typically assumed that it is easier for large firms to access other, non-intermediated forms of external finance, because the markets possess more information about these firms. Following monetary tightening, it is therefore relatively easy for large firms to substitute intermediated credit with other funds, whereas small firms are less flexible and hence face a restricted availability of funds.

Both channels are reflected in theories of credit market imperfections like those of Bernanke and Gertler (1989) and Kiyotaki and Moore (1997). Several publications like Christiano, Eichenbaum, and Evans (1996) or Gertler and Gilchrist (1994) have provided supportive evidence for the US economy: using firm size as a proxy for capital market access, they do indeed find that small firms are affected more strongly by monetary policy.

The strength of both transmission channels depends on the phase of the business cycle: theory predicts that both are stronger in a downturn. The balance sheet channel becomes more potent because net worth of firms falls in downturns, with a corresponding deterioration of balance sheet positions; the bank lending channel is strengthened because default probabilities rise in a downturn, thus increasing the cost of intermediated credit and starting a flight to quality, which restricts small firms even more than in booms.

Gertler and Gilchrist (1994) show that, indeed, small firms' reactions to shocks to the federal funds rate are dependent on the business cycle position. Perez-Quiros and Timmermann (2000) confirm that the stock returns of small firms are affected more strongly by tightening monetary conditions than those of large firms and that these effects are reinforced if the economy is in a recession.

Whereas the evidence for the US is generally supportive of these effects, the picture for Germany (and other European countries) is much less clear. The recent constributions by Kalckreuth (2003) and Chatelain et al. (2003) conclude that there is some scope for these channels in Germany, but that they are of secondary importance. By splitting firms according to a rating variable that measures their credit worthiness, distributional effects of monetary policy can be identified, whereas the size of firms appears uninformative in this respect. This is in contrast with Audrestsch and Elston (2002), who find firm size to be important. Finally, Siegfried (2000) cannot identify credit channel effects at all in his study.

The data underlying most of the existing studies has two drawbacks. On the one hand, there is often a compositional bias towards large firms. On the other hand, annual balance sheet data, which are often available for small firms, do not allow inference at higher frequencies. The present paper exploits a data set that is not subject to those shortcomings; it includes very small firms (1–49 employees) and is available at a monthly frequency.

A large part of the literature follows Fazzari et al. (1988) by comparing the sensitivity of investment to cash flow across firms with differing degrees of informational asymmetries. However, Kaplan and Zingales (1997) and Kaplan and Zingales (2000) argue that such investment-cash flow sensitivities do not provide useful measures of financing constraints. Rather, the reaction need not be monotonic in the degree of financial constraints. This can be the case if the finance premium of a strongly financially constrained firm reacts less than for a firm which is relatively less constrained. The approach taken in this paper differs from this indirect testing by comparing cash flow sensitivities and thus not prone to the Kaplan and Zingales critique. Although I will follow the literature and classify firms a priori according to the degree of financial constraints (using a size criterion), I will conduct a direct test as to how the firm (namely, its business conditions) is affected by monetary policy.

The remainder of this paper is organized as follows. The data set will be described in Sect. 2. Section 3 explains the testing strategy applied. The subsequent Sect. 4 explores whether small firms are affected disproportionately by monetary tightenings. Section 5 investigates whether the asymmetry arises due to demand or supply side factors. In a further step, Sect. 6 checks for business cycle asymmetries of monetary policy effects. Section 7 concludes.

2 Data Description

Each month, the German Ifo-Institute for Economic Research conducts a business survey among more than 8,000 firms. Of these, approximately 3,000 belong to the West German manufacturing industry and form the subsample used in this paper. Firms are invited to answer questions on their business and demand conditions in the following ways:

- "At present, we consider our business conditions to be i) good, ii) satisfactory (usual for the season), iii) bad"
- "Our demand situation, compared to the last month, has i) improved, ii) remained unchanged, iii) deteriorated"

Boxes are provided next to each answer; the firms have to tick the box according to their choice. For each question, all answers are aggregated to an index variable by subtracting the share of "−"answers (third option) from the share of "+"answers (first option). The indices can therefore take any value between +1 and −1, with the extreme cases occurring when all firms answer with "+" or "−".

The data can be broken down according to firm size, with the classifications depicted in Table 1.

The size sorted data are available from July 1981. The latest observation included in the analysis here is 1998:12, to avoid the problem of a changing monetary policy regime with the introduction of the euro. As an illustration, Fig. 1 shows the business conditions for the largest and smallest firms. Apparently, there is quite some variation of the series across size groups.

Table 1. Sample Breakdown

Size Class	1	2	3	4	5
Employees	1–49	50–199	200–499	500–999	≥1,000
% of Sample	16%	33%	23%	13%	15%

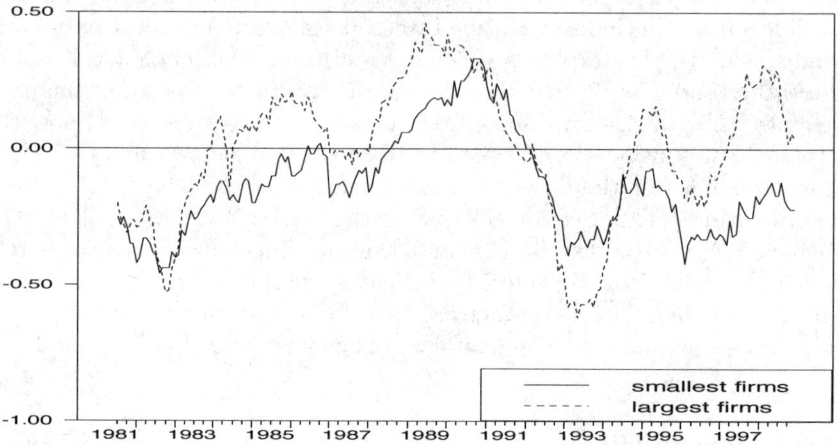

Fig. 1. Business Conditions of Firms of Size Class 1 (Smallest) and 5 (Largest)

Tables 2 to 4 provide some descriptive statistics of the series. They all exhibit a monotonic relationship between the size classes. This monotonicity will reappear in several results throughout the paper and suggests that size is an important factor in explaining firm behavior.

Table 2. Mean of Series

Size Class	1 (smallest)	2	3	4	5 (largest)
Business Conditions	-.118	-.064	-.048	-.020	-.006
Demand	-.091	-.050	-.019	-.013	.010

Table 3. Coefficient of Variation of Series

Size Class	1 (smallest)	2	3	4	5 (largest)
Business Conditions	-141	-323	-425	-1095	-3917
Demand	-109	-220	-568	-885	1240

A priori, it is not clear whether data series of this kind are actually suitable for an analysis of macroeconomic issues. Firstly, it can be argued that

Table 4. Correlation Coefficients for Different Size Classes

Business Conditions					Demand				
*sc*1	*sc*2	*sc*3	*sc*4	*sc*5	*sc*1	*sc*2	*sc*3	*sc*4	*sc*5
1					1				
97	1				.94	1			
.91	.96	1			.89	.92	1		
.90	.95	.98	1		.81	.86	.90	1	
.77	.84	.93	.94	1	.74	.79	.87	.87	1

the access to relevant information differs across size classes, thus leading to different response patterns. Secondly, the series contain only perceptions of firms, rather than "hard" and quantifiable facts. Nothing guarantees that the perceptions of firms are, even when aggregated, on average correct. However, there is evidence that the data are free of such biases.

The business conditions index is used, together with a series on firms' business expectations, to construct the "Ifo Business Climate Index", an indicator which is widely used in German business cycle analysis because of its good quality as a leading indicator. Indeed, as is shown in Table 6 in the appendix, the correlations of the data with the business cycle is striking and clearly shows a leading pattern. Business conditions lead deviations from trend in industrial production by one quarter, and have a correlation coefficient of 0.85 for most size classes. The high correlation of all series with the business cycle suggests that they draw a rather accurate picture of the actual business conditions.

Another potential problem with this data could arise if size were correlated with other features, like e.g. the industry affiliation. In such a case, the regressions might reveal industry effects of monetary policy rather than size effects. Although it might be the case that the size distribution differs across industries, it is comforting to know that most industries cover all size classes. Exceptions are 6 out of 27 industries, namely the wood industry, which comprises size classes 1 to 3 only, car manufacturing (size classes 2 to 5 only), ceramics (1 to 4), paper (1 to 4), "other production goods" (3 to 5), and "other consumer goods" (1 to 3). Most of these industries (with the exception of car manufacturing) have a relatively small share in the aggregate industrial production.

Since the data are aggregated across firms, it is not possible to estimate the individual firms' thresholds at which they would have changed their assessment of business conditions sufficiently to also change their answer to the survey. Whereas the series of a single firm follows a step function over time, changing between the three possible answers, this would only be the case for the aggregated series if the thresholds were identical across firms. The smoothness of the series reveals that the thresholds are different for the individual firms, however. The aggregated series can therefore not be used to estimate the threshold value for firms, and whether this depends on firm size, but instead to estimate whether a larger share of small firms experiences a change in business conditions that leads them to change their assessment in the survey.

In any case, the survey data cannot give an estimate of how strongly a firm is affected once it has passed the threshold level. The estimates in this paper might therefore underestimate the potential asymmetries, if not only more small firms are led to report a worsening of their conditions, but their actual conditions also deteriorate by even more than the threshold value.

The data are not only aggregated across firms, but also across the type of answers, since the share of negative answers is subtracted from the share of positive answers. In order to analyze whether this affects the results, all regressions have been performed on the share of positive and negative answers separately, too. All results in the paper are unaffected by this robustness check.

The business survey series are transformed according to $y^* = \ln\left(\frac{1+y}{1-y}\right)$, a monotonically increasing transformation that maps the data from the $[-1,1]$ interval to $[-\infty,+\infty]$; a more detailed explanation is provided in appendix A.1.

3 Testing Strategy

Tests of the balance sheet and bank lending channel need to identify the reaction of credit supply to a monetary policy shock. In this paper, as in Gertler and Gilchrist (1994), we will employ the heterogeneity of firms to do so. The underlying assumption, as mentioned in the introduction, is that small firms are more prone to asymmetric information problems and more dependent on bank loans than large firms. A monetary-policy-induced decrease of credit supply should therefore lead to a worsening of business conditions that is larger for small firms than for large firms. The main difficulty, however, is to ensure that the bank lending channel is the only possible explanation for such a differential reaction.

Gertler and Gilchrist analyse the reaction of sales to a monetary policy shock. A larger drop of sales in small than in large firms, however could also be explained by subcontracting: if large firms contract out to small firms when demand is high, but maintain the whole business in times of weak demand, then this could also imply a stronger drop of sales for small firms after a monetary tightening. Similarly, business conditions for small firms would deteriorate by more than those for large firms in such a case. To overcome this identification problem, Gertler and Gilchrist analyze the reaction of inventories: if financial frictions exist, then small firms should face more difficulties in smoothing production when sales decline and as such should be forced to shed inventories. In this paper, a different strategy is used. Since firms reveal their demand situation, the effects of subcontracting should be reflected in the demand situation of small firms. Once demand is controlled for, any additional disproportionate decrease in business conditions cannot be explained by subcontracting.

A similar identification problem arises if small firms are concentrated in cyclical industries. Again, this possibility is accounted for by the demand variable. Having controlled for demand, the cyclicality of the industry has been corrected for.

A third issue mentioned by Gertler and Gilchrist could arise if small firms have more flexible technologies. For their sales and inventories data, this is potentially interesting, since a more flexible firm can adjust inventories to movements in sales more quickly. For the business conditions, this is not an issue, since this scenario would imply that a small firm, with a faster adjustment, reports depressed business conditions for a shorter period only. This effect would therefore counteract the expected stronger reaction of small firms' business conditions.

As an additional check, Gertler and Gilchrist suggest testing for asymmetries across the business cycle. This approach will be implemented here as well. The credit constraints should be more important in recessions than in booms, which would imply that the reaction of small firms' business conditions is larger during recessions than it is during booms.

Although the Ifo survey contains data on inventories, they will not be exploited here, because the actual level of inventories, as analyzed in Gertler and Gilchrist, is conceptually different from the according survey data. In the survey, firms are asked whether they consider their level of inventories too small, sufficient, or too big. If a firm accumulates inventories, this can be an active process because it perceives the present level of inventories as too low, or because inventories are treated as some sort of residual: with decreasing demand, a firm might want to smooth production and therefore accumulates inventories. Although we would see an accumulation of inventories in both cases, the answers in the business survey would be different.

The next sections will first estimate whether business conditions show a differential response according to size classes. Subsequently, the control for demand will be introduced. Eventually, it will be analyzed whether the effects of monetary policy on business conditions differ across business cycle phases.

4 Monetary Policy and Business Conditions

The effects of monetary policy will be analyzed with Structural Vector Autoregressions (SVARs). In particular, the identification approach suggested by King, Plosser, Stock, and Watson (1991) (KPSW) will be employed. In their framework, monetary policy can be modelled in terms of shocks to cointegration relations and as such need not be restricted to shocks to single variables. As a matter of fact, a monetary policy shock will be modelled as a shock to the interest rate and (with opposite sign) to the money growth rate. A more detailed discussion of both SVAR models and the KPSW procedure is provided in appendix A.2.

4.1 The Baseline Model

The estimations start with a simple baseline model to understand how business conditions of firms are affected by monetary policy. Later on, the model will be extended to investigate the differential impact of monetary policy on firms of different size.

The baseline model consists of a four-variate VAR with

$$X_t = [Dm_t \quad bc_{i,t} \quad i_t \quad \pi_t]' ,$$

where X_t includes the growth rate of M3 (Dm_t), business conditions of size class i ($bc_{i,t}$), a three month's money market rate (i_t) and producer price inflation (π_t).[2] The data are monthly and range from 1981:7 to 1998:12, covering a sample of 210 observations. Since the aim of this paper is to identify effects over the business cycle, seasonality and long-run trends are eliminated by the inclusion of seasonal dummies and the use of detrended variables. The latter is achieved by simply regressing the data on a linear trend. Six lags are included in the models, which are estimated as Vector Error Correction models (VECMs) to allow for the possibility of cointegration. Stability tests on the VARs do not show any signs of structural breaks.

This model is estimated separately for the business conditions of each size class.[3] The cointegration analysis for this baseline model suggests the existence of cointegration relations (see Table 7 in the appendix). Three possible relations come to mind: the business conditions should be stationary, because they form a business cycle indicator and as such should be mean reverting; economic theory suggests furthermore that real interest rates are stationary. The third cointegrating vector assumes that in the long run, money growth (possibly money growth exceeding some constant rate) equals inflation, which imposes superneutrality of money.[4] A cointegration rank of 3 seems plausible a priori, and the test statistics can be read in this way. In the following, the existence of 3 cointegration relations is therefore assumed, with the cointegrating vectors formulated as follows:

	Dm_t	$bc_{i,t}$	i_t	π_t
β_1' :	0	1	0	0
β_2' :	0	0	1	-1
β_3' :	1	0	0	-1

[2] All variables, with the exception of interest rates, are in logarithms (the growth rates are annualized differences of the variables in logarithms). Producer price inflation was chosen because it is not affected by indirect tax increases. The consumer price index for Germany is greatly distorted by indirect tax increases and one-off effects of German unification, which would require the introduction of several dummy variables in a VAR.

[3] Although this could imply that each model estimates a different monetary policy shock, a direct comparison shows that they are nearly identically estimated.

[4] This is derived and shown to be empirically relevant in Crowder (1997).

This hypothesis cannot be rejected in a corresponding test, as shown in Table 8 in the appendix. With this specification of the cointegrating vectors, the impulse response analysis of the system can now be performed. The monetary policy shock will be identified within the transitory subsystem, because after some time all variables should return to baseline (note that this already implies an identification restriction).[5] To identify the monetary policy shock within this subsystem, it is assumed that it affects neither business conditions nor inflation within the same month.

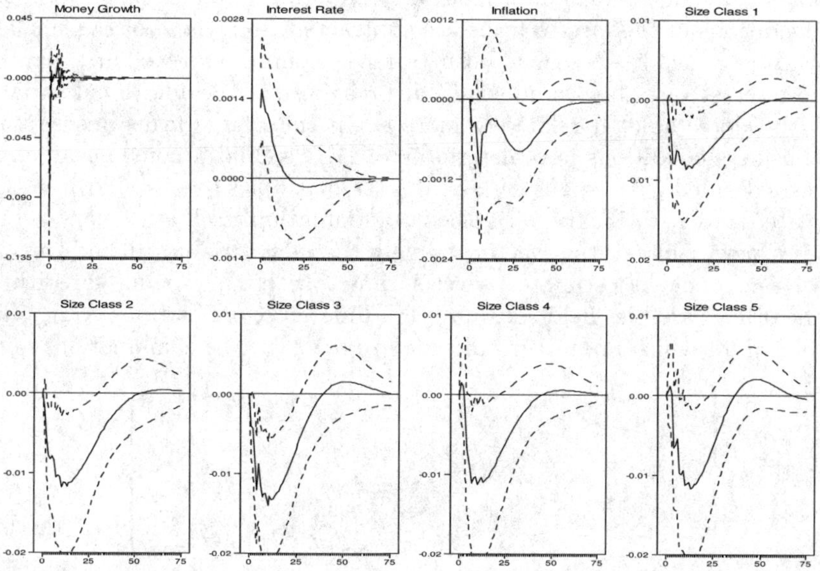

Fig. 2. Responses to a Monetary Policy Shock, Baseline Model

The resulting impulse responses, presented with 90% error bands, are provided in Fig. 2. The monetary policy shock is found to be a combination of a shock to the money growth rate and to interest rates: a decrease in money growth plus an increase in interest rates constitute a contractionary monetary policy shock. This shock decreases inflation and business conditions. All impulse responses are as expected a priori, which indicates that the base-

[5]Actually, the persistent shock is a nominal shock, too. It affects the nonstationary variables in the VAR, i.e. permanently alters the levels of inflation, money growth and/or interest rates. The interpretation of such a shock could be one of a changing inflation target of the Bundesbank. However, such a shock is difficult to reconcile with the actual pattern of the Bundesbank's monetary policy; I consider it more reasonable to assume that the nonstationarity of the series is a matter of the sample size rather than one of actual properties of the time series.

line model has succeeded in identifying monetary policy innovations.[6] However, these models cannot estimate whether a monetary tightening might have asymmetric impacts on firms of different size. An extended model is therefore called for.

4.2 Asymmetric Effects of a Monetary Tightening Across Size Classes

In order to test for possible asymmetries across size classes, the difference of responses is included as an additional variable. To give an example, the business conditions of the largest firms are subtracted from those of the smallest firms ($\Delta_{15,t} = bc_{1,t} - bc_{5,t}$). If both business conditions react in a parallel way to interest rate shocks, no significant response of the additional variable should be detectable. If relatively more small than large firms answer that their business conditions have deteriorated, $\Delta_{ij,t}$ should become negative.

The extended VAR spans $X_t = [\Delta_{ij,t} \quad Dm_t \quad ip_t \quad i_t \quad \pi_t]'$.[7] $\Delta_{ij,t}$ as the difference of two stationary variables is by definition itself stationary, which implies a new cointegrating vector, namely the new variables themselves. As before, the model is estimated several times, with $\Delta_{ij,t}$ being substituted and the other variables held constant. Ten different combinations of $\Delta_{ij,t}$ are possible, all of which are in turn included in a VAR. The combinations are:

$$\left\{ \begin{array}{rrrr} bc_{4,t} - bc_{5,t} & bc_{3,t} - bc_{5,t} & bc_{2,t} - bc_{5,t} & bc_{1,t} - bc_{5,t} \\ & bc_{3,t} - bc_{4,t} & bc_{2,t} - bc_{4,t} & bc_{1,t} - bc_{4,t} \\ & & bc_{2,t} - bc_{3,t} & bc_{1,t} - bc_{3,t} \\ & & & bc_{1,t} - bc_{2,t} \end{array} \right\}$$

The results of this exercise are reported in Fig. 3. A tightening of monetary policy leads to distributional effects which are, however, estimated only at low levels of significance. The business conditions of all size classes worsen (see above), but those of smaller size classes deteriorate more after approximately 18 months. The point estimates of responses of $\Delta_{ij,t}$ are then negative for every single measure. This implies that the business conditions of smaller firms take longer to return to baseline than those of larger firms, which would mean that the transmission lags of the balance sheet and bank lending channel are relatively long. This is not implausible, however, since both channels operate through the banking system, which might add further reaction and transmission lags.

[6]The results throughout this paper are robust to a substitution of M3 with M2, or the inclusion of exchange rates.

[7]Detrended industrial production, ip_t, replaces the business conditions, $bc_{i,t}$, used so far for two reasons: first, to have an identical output variable across models and second, to avoid using the business conditions of a size class twice, in $bc_{i,t}$ as well as in $\Delta_{ij,t}$. The results go through with using a $bc_{i,t}$-variable instead, too.

Additionally, the impulse responses evolve monotonically across size classes. Firms become more heterogeneous when moving from the left to the right in the matrix of responses, as well as when moving up from the bottom. In both directions, and for every single row and column, the point estimates of the impulse responses become more pronounced step by step.

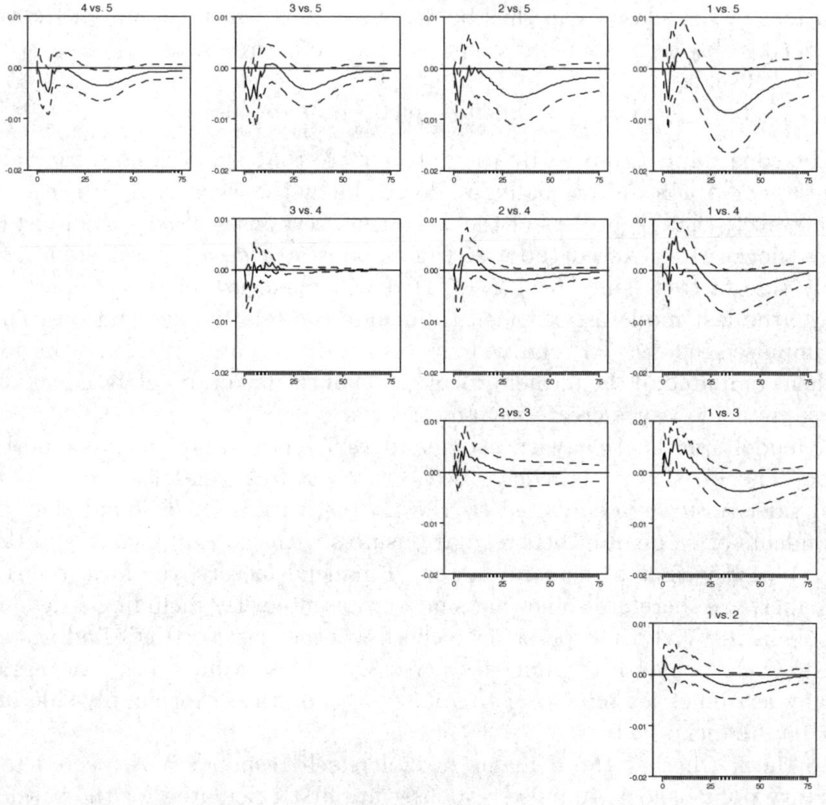

Fig. 3. Responses of the Relative Business Conditions of Firms ($\Delta_{ij,t}$) to a Contractionary Monetary Policy Shock

5 Demand Side Effects

The original hypothesis that small firms are affected more strongly by monetary policy shocks stems from capital market imperfection theories and as such is concerned with financial factors. The evidence found in the preceding section supports this hypothesis, but cannot reveal whether the asymmetry indeed arises due to financial factors. If the business survey included questions on the financial situation of firms, the hypothesis could be tested directly. Unfortunately, this is not the case. The survey question on the current demand situation of firms can be helpful to single out other potential explanations, however.

Potentially, both the supply side as well as the demand side situation of firms should enter the evaluation of current business conditions. The business conditions of size class i can thus be described as a weighted sum of the two factors (possibly with some intercept α_i and some error term $\varepsilon_{i,t}$):

$$bc_{i,t} = \alpha_i + \omega_i dem_{i,t} + (1 - \omega_i) sup_{i,t} + \varepsilon_{i,t}$$

The constraints imposed by the data set are that $sup_{i,t}$ is not observable – whereas $dem_{i,t}$ is. Additionally, we do not know the weights ω_i. It is easy to see, however, that regardless of the weighting, responses of $bc_{i,t}$ to monetary policy shocks that exceed those of the responses of $dem_{i,t}$ must stem from supply side factors (since $0 \leq \omega_i \leq 1$). I will make use of this property as follows: the last model is extended to include the relative demand positions. The impulse responses of relative business conditions and demand situations are then compared: if the former are bigger than the latter, it can be concluded that supply-side issues create asymmetry, too.

A model specification with a demand variable is useful for yet another reason. The Ifo survey data have been criticized for a bias towards the demand side. A survey conducted by the Ifo Institute in 1976 found that the respondents often deal in their regular business with the firm's sales, and thus give a biased weight to demand factors. Financial factors, the focal point of this paper, are therefore somewhat underrepresented. By including a demand variable in the VAR, it is possible to check whether last section's findings are robust. Once demand asymmetries across size classes have been accounted for, any asymmetries on top of this make a strong case for supply-side and probably financial factors.

To check whether the demand variable itself responds as expected to a monetary policy shock, impulse responses are first calculated for the baseline VAR $X_t = [Dm_t \quad dem_{i,t} \quad i_t \quad \pi_t]'$. $dem_{i,t}$ denotes demand and is varied to cover all five size classes. The results of the cointegration analysis and the tests of the restrictions on the cointegrating vectors can be found in the appendix. A cointegration rank of $r = 3$ is maintained for all models, with the cointegrating vectors being the demand variable, the real interest rate and superneutrality of money (see Tables 9 and 10). Figure 4 plots the impulse responses of this baseline VAR. Following a contractionary monetary policy shock, demand declines for firms of all size classes, as expected.

In order to test for asymmetric effects, the relative demand situation is included in the model of the preceding section. The VAR now comprises $X_t = [\Delta_{ij,Dt} \quad \Delta_{ij,t} \quad Dm_t \quad ip_t \quad i_t \quad \pi_t]'$, where $\Delta_{ij,Dt}$ denotes the relative demand position of firms, in contrast to $\Delta_{ij,t}$ which represents the relative

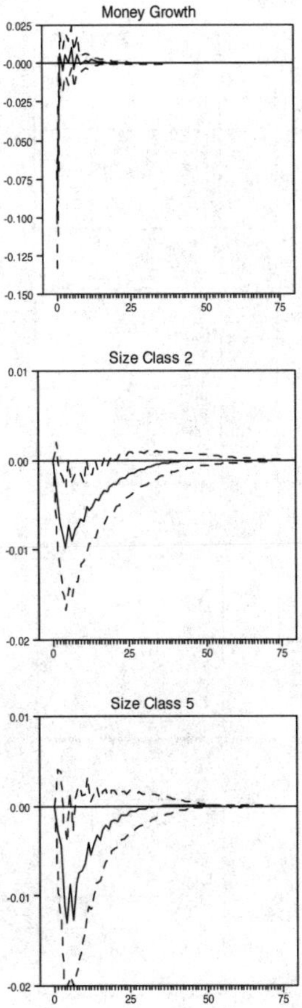

Fig. 4. Responses of Demand to a Monetary Policy Shock

business conditions of firms. The model is again estimated for all ten possible combinations of the delta-variables. The corresponding impulse responses can be found in Figs. 5 and 6. The relative demand positions of firms deteriorate after a monetary policy tightening, which means that again there is a bias which is unfavorable for small firms, although this specification has not been able to improve the significance of the findings. Again, each point estimate becomes more pronounced moving up the columns or moving to the right in the rows of Fig. 5.

How does the picture on the relative positions of firms change with respect to their business conditions? Comparing Fig. 5 with Fig. 6, it turns out that, indeed, the responses of relative business conditions are indeed much stronger than those of demand positions. Interestingly, the responses of relative business conditions hardly change when the model is extended: Figs. 3 and 6 are

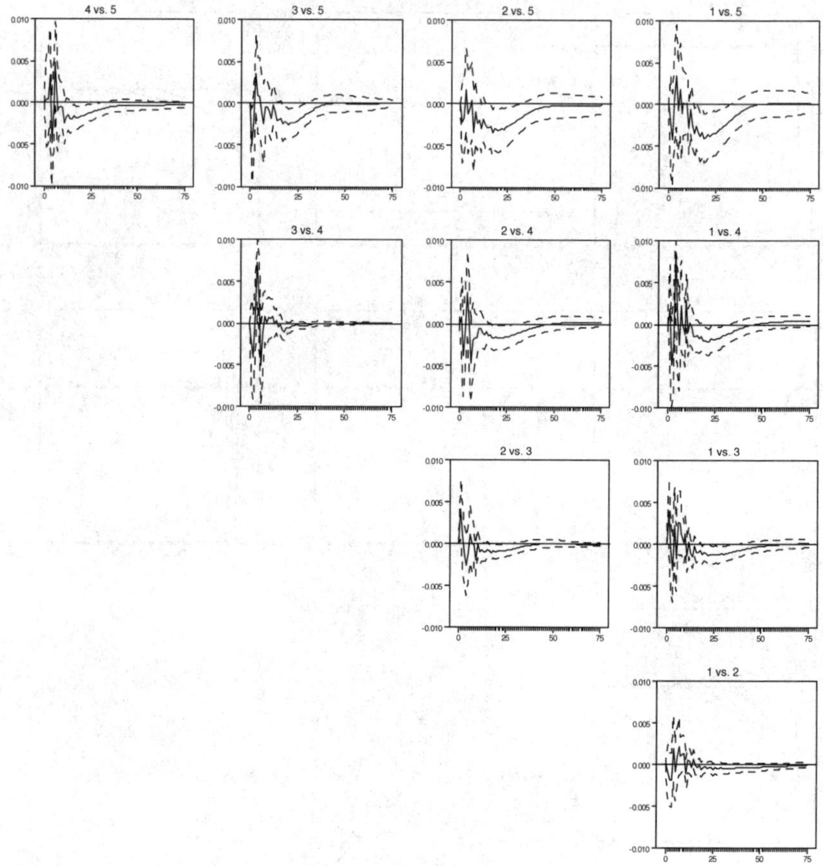

Fig. 5. Responses of the Relative Demand Positions of Firms ($\Delta_{ij,Dt}$) to a Contractionary Monetary Policy Shock

nearly identical. The conclusion from this exercise is that demand also reacts more strongly for small firms; however, demand tells only part of the story. We are left with another cause of asymmetry that must stem from the supply side.

6 Business Cycle Asymmetry

As stated in the introduction, theories of the credit channel maintain the hypothesis that the distributional effects of monetary policy actions should be more pronounced in business cycle downturns. In the following, I will test for these effects, but two caveats should be mentioned beforehand.

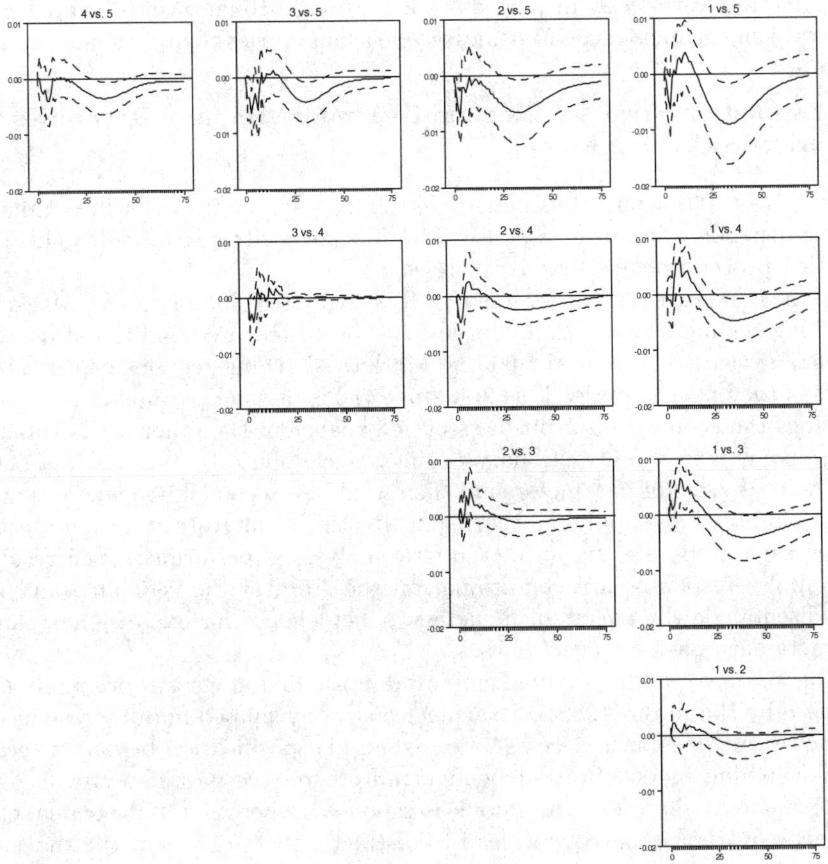

Fig. 6. Responses of the Relative Business Conditions of Firms ($\Delta_{ij,t}$) to a Contractionary Monetary Policy Shock in a Model with Demand

Firstly, the data sample ranges from 1981:7 to 1998:12 and inspection of Fig. 1 reveals that over this sample period the German economy went through roughly 1.5 cycles. The evidence to be extracted from this small sample has to be taken with caution.

Secondly, the German economy is often referred to as a bank-based system. Small firms in particular often have a close link to one bank, their "Hausbank". Theory suggests that small firms allow one single bank to gain such an influential position only because they expect advantages in other areas. For example, one of the possible gains a small firm might achieve in a close banking relationship is interest rate smoothing: a bank might be willing not to pass on a monetary-policy-induced interest rate increase to a close customer. This effect is probably strongest in times when the borrower would have difficulties with rising interest rates, i.e., in periods of low growth. Relationship lending can thus weaken the incidence of business cycle asymmetries to quite some extent.

6.1 Estimation Strategy: Regime-Dependent Impulse Responses in a Markov-Switching Model

In order to test for such business-cycle-related asymmetries, I will calculate regime-dependent impulse responses in a Markov-switching model.[8] This estimation procedure consists of two stages.

In the first stage, an unrestricted VAR is estimated that allows for Markov-switching regimes. Since the hypotheses to be tested are conditional on the business cycle, it is essential that the Markov-switching regimes capture the states of the business cycle. This first stage yields distinct parameter sets: one describes the economy in a business cycle expansion; the other set is valid if the economy is in a contractionary business cycle phase.

These two sets of parameters are then used in a second stage where structure is imposed by applying the usual identification restrictions, for each regime separately, and impulse response analysis is performed. The resulting impulse responses are conditional on the state of the economy, and as such disentangle the effects of monetary policy shocks for expansionary and contractionary business cycle phases.

The Markov-switching model employed in the first stage was originally introduced by Hamilton (1989) . To achieve distinctly shaped impulse responses for the two regimes, it is necessary to extend his specification beyond a mere mean-switching model. State-dependent autoregressive parameters will give rise to different shapes of the impulse responses, whereas a state-dependent variance–covariance matrix will lead to distinct impact effects of the shocks.

Impulse responses conditional on the state of the economy are of course a ceteris paribus experiment. The economy is in a given regime when the monetary policy shock hits the system, and the effects traced by looking at impulse responses assume that, throughout, the economy does not switch regimes.[9] In this way it is possible to test the theoretical predictions, which themselves are conditional: the transmission channels are claimed to be stronger during downturns than during expansions.

Of course, the analysis is a pure thought experiment. Given a probability of staying in one regime of, say, .95, the expected probability of still being in the same regime some 48 months later is merely .09 – so one would not really expect to stay in the same regime all the time for which the impulse responses are actually being calculated. The impulse responses are nonetheless a useful tool. As long as the economy stays in the same regime, they are valid – so

[8] See Ehrmann et al. (2003) for a more detailed exposition of the estimation strategy.

[9] This excludes any analysis of how effective a monetary policy shock can be in moving the economy from one state to the other.

even if the full trajectory is not being realized, the periods up to the change in regime are characterized by the conditional impulse responses.

6.2 Model Set-up

To keep the model as parsimonious as possible, the number of regimes chosen is two. In addition, the number of variables in the VAR is reduced. It is not feasible in this context to estimate large-dimensional systems as in the preceding sections. The reduction is carried out in two steps. Firstly, it turns out that a cointegrated VAR with $X_t = [bc_{i,t} \quad i_t \quad \pi_t]'$ with the KPSW identification scheme gives reasonable impulse responses, too: business conditions deteriorate after a shock to the interest rate, and inflation falls. The informational content has decreased of course, because now it is no longer possible to identify the liquidity effects of monetary policy.

A second reduction is possible because in the very special case analyzed here, where the variables of interest are stationary, the model specification can be reduced from a full-blown VECM with KPSW's identification scheme to a simple VAR with stationary variables only, where the identification scheme follows a Choleski decomposition. The two models simulate the same shocks in this case: A KPSW model simulates shocks to the cointegration relations

$$\beta' X_t = \begin{pmatrix} 1\,0\,0 \\ 0\,1\,\text{-}1 \end{pmatrix} \begin{pmatrix} bc_{i,t} \\ i_t \\ \pi_t \end{pmatrix}$$

where the monetary policy shock is a shock to the second cointegrating vector, i.e., to the real interest rate. An equivalent shock can be modelled in a VAR which includes $bc_{i,t}$ and the real interest rate r_t directly.

Both in KPSW with two cointegration relations and in the stationary VAR, one identification restriction has to be imposed. The restriction that a monetary policy shock cannot affect business conditions contemporaneously is imposed in a VAR with a Choleski decomposition by ordering real interest rates last.

The business conditions of firms define the business cycle; if they fall, the economy is in a contraction; if they rise, the business cycle position is expansionary. This implies that models for the different size classes would define a different business cycle. To ensure some stability, each model therefore includes the business conditions of the largest firms and additionally those of firms of a different size class. This leads to the model set-up

$$\begin{pmatrix} bc_{i,t} \\ bc_{5,t} \\ r_t \end{pmatrix} = \begin{pmatrix} \beta_1(s_t) \\ \beta_2(s_t) \\ \beta_3(s_t) \end{pmatrix} + B_1(s_t) \begin{pmatrix} bc_{i,t-1} \\ bc_{5,t-1} \\ r_{t-1} \end{pmatrix} + B_2(s_t) \begin{pmatrix} bc_{i,t-2} \\ bc_{5,t-2} \\ r_{t-2} \end{pmatrix} + \begin{pmatrix} \varepsilon_{1t} \\ \varepsilon_{2t} \\ \varepsilon_{3t} \end{pmatrix} \quad (1)$$

where $\varepsilon_t \backsim iid \quad N(0, \Sigma)$. The state transition probabilities are assumed to follow a first-order Markov chain:

$$p_{ij} = \Pr(s_{t+1} = j | s_t = i), \quad \sum_{j=1}^{2} p_{ij} = 1 \quad \forall i, j \in \{1, 2\} \tag{2}$$

Some restrictions are imposed to decrease the number of switching parameters: none of the autoregressive parameters in the interest rate equation is switching, and the variance–covariance matrix is not state-dependent.

6.3 Empirical Results

In such a set-up, it is a priori not sure whether the regimes picked by the algorithm are actually related to the business cycle. Any kind of regime that shows best fit, be it characterized by distinct intercepts, autoregressive parameters, or some combination, can emerge. Nonetheless, the regimes picked can indeed be characterized as business cycle downturns and expansions. To take an example, in the model with $bc_{2,t}$ and $bc_{5,t}$ the estimated mean for $bc_{5,t}$ is $-.23$ in regime one, and .09 in regime two ($-.21$ and .04 for $bc_{2,t}$). Figure 7 reports the according regime probabilities and compares them with the business conditions variable $bc_{5,t}$. The fit of regimes to expansions and contractions is relatively close: regime 1 spans from peaks to troughs and therefore indicates a business cycle contraction, whilst regime 2 is well characterized as an economic expansion. The characterization of business cycle regimes is very close to those found in other, univariate Markov-switching models, e.g. in Krolzig and Toro (2000). The matrix of switching probabilities is

$$P = \begin{pmatrix} 0.92 & 0.08 \\ 0.04 & 0.96 \end{pmatrix}.$$

Two lags prove to be sufficient to achieve a well-specified VAR. This shows that the fit of the models is much better in a Markov-switching framework than when neglecting it; in the standard VAR models, a lag length of six was needed. The results of mis-specification tests following Hamilton (1996) can be found in the appendix. The restrictions imposed on the autoregressive parameters of the interest rate equation are accepted with a p-level of 0.65.

In the second stage of the procedure, structure is given to the unrestricted MS-VAR. Figure 8 graphs the impulse responses to a monetary policy shock conditional on the state of the economy. In both regimes, a tightening of monetary policy leads to a deterioration of business conditions for firms of all size classes. Not unexpectedly, the impulse response functions are estimated rather imprecisely. This is especially the case for regime 1, which is estimated on very few observations. When interpreting the point estimates, however, it is interesting to compare the responses for a given size class across the two regimes. For some size classes, there does not seem to be any difference, whereas firms of size class one face a stronger deterioration of business conditions when the economy is in a downturn. The magnitude of the maximum effects more than

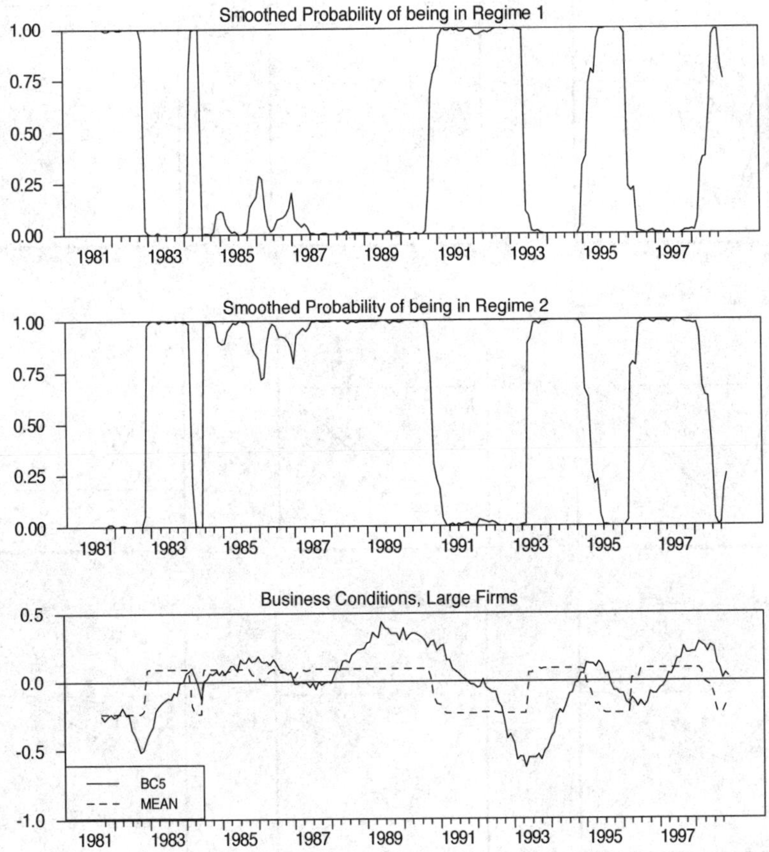

Fig. 7. Regime Probabilities for the Markov-Switching VAR with Business Conditions

doubles: from −3.5 to −7.7. A direct comparison across size classes is provided in the Table 5, which calculates the amplification of responses in contractions relative to expansions (in the example of size class one: $\frac{-7.7}{-3.5} = 2.2$). As predicted by theory, the effect of an interest rate shock on business conditions of the smallest firms is stronger in a downturn than in an expansion, although this finding is subject to a caveat regarding its statistical significance.

Table 5. Amplification of Responses in Business Cycle Downturns

Size Class	1	2	3	4	5
Amplification Factor	2.2	0.7	1.0	1.7	1.0

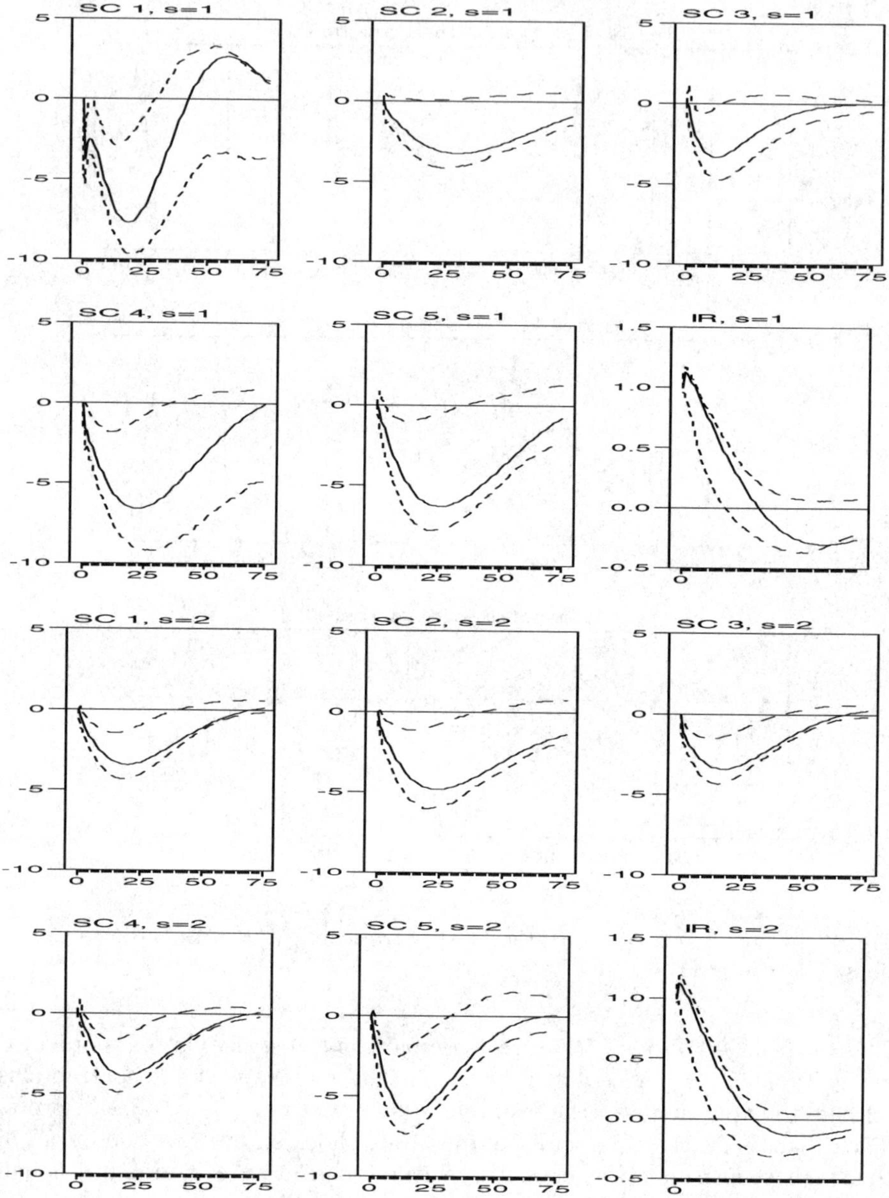

Fig. 8. State-Dependent Responses to a Monetary Policy Shock

7 Conclusion

This paper has provided empirical tests for hypotheses formulated in capital market imperfection theories, claiming a higher exposure of small firms to monetary policy tightenings when compared to large firms. The data set analyzed consists of firms' aggregated answers from a business survey. The data is sorted into size classes, ranging from firms with 1–49 employees to firms with more than 1,000 employees. Thus, a sample bias towards large firms which is present in many data sets is avoided. The business survey is conducted on a monthly basis, which allows for an analysis at a much higher frequency than the usual data sets on small firms (mostly annual balance sheet data or quarterly financial reports). The downside of the data set is possible ambiguities, because the survey questions concern non-quantifiable items such as the general assessment of business conditions. It has been shown, however, that the series possess good leading indicator qualities and correlate closely with the business cycle components of industrial production. Therefore, the data quality can be considered as adequate for research on macroeconomic issues.

The empirical results support theories of asymmetric monetary policy effects. The business conditions of all firms deteriorate after a monetary tightening, but those of small firms do so relatively more. As a consequence, small firms are hit disproportionately strongly by interest rate increases; this shift in their relative position causes distributional effects of monetary policy in that the burden of adjustments is unevenly shared between firms of different size. Although at modest levels of significance, it has furthermore been shown that these asymmetries are augmented in business cycle downturns. Compared to expansions, the distributional effects are more pronounced.

An analysis of demand-side factors has been performed in order to distinguish supply-side from demand-side effects. After accounting for differences in the relative demand situations of small vs. large firms, there are still distributional effects of monetary policy detectable. Demand-side factors can thus tell only part of the story, with the bulk being left for supply-side factors. Even though it was not possible to test the importance of financial issues with the available data, this is the main criterion that comes to mind when thinking about uneven effects of interest rate changes. The empirical findings of this paper therefore support theories which predict asymmetric effects of monetary policy and cannot reject theories that attribute such effects to financial factors.

A Appendix

A.1 Transformation of Business Survey Data for the Empirical Analysis

The transformation applied to the business survey data series is based on the assumption that the data follows a logistic model. Most of the time, it can be expected that the variables cluster around medium values in the range, say, of $[-.5, .5]$. Only if the macroeconomic conditions become very (un-)favourable can it be expected that the series come close to their extreme values of ± 1. In order to make 100% of all firms answer that times are worse/better, the conditions must be very severe, especially because the data are not disaggregated according to industry. Indeed, the actual range of the series is far from hitting the borderline cases. This means, however, that the trajectories of the business survey series follow the model

$$y_t = 2\frac{e^{x_t'\beta+\varepsilon_t}}{1+e^{x_t'\beta+\varepsilon_t}} - 1, \tag{3}$$

where the x_t are the usual explanatory variables of a regression model. The multiplication by factor 2 and the subtraction of 1 ensure that the data actually lie in the range $[-1, 1]$ (for $x_t'\beta + \varepsilon_t \to \infty$, $y_t \to 1$; for $x_t'\beta + \varepsilon_t \to -\infty$, $y_t \to -1$). Graphically, the model assumed for the business survey data looks as follows:

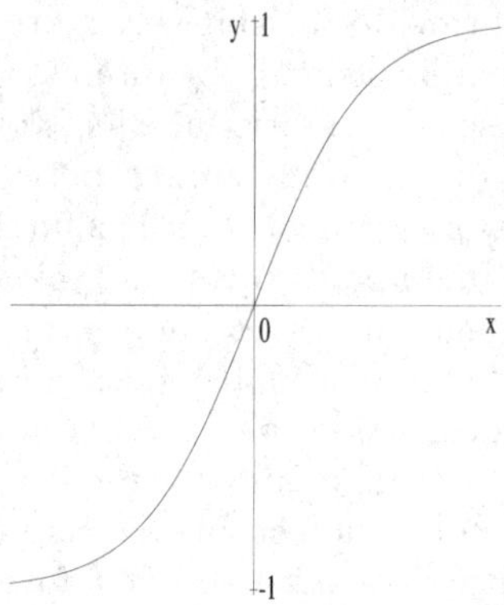

Let $a_t = e^{x_t'\beta+\varepsilon_t}$. Thus (3) simplifies to

$$\begin{aligned} y_t &= \frac{2a_t}{1+a_t} - 1 \\ y_t + y_t a_t &= 2a_t - 1 - a_t \\ a_t(1-y_t) &= 1 + y_t \\ a_t &= \frac{1+y_t}{1-y_t} \\ e^{x_t'\beta+\varepsilon_t} &= \frac{1+y_t}{1-y_t} \end{aligned}$$

By applying the transformation $y_t^* = \ln\left(\frac{1+y_t}{1-y_t}\right)$it is possible to estimate a linear regression model

$$y_t^* = x_t'\beta + \varepsilon_t \tag{4}$$

A.2 The KPSW-Approach to Identification in Structural Vector Autoregressions

Structural Vector Autoregressions (SVARs) go back to the seminal article by Sims (1980). They assume that the economy can be described by a dynamic, stochastic, linear model of the form:

$$A_0 X_t = A_1 X_{t-1} + ... + A_k X_{t-k} + \mu_t = A(L) X_{t-1} + \mu_t \tag{5}$$

with $\mu_t \sim iid \quad N(0, \Sigma_\mu)$, where X_t represents an $nx1$-vector of endogenous variables, including one or several instrument variables, and L denotes the lag operator. The estimation proceeds with the reduced form

$$X_t = C_1 X_{t-1} + ... + C_k X_{t-k} + \varepsilon_t = C(L) X_{t-1} + \varepsilon_t \tag{6}$$

with $C_i = A_0^{-1} A_i$ and $\varepsilon_t = A_0^{-1} \mu_t$. Estimates can be found for the coefficient matrices C_i and the variance–covariance matrix of the disturbances ε_t, Σ_ε. However, of interest are the parameters in the matrices A_i and Σ_μ, which are exactly identified if n^2 parameters are restricted. A first set of restrictions is found by the assumption of uncorrelated structural errors (i.e., Σ_μ diagonal) and by normalising the diagonal elements to unity, yielding $\Sigma_\mu = E(\mu_t \mu_t') = I_n$, which imposes $n(n+1)/2$ restrictions. Hence, further $n(n-1)/2$ restrictions are needed. Sims (1980) used a recursive structure to achieve identification, whereas subsequent contributions extended the range of identification schemes by restricting parameters in various matrices of the system. Amongst these are King, Plosser, Stock, and Watson (1991). They have shown that cointegration properties of the data can be used for identification purposes. A cointegrated VAR model, which is in its Vector Error Correction format (See Johansen (1995), pp. 45–49):

$$\Delta X_t = \alpha\beta' X_{t-1} + \sum_{i=1}^{k-1} \Gamma_i \Delta X_{t-i} + \varepsilon_t \tag{7}$$

has the Granger representation

$$X_t = C \sum_{i=1}^{t} \varepsilon_i + C^*(L)\varepsilon_t + A \tag{8}$$

where A depends on initial values, $\beta' A = 0$, and $C = \beta_\perp(\alpha_\perp' \Gamma \beta_\perp)^{-1} \alpha_\perp'$ with $\Gamma = I - \sum_{i=1}^{k-1} \Gamma_i$. Equation (8) shows that the representation in levels is composed of two parts, the non-stationary common trends $\alpha_{\perp}^{'}\sum_{i=1}^{t}\varepsilon_i$ and the stationary part of $C^*(L)\varepsilon_t$.

The idea behind KPSW is to decompose the shocks ε into r shocks that have only transitory effects (on the levels of the variables), and $n-r$ shocks with permanent effects (with r denoting the number of cointegration relations). This is achieved by rotating the system by premultiplying certain matrices. The new set of variables Y is

$$Y_t = \begin{pmatrix} SX_t \\ \beta' X_t \end{pmatrix}. \tag{9}$$

The matrix S has to satisfy $SC \neq 0$. It follows that the new set of variables consists of $n-r$ non-stationary and r stationary variables. The stationary variables are identical to the cointegrating vectors; their stationarity follows because $\beta' C = 0$ and $\beta' A = 0$:

$$\beta' X_t = \beta' \beta_{\perp}(\alpha_{\perp}^{'} \Gamma(1) \beta_{\perp})^{-1} \alpha_{\perp}^{'} \sum_{i=1}^{t} \varepsilon_i + \beta' C^*(L)\varepsilon_t + \beta' A = \beta' C^*(L)\varepsilon_t. \tag{10}$$

This system need not be identified fully; partial identification of either the transitory or the persistent shocks is also possible. This amounts to the imposition of $r(n-r)$ identification restrictions by setting the according covariances of the shocks to zero. These restrictions have been tested for by the test for the cointegrating rank. Instead, however, a different kind of identification restriction is needed, namely a decision as to which part of the system the supposed shock is to be found (like in the context of the present paper, where the monetary policy shock is identified in the transitory subsystem). This restriction cannot be tested and has to be justified by economic theory.

To identify the subsystems, additional untested identification restrictions are necessary. If only the shocks with permanent effects are of interest, then $(n-r)(n-r-1)/2$ additional identification restrictions are needed. In particular, where there are $r = n-1$ cointegration relations, no additional identification restrictions have to be imposed. Should the shocks of interest be the transitory ones, then $r(r-1)/2$ additional restrictions are sufficient.

A.3 Test Statistics

Table 6. Cross-Correlation of Business Conditions with Industrial Production, Quarterly Bandpass-Filtered Variables

	-6	*-5*	*-4*	*-3*	*-2*	*-1*	*0*	*1*	*2*	*3*	*4*	*5*	*6*
bc1	-.69	-.66	-.52	-.26	.08	.42	.67	**.78**	.74	.60	.43	.27	.15
bc2	-.46	-.30	-.08	.20	.48	.70	.83	**.85**	.76	.61	.43	.24	.08
bc3	-.51	-.36	-.13	.15	.44	.68	.82	**.85**	.78	.64	.47	.30	.16
bc4	-.56	-.42	-.19	.10	.41	.67	.82	**.85**	.78	.64	.47	.30	.14
bc5	-.58	-.45	-.22	.08	.40	.67	.83	**.85**	.76	.61	.43	.26	.11

For lag k, the correlations are defined between output_t and business conditions_{t-k}. Hence, a positive k indicates the lead of a variable with respect to the business cycle. The variables are: business conditions for firms of size class 1 (bc1) to 5 (bc5), where 1=smallest, 5=largest.

Table 7. Trace Statistics for the Test of Cointegration Rank of the Baseline Model

Model	$bc_{1,t}$	$bc_{2,t}$	$bc_{3,t}$	$bc_{4,t}$	$bc_{5,t}$
$r = 0^a$	92.14	90.61	97.30	94.73	99.08
$r = 1^b$	50.87	48.08	51.12	49.84	56.60
$r = 2^c$	21.70	20.66	24.72	23.07	27.22
$r = 3^d$	4.37*	4.83*	5.70*	7.30*	6.19*

[a] critical values 95%: 53.42; [b] 34.80; [c] 19.99; [d] 9.13

Table 8. Test for Three Cointegrating Vectors in the Baseline Model: $bc_{i,t}$, Real Interest Rates and Superneutrality of Money

Model	$bc_{1,t}$	$bc_{2,t}$	$bc_{3,t}$	$bc_{4,t}$	$bc_{5,t}$
$\chi^2(3)$	6.80	5.81	4.52	3.49	5.83
p-value	0.08	0.12	0.21	0.32	0.12

Table 9. Trace Statistics for the Test of Cointegration Rank of the Baseline Model with Demand Variables

Model	$dem_{1,t}$	$dem_{2,t}$	$dem_{3,t}$	$dem_{4,t}$	$dem_{5,t}$
$r = 0^a$	87.18	85.89	93.72	89.81	85.40
$r = 1^b$	45.87	42.28	50.30	47.03	43.72
$r = 2^c$	22.04	21.91	23.39	22.23	22.57
$r = 3^d$	4.09*	4.56*	6.69*	5.93*	5.97*

^{a} critical values 95%: 53.42; ^{b} 34.80; ^{c} 19.99; ^{d} 9.13

Table 10. Test for Three Cointegrating Vectors in the Baseline Model with Demand Variables: Demand, Real Interest Rates and Superneutrality of Money

Model	$dem_{1,t}$	$dem_{2,t}$	$dem_{3,t}$	$dem_{4,t}$	$dem_{5,t}$
$\chi^2(3)$	8.48	7.01	6.05	6.45	6.13
p-value	0.04	0.07	0.11	0.09	0.11

Table 11. Mis-Specification Tests for the MS-VAR Model on Business Conditions: $bc_{2,t}, bc_{5,t}, r_t$

	Autocorrelation	ARCH	Markov chain
Equation 1	1.20 (0.31)	0.02 (0.89)	1.41 (0.23)
Equation 2	2.09 (0.08)	3.22 (0.07)	0.03 (1.00)
Equation 3	0.37 (0.83)	1.50 (0.22)	3.03 (0.02)*
System	1.03 (0.42)	1.32 (0.12)	2.01 (0.05)

Tests are for omitted autocorrelation, omitted ARCH and mis-specification of the Markovian dynamics. Numbers in brackets are p-values.

References

AUDRESTSCH, D., AND J. ELSTON (2002): "Does Firm Size Matter? Evidence on the Impact of Liquidity Constraints on Firm Investment Behavior in Germany," *International Journal of Industrial Organization*, 20, 1–17.

BERNANKE, B., AND M. GERTLER (1989): "Agency Costs, Net Worth, and Business Fluctuations," *American Economic Review*, 79, 14–31.

CECCHETTI, S. (1995): "Distinguishing Theories of the Monetary Transmission Mechanism," *Federal Reserve Bank of St. Louis Review*, 77, 83–97.

CHATELAIN, J., A. GENERALE, I. HERNANDO, AND U. V. P. VERMEULEN (2003): "Firm Investment and Monetary Policy Transmission in the Euro Area," in *Monetary Policy Transmission in the Euro Area*, ed. by I. Angeloni, A. Kashyap, and B. Mojon, pp. 133–161. Cambridge University Press.

CHRISTIANO, L., M. EICHENBAUM, AND C. EVANS (1996): "The Effects of Monetary Policy Shocks: Evidence from the Flow of Funds," *Review of Economics and Statistics*, 78, 16–34.

CROWDER, W. (1997): *The Liquidity Effect: Identifying Permanent and Transitory Components of Money Growth.* mimeo, University of Texas at Arlington.

EHRMANN, M., M. ELLISON, AND N. VALLA (2003): "Regime-Dependent Impulse Response Functions in a Markov-Switching Vector Autoregression Model," *Economics Letters*, 78, 295–299.

FAZZARI, S., R. HUBBARD, AND B. PETERSEN (1988): "Financing Constraints and Corporate Investment," *Brookings Papers on Economic Activity*, pp. 141–195.

GERTLER, M., AND S. GILCHRIST (1994): "Monetary Policy, Business Cycles, and the Behavior of Small Manufacturing Firms," *Quarterly Journal of Economics*, 109, 309–340.

HAMILTON, J. (1989): "A New Approach to the Economic Analysis of Non-Stationary Time Series and the Business Cycle," *Econometrica*, 57, 357–384.

——— (1996): "Specification Testing in Markov-Switching Time-Series Models," *Journal of Econometrics*, 70, 127–157.

JOHANSEN, S. (1995): *Likelihood-Based Inference in Cointegrated Vector Autoregressive Models.* Oxford University Press, Oxford.

KALCKREUTH, U. V. (2003): "Investment and Monetary Transmission in Germany: A Microeconometric Investigation," in *Monetary Policy Transmission in the Euro Area*, ed. by I. Angeloni, A. Kashyap, and B. Mojon, pp. 133–161. Cambridge University Press.

KAPLAN, S., AND L. ZINGALES (1997): "Do Investment-Cash Flow Sensitivities Provide Useful Measures of Financing Constraints?," *Quarterly Journal of Economics*, 112, 169–215.

——— (2000): "Investment-Cash Flow Sensitivities Are Not Valid Measures of Financing Constraints?," *Quarterly Journal of Economics*, 115, 707–712.

KING, R., C. PLOSSER, J. STOCK, AND M. WATSON (1991): "Stochastic Trends and Economic Fluctuations," *American Economic Review*, 81, 819–840.

KIYOTAKI, N., AND J. MOORE (1997): "Credit Cycles," *Journal of Political Economy*, 105, 211–248.

KROLZIG, H., AND J. TORO (2000): "Classical and Modern Business Cycle Measurement: The European Case," Economic Discussion Paper No. 60, University of Oxford.

PEREZ-QUIROS, G., AND A. TIMMERMANN (2000): "Firm Size and Cyclical Variations in Stock Returns," *Journal of Finance*, 55, 1229–1262.

Siegfried, N. (2000): “Microeconometric Evidence for a German Credit Channel,” Macroeconomics Working Paper No. 1/2000, University of Hamburg.
Sims, C. (1980): “Macroeconomics and Reality,” *Econometrica*, 48, 1–48.

The Role of the Ifo Business Climate Indicator and Asset Prices in German Monetary Policy

Elmer Sterken *

University of Groningen, Department of Economics, P.O. Box 800, 9700 AV Groningen, The Netherlands and CESifo, Munich, Germany.
e.sterken@eco.rug.nl

1 Introduction

No matter whether an instrument or a targeting rule is used, monetary policy makers are concerned about the short-run future development of e.g. inflationary expectations and/or the expected output gap. The forward looking nature of monetary policy is widely acknowledged in theory, see e.g. Walsh (2003), but still creating problems in empirical analysis. In most of the nowadays popular time-series studies, Christiano, Eichenbaum, and Evans (1999), it has become apparent that it is hard to use reliable indicators of expected output and price developments. As Orphanides (2001) argues, the use of e.g. real-time output data can change for instance the role and interpretation of a Taylor rule in the US case.[1] In this paper we present a double answer to the forward looking problem problem. We will use a business cycle indicator as a proxy to measure current real economic activity. Moreover, we will use asset prices as indicators of expectations of all future economic variables. The goal of the paper is twofold. First, we want to illustrate that misspecification issues are less likely to occur if one takes these kind of forward looking variables into account. Secondly, we will show that central banks do indeed respond to information embedded in these forward-looking variables. This sheds some new light on the interpretation of monetary policy.

In the end the effectiveness of monetary transmission, by whatever channel, depends on the rigidity of prices and wages and on the transmission into real expenditure categories. Traditionally, the so-called interest rate channel is held

*I thank Bob Chirinko and Leo de Haan for sharing their knowledge, Jan Jacobs for helpful remarks and especially Frank Westermann for essential suggestions. This paper is sponsored by CESifo. I gratefully acknowledge the support of Timo Wollmershäuser and Jan-Egbert Sturm.

[1]Adema (2003) on the other hand illustrates that this problem is less relevant for the euro area, because the European Central Banks focuses more on the control of inflation.

responsible for transmission of monetary policy shocks. Nowadays the working of the whole financial system is believed to be relevant. Due to informational problems the credit market has a special role in propagating monetary shocks, see Bernanke and Blinder (1988). But revaluation of all assets and liabilities (resulting in net wealth positions) seems to determine the ultimate impact. The financial structure, as described by Tobin in his general equilibrium view on the financial sector, see Brainard and Tobin (1968), is crucial in transmission. See also the financial accelerator approach by Bernanke, Gertler, and Gilchrist (1999).

As Lettau et al. (2002) show for the US, equity, housing and liquidity are considered to be the three key financial markets in transmission (apart from the money and credit markets). Liquidity in various forms is essential to consumption and investment decisions (but we will not elaborate on this well-developed literature here). Lettau et al. argue that the housing market is central in monetary transmission. An interest rate increase will increase the costs of mortgages. The fall in demand for housing will reduce the collateral value of existing houses, lower borrowing capacity for its owners and thus start a downturn in a credit cycle, Kiyotaki and Moore (1999). The direct wealth effects of housing market crashes are well known and by far more substantial than any other revaluation effect. Equity markets on the other hand have a leading role in expected future growth and inflation forecasting. The informational contents of equity is relevant to forward-looking decisions. As Bernanke (2003) argues monetary economists need to understand how strong monetary policy changes affect equity prices (the equity price-interest rate elasticity is believed to be about 3 to 6 for the US) and more important, why equity prices are influenced. With this knowledge one can analyze transmission of asset price changes into real decisions and infer consequences for monetary policy.

Asset prices contain more information than any other economic variable: e.g. equity prices are believed to signal future business cycle developments. Until the last recession in 2001 in the US, the SP-500 has shown to be a leading indicator of GDP growth. This leading property of asset prices has two major consequences. First, monetary authorities will use asset price information to derive inflationary and output gap expectations. The Bundesbank was believed to pursue a monetary strategy focused on inflation, Bernanke and Mihov (1997b), and thus would have been eager to follow asset price inflation. Secondly, private agents will use the information embedded in asset prices (or revaluations) into their decision making process. So the leading informational contents of asset prices might change our view on the effectiveness of monetary policy. If we observe that central banks care about expectations, we should also incorporate growth expectations. Are central bankers interested in lagged real growth or output gaps in steering monetary policy or do they take care of expected business cycle developments? We advocate the latter in this paper and combine the role of the role of asset prices and expected output developments. It is most likely that business cycle indicators will not be determined by asset price bubbles (as the US was in 2001) and will therefore be valuable contributors in our analysis.

We take Germany as an example because of two main reasons. First of all, the German financial system and the role of the housing market are special. Germany is known for being a bank-based economy, see e.g. Kakes and Sturm (2002). This leads to the expectation that housing price transmission may be important. With the Netherlands, Germany has the highest share of mortgage loans to GDP in the EU. This could lead to vulnerability to interest rate shocks. Moreover, the term of the mortgage contracts is typically long (25 to 30 years, as in Austria and The Netherlands). On the other hand the owner occupation rate in Germany is relatively low (40 percent, while 63 for the EU) while the private rental occupation rate is high. So it remains an empirical problem to establish the precise impact of house prices. Secondly, we take Germany as an example since it has a consistent historical experience in using business cycle indicators. We will return to this issue later on when discussing the data we use.

There are several interesting issues to be addressed. First, how is the monetary transmission mechanism affected by asset prices? Does neglecting asset price developments lead to the "wrong" conclusions with respect to output and inflation-sensitivity to monetary policy changes? Secondly, how big is the impact of asset price shocks on GDP? How should we cope with a contemporaneous measurement of GDP, knowing that official publication of GDP lags at least one year? And thirdly, did monetary authorities respond to asset price changes in the past? We do not go into the problem how central banks should respond to asset price changes. The latter problem requires the specification of a social welfare function, which is out of the scope of this paper.

In the next section we provide a short description of the theoretical context of our study. Our main argument in Sect. 2 is that it is generally believed that positive asset price shocks should stimulate real expenditure. In Sect. 3 we briefly compare the German housing and equity markets to those in France, Italy, Japan, the UK and US. We show that housing is relatively important in Germany. We proceed in Sect. 4 by reviewing the literature on Vector AutoRegression (VAR) models. We describe the methodology, the major results on monetary policy identification and VAR models that focus on Germany and/or asset prices. Next we specify a basic VAR model of the German economy. We show that including the Ifo indicator instead of real GDP growth in the base model leads to a more interesting interpretation of monetary policy. Next we show that including asset prices also provides a richer view. We compare the major findings of the models in terms of structural factorizations of impulse response functions and variance decompositions of the interest rate equation (which we assume to be the monetary policy rule). In Sect. 6 we summarize and conclude.

2 Theory

The literature on the theory of monetary transmission and monetary policy rules is enormous, see e.g. Walsh (2003). For our paper two strands of this literature are relevant. First, the role of the measurement of real activity. Secondly, the role of asset prices. In the discussion on monetary policy rules measurement of expected real activity is one of the recent issues of debate. Orphanides (2001) discusses the role of so-called real-time indicators of output gaps and concludes for the US that using real-time data matters in designing rules. Sauer and Sturm (2003) and Adema (2003) do not find that the use of real-time data matters to the ECB's monetary policy design. In general though, the literature is convinced of the forward-looking nature of monetary policy, see Clarida and Gertler (1997). So including more timely measures of output or output gaps is necessary in designing rules.

Our second theoretical item, the role of asset prices in monetary transmission, deserves a little more attention. We discuss the role of asset prices in general, and house and equity prices in particular. Housing and equity differ in two important aspects. First, housing provides direct consumer services and enters the utility function, see e.g. Aoki, Proudman, and Vlieghe (2002). Second, price changes of housing can be observed less frequently. This implies that the informational content of housing prices is typically less than the one carried by equity.

Standard classical monetary theory focuses on the interest rate channel. In the tradition of Wicksell (1907), a lower banking rate (below the natural rate of interest) has an impact on spending (investment in particular) which will lead to higher output if prices are sticky. Starting with Bernanke and Blinder (1988), the credit channel has become an important second line of transmission. Information asymmetries in the credit market will lead to equilibrium rationing and so transmit initial monetary shocks via credit to output. In the same spirit Bernanke and Gertler (1995) extended the credit channel to a credit view by allowing the so-called financial accelerator: revaluation of assets affects spending.

How should we treat asset price changes in this respect? First, since asset prices reflect expected discounted future payoff streams, an adjustment of a (stochastic) discount factor will lead to a revaluation. To what extent precisely monetary policy changes affect these stochastic discount factors (are risk premia embedded?) is unknown, but a positive shock to money market rates is likely to have a negative direct revaluation of assets. If asset prices change, how will this influence real expenditure? Here we can think of four basic mechanisms, see Chirinko, de Haan, and Sterken (2003).

First, there is the classical Modigliani life-cycle model, which leads to the wealth channel. Higher asset values will increase lifetime wealth and therefore positively affect e.g. private consumption. It is an empirical matter to what extent various assets will (temporarily) affect lifetime wealth. Equity price changes might be transitory and interpreted in this way, while house price changes for instance might be considered to be more permanent (or sticky at least). Moreover, an asset like housing provides direct consumer services and enters a utility function, see e.g. Aoki, Proudman, and Vlieghe (2002). If asset components and consumption are substitutes, an increase in e.g. housing wealth might lead to substitution out of consumption. So the wealth channel is not completely clear about the impact of asset price changes on real expenditure.

Secondly, in relation to the financial accelerator, we have the balance sheet channel. Both consumers and firms can be exposed to financing constraints, due to informational problems. If external finance is more expensive than internal sources of finance it is likely that financial structure of households or firms is relevant. Positive revaluation of assets can alleviate these constraints, see Hubbard (1998).

Third, positive shocks to e.g. equity prices might lower the equity financing costs (and to some extent the same argument holds for housing). If the current equity price falls below the fundamental value, equity financing gets cheap. This so-called equity-financing channel might not lead to a positive impact on real expenditure if managers use the proceeds from emissions to invest in financial transactions. So the sign of the equity channel is not clear a priori.

Fourth, in the spirit of Brainard and Tobin (1968) there might be an allocation channel. If there is an initial shock to some asset price, imperfect substitutable assets will be exchanged, leading to revaluation of other assets. It will be hard to align market and fundamental values, which might lead to misallocation. This misallocation might even stretch out to real investment.

The bottomline of these four channels is that it is likely that there will be positive impact of a policy interest rate decrease, but there is no absolute guarantee. It remains an empirical issue to what extent asset price changes will affect real expenditure.

3 The German Equity and Housing Markets in a Birds-Eye View

The German financial system is different from its UK and US equivalents, Allen and Gale (2000). We do not discuss this general feature in detail, but provide Table 1 with some basic key indicators for France, Germany, Italy, Japan, the UK and US (from the World Bank source on Financial Structure Indicators). We can observe the relative overhang to bank loans in Germany opposed to the more equity-markets-based Anglo-Saxon economies. Knowing this general feature of the German financial system, we provide some more detail on housing and equity markets. Table 2 provides information of the relative shares of equity and housing values in a subset of the countries (using our database EUROMON, produced by De Nederlandsche Bank). Here we see that housing wealth is relatively large in Germany. Equity markets are relatively larger by this measure in the UK and US (as one would expect from

Table 1). The wealth components are computed from the capital stock of the corporate sector and the general stock price index for the equity variable and the stock of owner occupied houses and the general housing price index for the housing variable. From Table 2 we conclude that the role of the housing market is relatively important in Germany.

Table 1. Financial System Indicators

	France	Germany	Italy	Japan	UK	US
Private credit by deposit money banks to GDP	80.9	93.6	53.1	102.4	79.1	64.3
Concentration of banks	34.5	38.6	30.6	18.3	45.0	21.1
Net Interest Margin	3.3	2.9	3.9	2.0	2.3	4.4
Stock market capitalization to GDP	22.6	19.1	13.6	68.0	82.6	64.9
Stock market total value traded to GDP	11.1	18.3	6.5	34.7	38.0	46.0
Stock market turnover ratio	39.7	85.7	38.8	48.6	40.3	62.8
Private bond market capitalization to GDP	42.5	48.1	30.4	43.2	16.6	79.5
Public bond market capitalization to GDP	32.7	22.9	91.2	52.3	30.2	56.1

Source: World Bank web-page:
http://www.worldbank.org/research/projects/finstructure/index.htm Financial Structure Indicators, averages over 1978–98.

Table 2. Housing and Equity Wealth Indicators (Percentages of GDP)

	France	Germany	Italy	Japan	UK	Japan
Housing	377.0	686.4	514.9	309.1	407.0	426.4
Equity	529.9	532.1	547.5	374.3	602.4	616.4

Source: EUROMON Database, De Nederlandsche Bank. The housing wealth is computed as the rebuilding value of the stock of private owner occupied houses (assuming a lifetime of 50 years). The equity wealth is computed as the value (traded and non-traded) of the capital stock (not owned by debt-holders). Here we assume an annual depreciation of 6 percent per year. The figures are averaged over 1978–2000.

For both markets it is interesting to know more about ownership, because ownership is relevant to the effectiveness of transmission. For the equity market it is hard to get an idea of the ownership structure though. La Porta, de Silanes, and Shleifer (1999) provide information on the ownership of listed firms for both medium-sized and large publicly traded firms. We give the data for the six economies of interest in Table 3. From this table it can be seen that public ownership is less widespread in Germany than in market-based economies. Medium-sized firms are owned by controlling families. Large firms are owned more often by financial institutions and the government.

Table 3. Equity Ownership Indicators (Fractions)

	France	Germany	Italy	Japan	UK	US
Medium-sized firms						
Widely held	0	0.1	0	0.3	0.6	0.9
Family	0.5	0.4	0.6	0.1	0.4	0.1
State	0.2	0.2	0	0	0	0
Widely held financial	0.2	0.1	0	0	0	0
Widely held corporate	0	0.1	0.1	0	0	0
Miscellaneous	0.1	0	0.3	0.6	0	0
Large publicly traded firms						
Widely held	0.6	0.5	0.2	0.9	1	0.8
Family	0.2	0.1	0.15	0.05	0	0.2
State	0.15	0.25	0.4	0.05	0	0
Widely held financial	0.05	0.15	0.05	0	0	0
Widely held corporate	0	0	0.1	0	0	0
Miscellaneous	0	0	0.1	0	0	0

Source: La Porta, de Silanes, and Shleifer (1999).

Finally, we provide some institutional data on the housing market in Table 4, see Giuliodori (2003). We provide information on the ownership structure in the upper panel. We can observe that relatively few houses are occupied by owners in Germany, and there is more rental activity. In principle this will complicate a housing price channel, but it is not said that house-owners will not transmit revaluation into rental tariffs. In the lower panel we give some mortgage system information. Germany has a relatively large fraction of mortgage loans, the contracts are typically longer, but the mortgage loan costs are comparable to the foreign equivalents.

4 Literature on Vector Autoregression Models

In this section we review the relevant literature on Vector Autoregression (VAR) models. We start with a discussion of the most important contributions in this field. Next we discuss how monetary policy shocks are identified in VAR models, and review the role of asset prices. Finally we give an overview of VAR models of the German economy.

Table 4. House Market Indicators

Variable	France	Germany	Italy	UK
Housing Tenure Structure				
Owner occupation rate	54	40	75	67
Social rental occupation rate	21	20	3	23
Private rental occupation rate	17	40	22	10
Other	8	0	0	0
Mortgage Systems				
Residential mortgages/GDP	21	51	7	57
Typical term	17.5	27.5	10	25
Typical Loan-to-Value ratio	75	70	50	92.5
Transaction costs	7.5	7.1	7.4	1.5

Source: Giuliodori (2003).

4.1 The History of VAR Methodology

Vector autoregressions have become an important tool since Sims (1980) criticized large-scale macroeconometric models for assuming unfounded identifying restrictions. One of the main issues in the analysis of properties of vector autoregressions is the (use of theory in order to come to) identification of so-called structural shocks. Sims suggested solving the identification of the contemporaneous structure of the model by using a recursive (orthogonalized) structure. This implies that there is no contemporaneous feedback from the variables mentioned at the end of the ordering on the variables on top. Although theory can play a role in such a recursive scheme, the lack of simultaneity led Bernanke (1986), Blanchard and Watson (1986) and Sims (1986) to propose a larger role for economic theory in formulating plausible restrictions on contemporaneous interactions among variables. This implies that the recursivity can be replaced by other more simultaneous structures (at least conserving the number of identifying restrictions). This class of models is labelled Structural VAR (SVAR) models. Blanchard and Quah (1989) and Gali (1992) suggested to impose so-called long-run restrictions on impulse response functions to allow, for instance, for inflation not to have an impact on output. But, as Faust and Leeper (1997) argue, imposing long-run restrictions of this type requires the VAR to satisfy strong dynamic restrictions.

Pesaran and Shin (1998) criticized the orthogonal impulse-response analysis (Cholesky decomposition) and advocated using so-called generalized impulse-response analysis. These generalized impulse responses from an innovation to the jth variable are generated by applying a variable specific Cholesky factor computed with the jth variable at the top of the ordering. These impulses therefore do not depend on the initial ordering of the variables. A major disadvantage of the generalized impulse response analysis is that the results are completely a-theoretical and lack any obvious interpretation. The major advantage is that the shock patterns observed appeal more to historical data and covariations.

Following the Granger representation theorem vector autoregressions can easily be transformed into a so-called Vector Error Correction model, see Garratt, Lee, Pesaran, and Shin (2003). In a VECM apart from the standard lagged differenced dependent vectors, stationary linear combinations of the levels of the variables are added. These cointegrating vectors describe the long-run equilibrium of the model. It is obvious that economic theory is needed to identify these long-run vectors. Garratt, Lee, Pesaran, and Shin (2003) show that it is possible, at least in principle, to combine long-run VECM restrictions and short-run theoretical restrictions in the so-called SVAR.

There is a debate on the use of cointegrating relations in VAR models. As Sims, Stock, and Watson (1990) showed, a VAR model of $I(1)$-variables can be estimated unrestricted (at least asymptotically) if there are sufficient cointegrated relations. Estimating a VECM with ill-specified (or arbitrarily chosen) long-run vectors will lead to biased impulse-response functions. Estimating the VAR in first-differenced stationary variables leads to a loss of information though. So the final choice between a model in $I(1)$- or $I(0)$-form depends on making the rather subjective trade-off between a loss of information using $I(0)$-variables versus the chance of including meaningless long-run vectors.

4.2 Identifying Monetary Policy Shocks

Identifying monetary policy shocks using times series information is not straightforward. One could simply observe the actions of monetary policy makers (e.g. policy interest rate increases), but policy makers respond to non-monetary developments. If the demand for goods increases and supply is fixed (as will be likely in the short run), an interest rate increase will reflect this demand change and not so much a monetary contraction. So one needs to know the structure of the economy in order to understand and interpret monetary shocks.

As Christiano, Eichenbaum, and Evans (1999) argue the literature explores three general strategies to isolate monetary policy shocks. The first uses economic identification to estimate central banks' feedback rules. Here one assumes that the monetary policy instrument, e.g. the policy interest rate, is well known and accepted, that the contemporaneous determinants of this policy rate are known, and that the dynamics of interaction between the policy rate and the other variables can be traced. One can directly estimate a forward-looking monetary policy reaction function, like Rudebusch (1998) does for a Taylor rule, or estimate a prototype VAR. Identification of monetary policy shocks can be performed by assuming orthogonalized shocks or by imposing structure in a SVAR, see Sims and Zha (1995), or Bernanke and Mihov (1997a). A second way to identify monetary policy shocks is to look at data like board meetings to try to distillate policy shocks, see Romer and

Romer (1989). A third method to identify shocks is to assume that they don't affect real variables in the long run, see Gali (1992). As explained above, this approach has been criticized. In long-run models, like VECMs, no attention to monetary shocks is given.

There are numerous VAR studies on monetary transmission. The basic interest in VAR models originated indeed from the interest in monetary transmission and the Lucas-critique on large-scale structural modelling (all the references given above apply to this field). As Christiano, Eichenbaum, and Evans (1999) argue the models can be classified according to the specification of the monetary reaction function. Central banks can focus on monetary aggregates (M2, M3), interbank aggregates – like (non)-borrowed or total reserves, see Bernanke and Mihov (1997a) –, interest rates – like the Taylor-rule, Taylor (1993) – or even on the interaction between interest and exchange rates, see for instance Kim and Roubini (2000), Cushman and Zha (1997), and Clarida and Gertler (1997).

In general terms one can argue that misspecification is a common theme in VAR models. Misspecification can originate from a wrong interpretation of the art of monetary policy to the lack of including relevant variables. One of the common features of monetary VAR models is the so-called price puzzle. In lots of postwar business cycles a rise in inflation was preceded by an increase in interest rates and commodity prices, see Eichenbaum (1992). Leaving commodity prices out or ignoring indicators of future inflation leads to substantial price puzzles in numerous VAR models. Barth and Ramey (2000) argue that the cost channel may be an important part of the monetary transmission mechanism. They argue that if working capital is an essential component of production and distribution, monetary contractions can affect output through a supply channel as well as the traditional demand-type channels. An increase in the interest rate will increase production costs and lower output. So, generally spoken, modern VAR studies are not so much troubled by the price puzzle (after controlling for other demand and supply shocks).

4.3 VAR Models and Asset Prices

Both VAR models and Equilibrium Business Cycle models report substantial asset price (wealth) effects. For instance Lettau, Ludvigson, and Steindel (2002) report a strong wealth effect on consumption in the US using an SVAR model. The IMF (2000) reports a robust international wealth effect, especially via equity prices in market-based economies. Bernanke, Gertler, and Gilchrist (1999) present a theoretical model that includes a so-called financial accelerator that can support the empirical findings. This model is extended with an equity market in Bernanke and Gertler (1999), while Aoki, Proudman, and Vlieghe (2002) include a housing market.

Besides the broad establishment of wealth effects there is a lively debate on the role of asset prices in monetary policy. The general notion in favour of including asset price fluctuations in monetary policy rules is that an asset price bubble is socially undesirable. The disruptive effects of the bursting of the bubble lead to real effects of various kinds (economic growth, investment, income distribution, soundness of the financial system), which should be avoided by a central bank. There are disadvantages of using monetary policy in trying to avoid bubbles though. As Dornbusch (1999) argues there are two major disadvantages. First, there is a tendency towards an asymmetric response to asset price changes. A sudden widespread slump in asset prices will lead to a large provision of liquidity. A central bank is concerned about trust in the financial system and wants to provide stability. An asset price boom should then lead to an increase in interest rates, but the general public will typically not appreciate this. Knowing the likely reaction of central banks, there will be a moral hazard problem that leads to overly risky investment, possibly creating a bubble. Secondly, the credibility of a central bank might be lowered. Asset prices are volatile and typically hard to predict. Responding on a day-to-day basis may reduce credibility.

The following items seem to be relevant in this discussion:

1. Should measures of the general price level include asset prices?
2. Should there be target levels for asset prices?
3. Should asset prices be included as indicators in a direct inflation strategy?
4. Should monetary policy makers react stronger to asset prices than item 3 prescribes?

The majority of opinions says no to the first two items. It is very hard to estimate the true value of individual stock for instance, so how could a central bank be able to value all assets appropriately? In the System of National Accounts it is common to measure price indices based on flow transactions in goods. Including prices of stocks of assets would blur this approach. Moreover, one could argue that if asset prices were relevant, they would be leading indicators in decisions. Moreover they can be leading indicators without being included in the indicators of the current general price level.

The empirical research on the third and fourth item can be divided into two competing views. On the one hand, papers by Bernanke and Gertler (2001) argue that a central bank should not respond to asset price fluctuations. On the other hand, Cecchetti, Genberg, and Wadhani (2002) and Filardo (2001) come to the opposite conclusion. Bernanke and Gertler analyze the role of an exogenously determined flexible inflation-targeting rule in a sophisticated dynamic new-Keynesian model with credit market frictions. Their main idea is that if asset price changes are important they should translate into changes in expected inflation and via that channel have their impact on monetary policy. A central bank should not try to target asset prices. Cecchetti et al. argue that one should use an optimal monetary policy rule that takes into account all information. Ignoring asset price changes will lead to sub-optimal outcomes. But a central bank should be able to distinguish asset price bubbles in the Cecchetti et al. model. Filardo argues that a central bank should respond to asset price movements as long as they provide some information about inflation or output, even if the prices are driven by bubbles or not. It should be clear though in the Filardo-model how asset price fluctuations affect real variables. If this is not clear, the expected costs of responding to asset price changes might be too high.

So both wealth effects and monetary policy reactions to asset price changes are found to be relevant and could possibly lead to better specifications of VAR models. In principle three assets are used in empirical studies: equity, housing and liquidity. We do not focus on liquidity here, but review some of the results found for equity transmission and housing market studies.

Ludvigson and Steindel (2002) analyze the impact of wealth on consumption. Using a VAR model they find that there is a contemporaneous impact from wealth on consumption. Lettau, Ludvigson, and Steindel (2002) construct an SVAR for the US and include household asset wealth in a consumption model. They conclude that the impact of shocks to the Federal Funds Rate via wealth components is not so strong, but direct interest rate effects are. Asset values can be influenced by other sources (like price increases or upturn of the business cycle) and can be amplified into consumption.

Lastrapes (2002) estimates the dynamic response of aggregate owner-occupied housing prices to money supply shocks and interprets these responses using a dynamic equilibrium model of the housing market that relies on the asset view of housing demand. Money supply shocks are identified empirically from a vector autoregression. Using monthly data, he finds that money shocks have real effects on the housing market: both real housing prices and housing sales (new starts and existing homes) rise in the short-run in response to positive shocks to the money supply. Giuliodori (2003) gives an extensive overview of the role of house prices in the euro countries. He estimates SVAR models for several countries (Belgium, Finland, Ireland, Italy, the Netherlands, Spain, Sweden and the UK) and links the results to facts of financial structure, like Cecchetti (1999). Giuliodori includes inflation, GDP, real house prices, the interest rate and the exchange rate as the key variables. Iaccoviello (2000) estimates VAR models for six European economies to explain house price movements. He finds a substantial impact of monetary policy on house prices. Using a sample of France, Germany, Italy, Spain, Sweden and the UK, Iacoviello specifies a five-dimensional VAR with output, real house prices, real money, a short-term interest rate and inflation. He finds that a contractionary monetary policy has a negative impact on real house prices (to a similar extent as output), especially in the UK and Italy (while moderate effects appear for Germany).

There are not so many VAR studies that include equity prices. Goodhart and Hofmann (2001) is an exception. They assess the role of asset prices as information variables for aggregate demand conditions and in the transmission of monetary policy. By looking at reduced form coefficient estimates and VAR impulse responses Goodhart and Hofmann derive Financial Conditions Indices, weighted averages of the short-term real interest rate, the effective real exchange rate, real property and real share prices, for the G7 countries. They find that house and share prices receive a substantial weight in such an index and that the derived Financial Conditions Indices contain useful information about future inflationary pressures. Elbourne and Salomons (2003) estimate an 8-variable VAR for developed economies and find no substantial equity wealth effects (except for the UK and Japan).

4.4 VAR Models of Germany

Many VAR models for Germany have been developed. We limit ourselves here to review SVAR models and models that focus on monetary transmission. In an early study Weber (1996) analyzes the determinants of the post-unification downturn in Germany using an SVAR model. The results suggest that German business cycles were not all alike. Whilst adverse supply shocks clearly mattered before unification, it is primarily adverse aggregate demand shocks and a too tight monetary policy which dominate the German post-unification decline in output growth rates. Bernanke and Mihov (1997b) apply a structural VAR to determine the historical optimal indicator of German monetary policy and find that the Lombard rate has historically been a good policy indicator. Peersman (2002) estimates an SVAR model that links short and long run interest rates in Germany. He finds a positive correlation after a supply and demand shock and a negative correlation after a monetary policy shock. Kakes and Sturm (2002) analyze monetary policy transmission according to the credit channel by assuming heterogeneity between banks. Banks hold important positions in the German economy, which justifies such an approach.

There have been a number of VAR studies on the EU level that include the German case. In the Monetary Transmission Network of the European Central Bank, Mojon and Peersman (2003) review VAR models for 10 EU-countries. They classify the countries according to their monetary integration with Germany. Apart form the first class, Germany itself, there are core-Germany countries, like the Netherlands or Austria, and other EU countries. Mojon and Peersman find output effects from a tighter monetary policy, falling prices and a rather common pattern across countries. Peersman and Smets (2001) estimate an area-wide identified VAR for the euro area. They find for the EU similar effects as have been found in the analysis of US monetary policy. On the G-7 level Canova and de Nicolo (2002) examine the importance of monetary disturbances for cyclical fluctuations in real activity and inflation. They employ a novel identification approach, which uses the sign of the cross-correlation function in response to shocks to assign a structural interpretation to orthogonal innovations. They find that identified monetary shocks significantly contribute to output and inflation cycles in all G-7 countries.

5 Vector Autoregression

In this section we present our different Vector AutoRegressions (VARs). We first construct a basic VAR model, including output, prices, credit, the exchange rate and the interest rate as the key endogenous variables. Next we switch output for the Ifo business climate indicator and add asset prices to illustrate their contribution. Overall, we follow the same methodology in the models. We estimate the VAR models using quarterly data from 1978.4 to 1989.4 and 1992.1 to 1998.4. So we exclude the German reunification period and end our sample at the start of the European Central Bank. We estimate Structural VAR (SVAR) models in all cases. We focus on the interpretation of the Impulse Response Functions as far as the impact of interest rate and asset prices shocks and variance-decompositions of the interest rate residuals concerning monetary policy. Data are taken from EUROMON, produced by the Dutch central bank (see the appendix for a description of the data.)

5.1 A Basic VAR Model

First we estimate a basic five-variable VAR model of the German economy for the 1978.4–1998.4 sample (excluding the reunification period 1990.1–1991.4). This period covers the basic EMS period. This VAR model includes reference series like GDP (Y), the CPI (P), real domestic credit to the private sector (CR, as the indicator of monetary stance), the nominal trade weighted exchange rate (E), and the short-term money market interest rate (R_S). We use the latter variable as the indicator of monetary policy. Identified shocks to the interest rate will be interpreted as monetary policy changes. Officially, this might not have been the monetary strategy of the Bundesbank, but de facto interest rate was used in the EMS period as monetary policy variable. See also Bernanke and Mihov (1997b).

The dependent vector is $[Y, P, CR, E, R_S]$. All variables are in logs. We tested for stationarity of the series using a larger sample available in the data set: 1970.1–2000.4. Most series are found to be of order I(1), although the first difference of the log of the price level is a borderline case (see Table 5). The interest rates are stationary in the sample 1970.1–2000.4, but non-stationary in the sample 1978.4–1998.4 (e.g. the German interest rate has a p-value of 0.139). Next we test for the number of cointegrating vectors. If we find a near to full rank we could follow the Sims et al. (1990) principle and estimate the model in levels. Both the Trace and the Maximum Eigenvalue test indicate two co-integrating vectors at the one percent confidence level. Given the fact that our sample is small we need to use the one percent levels to test for co-integration, see Cheung and Lai (1993). This finding leads us to use a model in differences. We use the annual difference operator: $\Delta_4(x) = x - x_{-4}$. All variables are stationary in this form (results not reported here, but available upon request), except again for the inflation rate (p=0.188). Proceeding with the model in differences we loose some information by not using the levels. We included three exogenous variables in the VAR in order to capture world economic development: relevant world trade growth ($\Delta_4(WT)$), world commodity inflation ($\Delta_4(P_C)$), and annual change of the log of the US short-term interest rate ($\Delta(R_{US})$). Although Germany is a large economy, it will be dependent on world developments. Moreover, we might reduce the so-called price puzzle including a world commodity price index.

Table 5. Unit Root Test Results

	Levels			Differences		
Variable	ADF	(c,t,n)	p-value	ADF	(c,t,n)	p-value
Y	-2.893	$(c,t,4)$	0.169	-4.294	$(c,3)$	0.001
P	-2.707	$(c,t,4)$	0.236	-1.271	(3)	0.187
CR	-2.059	$(c,t,1)$	0.563	-10.069	$(c,1)$	0.000
P_H	-2.346	$(c,t,5)$	0.405	-4.294	(4)	0.002
P_{EQ}	-2.483	$(c,t,1)$	0.336	-4.294	$(c,0)$	0.000
E	2.184	(1)	0.993	-4.294	(0)	0.000
R_S	-2.970	$(c,1)$	0.041			
W_T	-1.820	$(c,t,2)$	0.687	-4.261	$(c,1)$	0.001
P_C	-2.893	$(c,t,4)$	0.169			
R_{US}	-3.051	$(c,5)$	0.033			
IFO	-3.587	$(c,1)$	0.008			

Sample: 1970.1–2000.4. c = intercept, t = trend, n = number of lags (following the Schwartz-criterium).

The ordering of the variables is relevant in a Cholesky factorization of the variance-covariance residual matrix. We assume that shocks to output are basically driven by supply elements, that prices are rather sticky, credit largely dependent on output changes and the single asset price, the exchange rate, endogenous to a large extent. The policy interest rate is assumed to be responding to all other variables in the system. Experimenting with the lag structure we found three lags. It is good to note that the lag-length criteria did not hint at one specific lag length due to the flatness of the optimization surface.

As explained above, there are various ways to represent the analysis of shocks in a VAR model:

- One can compute the orthogonalized Impulse Response Functions. This is the solution offered by Sims (1980) and is labelled the Cholesky decomposition.

- One can impose theoretical structure on the short-run contemporaneous impact and restrict the B_0-matrix to an identified matrix. This approach is known as the SVAR, see Bernanke (1986).
- One can impose theoretical structure on the long-run impact of contemporaneous shocks. This is the approach proposed by Blanchard and Quah (1989) and Gali (1992), but criticized by Faust and Leeper (1997).
- One can impose 'realistic' shocks by so-called Generalized Impulse Response functions, see Pesaran and Shin (1998). Realistic shocks are taken from the estimated variance-covariance matrix of the residuals. Using GIRs the ordering of the variable in the VAR becomes irrelevant.

Inspecting the variance-covariance matrix of the estimated residuals the covariance of the interest rate residuals with all other variables are rather large (especially the exchange rate residuals). This implies that imposing a structure on the B_0-matrix will change the IRF's. Ideally one would like to derive restrictions from a fully-fledged macroeconomic system. In practice however this is done infrequently (Gali (1992) and Sims and Zha (1995) being exceptions). Instead, the more widely used approach is to present commonly accepted restrictions based on broad classes of models. As a metric of appropriateness one uses the economic plausibility of the dynamic responses to shocks imposed.

We assume that output is fully determined by supply shocks – as can be found in Gali (1992) and Kim and Roubini (2000). Output does not respond to any financial variable, because in the short-run only technology will have an impact on production:

$$\epsilon_Y = \alpha_{11} u_Y \tag{1}$$

For inflation we assume that output and foreign price developments (e.g. via oil prices and changes in world economic) activity affect the domestic price development instantaneously. Inflation responds slowly to all other variables in the model. The latter assumption is also made by e.g. Kim and Roubini (2000), where domestic output affects inflation contemporaneously. Financial variables do not have a contemporaneous effect on output.

$$\epsilon_P = \alpha_{21} u_Y + \alpha_{22} u_P \tag{2}$$

Credit is assumed to be determined by demand for credit in the short run. A standard credit demand function is based on transactions and portfolio motives, here represented by output and the impact of the interest rate. Demand for credit is mainly based on domestic arguments, so we assume no contemporaneous influence of the exchange rate.

$$\epsilon_{CR} = \alpha_{31} u_Y + \alpha_{33} u_{CR} + \alpha_{35} u_R \tag{3}$$

The exchange rate is determined by output and interest rate shocks. Like Kim and Roubini (2000) we assume that interest rate and exchange rate shocks should be modelled interactively. We assume that the exchange rate does not respond to changes in domestic inflation instantaneously, since this information will be transmitted via the interest rate. Domestic output changes are used as signals of real activity and do have a contemporaneous impact, see Kim and Roubini (2000). Domestic credit conditions typically have no impact on the exchange rate.

$$\epsilon_E = \alpha_{41} u_Y + \alpha_{44} u_E + \alpha_{45} u_R \tag{4}$$

Finally we assume that the Bundesbank responded to shocks in output, assets, and inflation via a so-called Taylor rule, see Taylor (1993):

$$\epsilon_R = \alpha_{51} u_Y + \alpha_{52} u_P + \alpha_{53} u_{CR} + \alpha_{54} u_E + \alpha_{55} u_R \tag{5}$$

We summarize (1) to (5) in a system $\epsilon = B_0 u$:

$$\begin{pmatrix} \epsilon_Y \\ \epsilon_P \\ \epsilon_{CR} \\ \epsilon_E \\ \epsilon_R \end{pmatrix} = \begin{bmatrix} \alpha_{11} & 0 & 0 & 0 & 0 \\ \alpha_{21} & \alpha_{22} & 0 & 0 & 0 \\ \alpha_{31} & 0 & \alpha_{33} & 0 & \alpha_{35} \\ \alpha_{41} & 0 & 0 & \alpha_{44} & \alpha_{45} \\ \alpha_{51} & \alpha_{52} & \alpha_{53} & \alpha_{54} & \alpha_{55} \end{bmatrix} \begin{pmatrix} u_Y \\ u_P \\ u_{CR} \\ u_E \\ u_R \end{pmatrix} \tag{6}$$

Note that the structural model is overidentified with 1 degree of freedom. We can accept the overidentification using a χ^2-test: the p-value is 0.564. We do not give an interpretation to the parameters of the B_0-matrix, since the estimation itself cannot identify precise values in such a simultaneous system.

We analyze the results of this model in two ways. First, we calculate the Impulse Response Functions to structural shocks. We give the results in Fig. 1. In Fig. 1 u_Y is represented by shock1, u_P by shock2, etc. From Fig. 1 one can observe that a structural interest rate shock only affects credit, and not output or inflation. Credit shocks affect output and inflation. The interest rate responds to shocks in output and credit.

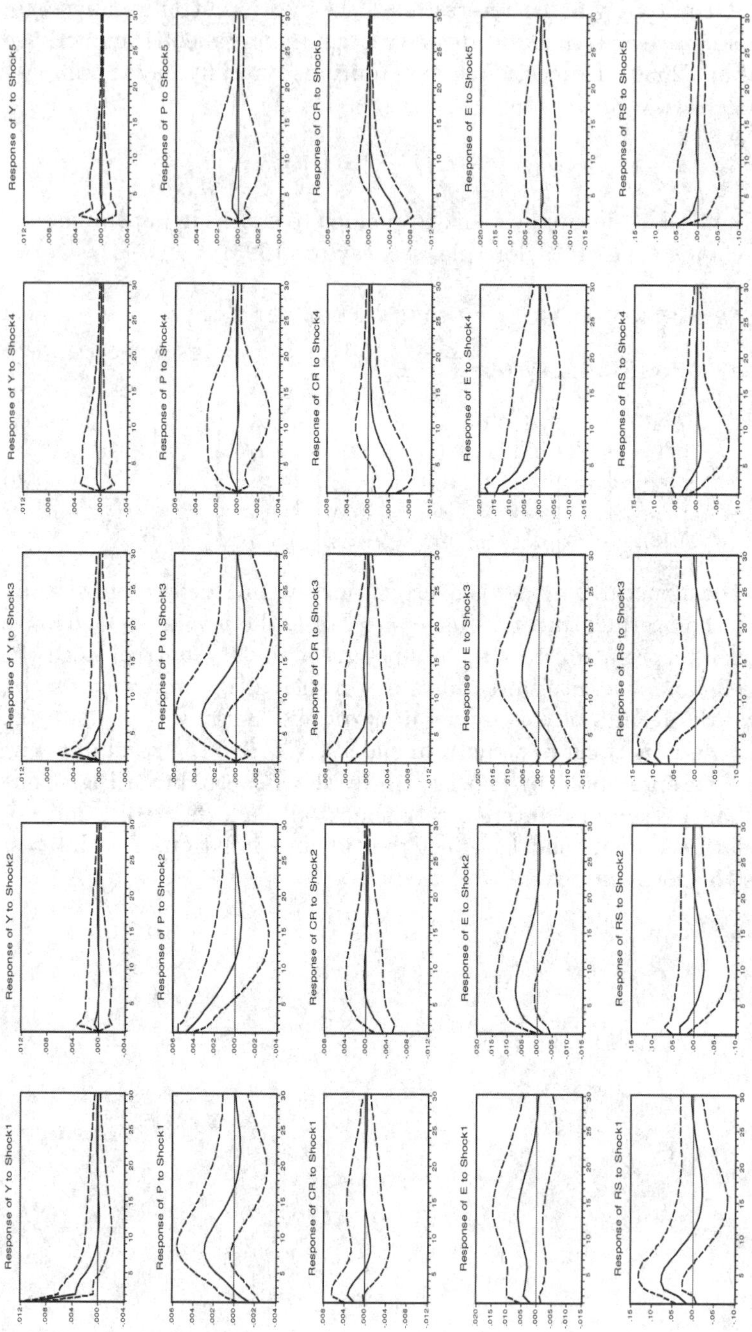

Fig. 1. Impulse Response Functions of the 5-Variable Model

Next we present the variance decomposition of the structural factorization for the interest rate shocks: these results shed light on the role of the variables in monetary policy (see Table 6). We can observe that output and credit are the crucial factors explaining the interest rate changes. This may be seen as a surprise, since it is widely accepted that the Bundesbank was more focused on inflation than on output. Apparently, credit takes the role of the monetary aggregate in describing monetary policy.

Table 6. Variance Decomposition of Interest Rate Residuals (SVAR)

Period	Y	P	CR	E	R_S
1	2.24	9.76	58.64	10.58	18.79
4	22.79	4.82	63.05	4.10	5.24
8	32.05	3.94	57.71	2.96	3.34
12	31.72	6.09	55.93	3.03	3.23
20	31.98	6.82	55.45	2.77	2.98

5.2 The Role of the Ifo Business Climate Indicator

One of the basic issues in monetary VAR models is the role of expectations. How does the central bank assess inflationary conditions and use its monetary policy instruments to correct any undesired developments? Suppose that, as Bernanke and Mihov (1997b) argue, the Bundesbank followed an inflation targeting approach. In that case it is likely that it will have used not only inflationary forecasting devices, but also indicators of real economic activity, like the output gap. Following Taylor (1993) central banks are believed to respond on output gap and inflationary developments (the latter being more important in the German setting than in e.g. the US). Given the information lag in (mostly revised) figures, see Orphanides (2001), it is rather unlikely that the GDP series takes this informational role. As Flaig and Plötscher (2001) illustrate, the Ifo indicator does carry an informational role in describing and predicting the German output gap.

In order to test for the value added of the Ifo indicator we switch this variable for $\Delta_4(Y)$ in the base model. We again estimated the Structural VAR used above. The fit of the model improves (the p-value of the overidentification test increases to 0.747). The Impulse Response Functions resemble those reported in Fig. 1 closely and are not reported here. We confine ourselves to the variance decompositions in order to assess the role of the Ifo business climate indicator. In Table 7 it can bee seen that the Ifo indicator gets a larger share in the decomposition than real GDP growth in the previous model. The role of credit is reduced and inflation gets more important. This finding seems to be more plausible. So, although the fit and the Impulse Response Functions of this model and the base model are comparable, the Ifo model should be preferred.

Table 7. Variance Decomposition of Interest Rate Residuals (SVAR)

Period	Y	P	CR	E	R_S
1	0.05	8.98	62.81	10.70	17.47
4	21.10	6.16	61.96	4.60	6.17
8	43.26	9.18	38.90	5.16	3.50
12	35.92	22.15	32.84	5.86	3.23
20	40.40	20.09	32.78	4.55	2.19

5.3 Extending the Model with Housing and Equity Prices

Knowing the properties of the base model we extend the VAR model with two additional variables: the house price index P_H and the equity price P_{EQ}. Both housing and equity will affect consumption and investment behaviour (which we will roughly proxy here by GDP). So we extend our dependent vector to: $[Y, P, CR, P_H, P_{EQ}, E, R_S]$. We treat housing and equity similar to the asset price included in the model: the exchange rate. The other model properties remain the same: we use three lags, include the world commodity price index, the world trade index and the US interest rate as exogenous variables. Testing for integration of the asset prices leads to the conclusion that both are stationary after differencing (see Table 5). Testing for cointegration reveals two co-integrating vectors at the 1 per cent confidence level, so we again estimate the model in annual differences using the 1978.4–1998.4 sample (skipping the reunification period). In the SVAR we treat the asset prices similar to the exchange rate in the base model, except for the contemporaneous impact of the housing and equity prices on real credit. Moreover we assume that housing, equity prices and the exchange rate are recursively influenced. This leaves a model with one overidentifying restriction (testing for overidentification yields a p-value of 0.288).

$$\begin{pmatrix} \epsilon_Y \\ \epsilon_P \\ \epsilon_{CR} \\ \epsilon_{PH} \\ \epsilon_{PEQ} \\ \epsilon_E \\ \epsilon_R \end{pmatrix} = \begin{bmatrix} \alpha_{11} & 0 & 0 & 0 & 0 & 0 & 0 \\ \alpha_{21} & \alpha_{22} & 0 & 0 & 0 & & \\ \alpha_{31} & 0 & \alpha_{33} & 0 & 0 & 0 & \alpha_{37} \\ \alpha_{41} & 0 & \alpha_{43} & \alpha_{44} & 0 & 0 & \alpha_{47} \\ \alpha_{51} & 0 & \alpha_{53} & \alpha_{54} & \alpha_{55} & 0 & \alpha_{57} \\ \alpha_{61} & 0 & 0 & \alpha_{64} & \alpha_{65} & \alpha_{66} & \alpha_{67} \\ \alpha_{71} & \alpha_{72} & \alpha_{73} & \alpha_{74} & \alpha_{75} & \alpha_{76} & \alpha_{77} \end{bmatrix} \begin{pmatrix} u_Y \\ u_P \\ u_{CR} \\ u_{PH} \\ u_{PEQ} \\ u_E \\ u_R \end{pmatrix} \tag{7}$$

We analyze the model again in two ways. First, we plot the impulse response functions of the reactions to housing, equity, and interest rate shocks.

Figures 2 to 4 present the responses to these shocks. From the housing price shock we observe a (non-significant) positive impact on output and the price level. It can also be observed that the interest rate increases, which reduces credit. The response to an equity price shock is quite different. Output and the price level stay rather constant; there is no interest rate response, and credit even increases (probably to finance equity investment). Finally, we can clearly observe a contractionary response to an interest rate shock. If we compare this result with the results of the base model, the model extended with asset prices clearly gives more stylized results. Especially house prices suffer from an interest rate shock. Overall, there does not seem to be an equity channel in Germany.

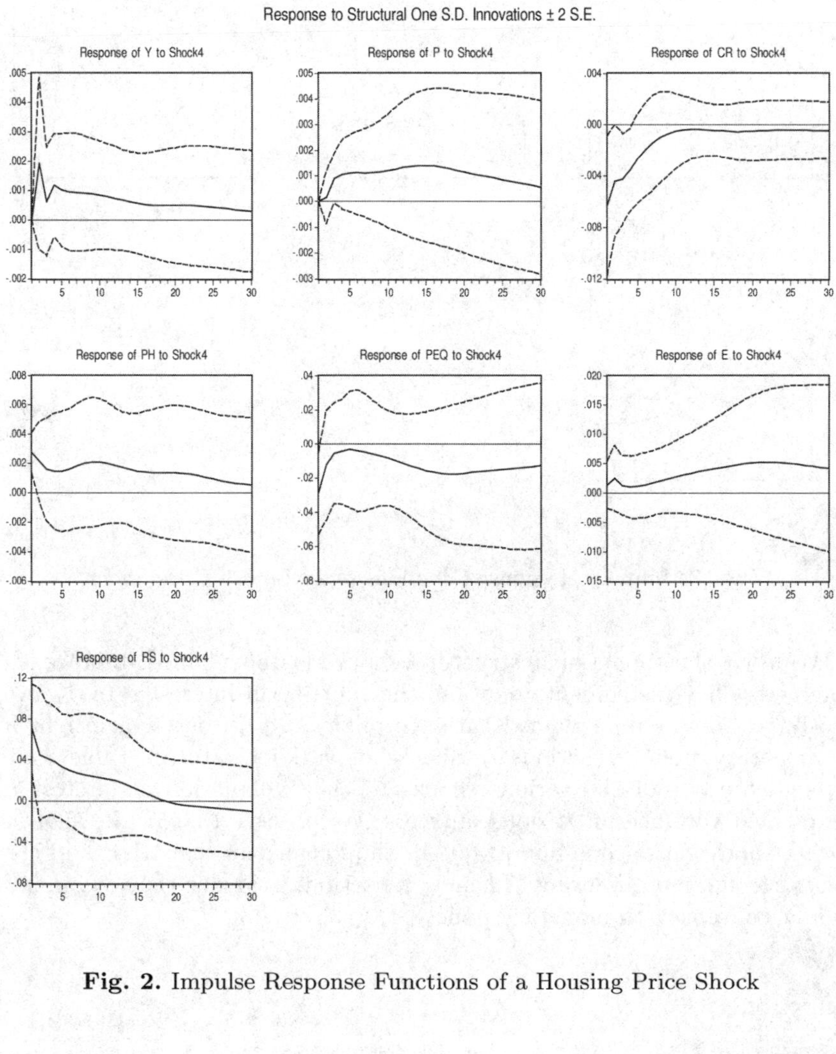

Fig. 2. Impulse Response Functions of a Housing Price Shock

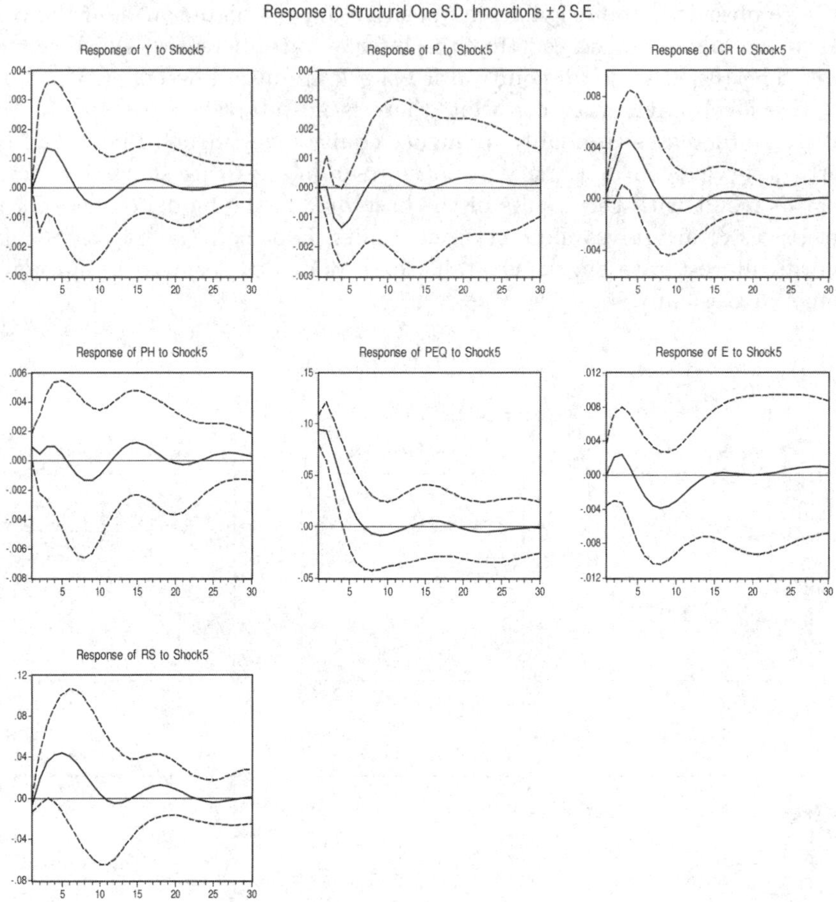

Fig. 3. Impulse Response Functions of an Equity Price Shock

We derive the impact of all structural shocks to unexplained variance of the monetary policy instrument equation: the short-term interest rate. Knowing the sources of this unexplained variance might help in deriving insight into the monetary policy reactions to shocks of various natures. Table 8 gives the contributions of the various shocks to the explanation of interest rate unexplained variance for various quarters. We observe that in the short run housing shock variance is important. In the longer run real GDP and credit shocks become more relevant. There is no serious evidence that e.g. inflation has a large impact on monetary policy.

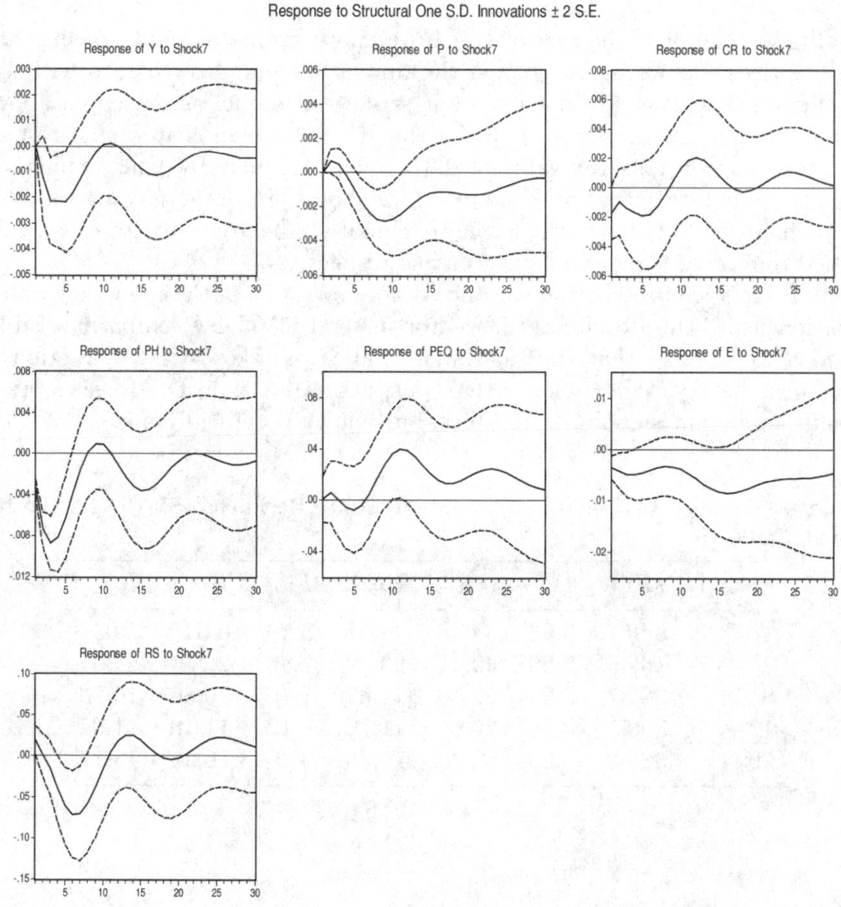

Fig. 4. Impulse Response Functions of an Interest Rate Shock

Table 8. Variance Decomposition of Interest Rate Residuals (SVAR)

Period	Y	P	CR	P_H	P_{EQ}	E	R_S
1	0.54	5.08	41.06	48.65	0.27	0.92	3.50
4	14.42	2.10	45.53	22.65	7.83	2.67	4.81
8	38.66	1.30	24.08	14.93	9.77	9.46	21.34
12	31.83	2.55	22.54	15.76	9.23	9.75	21.77
20	24.37	3.60	22.72	15.52	9.28	9.33	22.16

5.4 Using the Ifo Business Climate Indicator and Asset Prices

Finally, we combine the use of the Ifo climate indicator, and housing and equity prices. So we again change the annual output growth rate with the Ifo climate indicator. We use the same structural model as presented above. The fit of the model improves using the Ifo climate indicator (the test on overidentification gets a p-value of 0.375). The Impulse Response Functions of housing, equity prices and interest rate shocks are largely comparable to the plots presented above. Using the Ifo climate indicator does not change the alleged role of housing and equity in this respect.

In Table 9 we present the variance decompositions of the monetary policy equation using the Ifo climate indicator instead of GDP. Comparing Tables 9 and 8 we observe that the Ifo climate indicator takes a larger fraction to explain monetary policy shocks than output (as we expect). Housing prices remain important signalling variables, but equity is typically not.

Table 9. Variance Decomposition of Interest Rate Residuals (SVAR) for the Ifo-Climate Indicator

Period	IFO	P	CR	P_H	P_{EQ}	E	R_S
1	0.96	5.06	44.48	46.91	0.00	0.54	2.03
4	16.45	2.89	49.47	23.20	2.86	2.81	2.30
8	38.87	3.99	22.16	11.62	1.76	10.86	10.73
12	39.51	3.76	20.64	11.72	2.12	11.18	11.07
20	38.63	3.35	18.43	10.35	3.80	10.26	13.17

6 Summary and Conclusions

In this paper we analyze the role of the Ifo climate indicator and asset prices in German monetary policy. The Ifo climate indicator is a forward-looking indicator of output and should perform better than output itself in an analysis of monetary policy. Asset prices are believed to contain a large set of information and monetary policy should therefore include asset price information. We present a review of the theory of asset price transmission. Moreover, we illustrate that the German case is interesting to review, especially in terms of housing. The German housing market is relatively large compared to housing markets in other economies.

Using Structural Vector AutoRegression models we analyze the role of the Ifo climate indicator and asset price shocks. First we show that the Ifo indicator contributes to describing monetary policy performed by the Bundesbank. Generally we find that the expected negative impact of an interest rate shock on output and the CPI is found in the model with asset price effects (and not so much in the model without). Analyzing housing and equity shocks reveals that house price shocks have a substantial impact on monetary responses. Equity price shocks are rather irrelevant in the German case, which comes as no surprise, given the institutional ordering of the German financial system. These conclusions hold for the model with GDP and the model with the Ifo business climate indicator. Analyzing the variance decompositions of the various models shows that house prices have a serious impact on monetary policy. This impact is enforced using the Ifo business climate indicator, which in itself explains more of monetary policy changes than output.

How should we take account of these results? First of all our results might contribute to the discussion on the use of instrument rules versus targeting rules. As Bernanke and Mihov (1997b) show, it seems that the Bundesbank used some kind of inflation targeting strategy. Our results basically confirm this view and point at house prices being a crucial variable. This result weakens the role of Taylor rules, in which the full attention is given to output gaps and inflation itself in explaining monetary policy reactions.

Secondly and in line with the previous conclusion, one should have some concern about the large variety of variables influencing monetary policy in terms of the modelling strategy to analyze these effects. One cannot use a VAR model of 20 variables over such a short time span. A suggestion made by Giannone, Reichlin, and Sala (2002) is to use factor analysis prior to going to a VAR model. It is rather unlikely that in a high-dimensional VAR all the shocks will be independent. So Giannone et al. advocate using the principal components of all shocks. As we show in the German case, including a housing variable as one of the key shocks seems to be relevant.

Finally, a future avenue of research would be to analyze the housing market more in depth than we do in our reduced form model. Here one can think of a model in the spirit of Aoki, Proudman, and Vlieghe (2002), who present a dynamic stochastic general equilibrium model. This type of model could underpin the structure to identify the shocks in the short run, but also give directions to identify likely long-run effects.

A Data Appendix

We describe in short the sources of the data. For more information see Chirinko et al. (2003).

- *CR*: *Bank credit to the private sector.* In constant prices of 1990. IMF, *International Financial Statistics.* Nominal figures have been deflated by the private consumption deflator *P*.
- *E*: *Nominal effective exchange rate.* Index 1990=100. Exchange rates from *Datastream.* Weighted using calculated trade weights of 1990.

- I_B^R: *Investment in fixed assets of the business sector.* In constant prices of 1990. Calculated as total investment in fixed assets minus residential investment and government investment. Source: *OECD National Accounts* and *Quarterly National Accounts.* We interpolated annual data for government investment and residential investment.
- IFO: *IFO business climate index.* See www.cesifo.de.
- I_H^R: *Residential investment.* In constant prices of 1990. *OECD Quarterly National Accounts.* We interpolated annual data.
- K_B: *Market value of equity of the business sector.* $K_B = K_B^R \frac{P_{EQ}}{100}$.
- K_B^R: *Real value of equity of the business sector.* $K_B^R = K_B^R(-1) + I_B^R - \delta K_B^R(-1)$, where we used an annualised depreciation rate δ=0.06. Starting value derived from the sources of the *OECD, flows and stocks of fixed capital.*
- K_H: *Market value of stock of private owner occupied houses.* $K_H = K_H^R \frac{P_H}{100}$.
- K_H^R: *Rebuilding value of stock of private owner occupied houses.* $K_H^R = K_H^R(-1) + I_H^R - \delta K_H^R(-1)$, where we used an annualised depreciation rate $\delta = 0.02$. Starting value derived from *OECD, Flows and stocks of fixed capital.*
- P: *Deflator private consumption.* Index 1990=100. Source: *OECD National Accounts.*
- P_C: *Price of commodities.* In own currency, index 1990=100. Pre-denominated in dollars converted into national currencies using dollar exchange rates.
- P_{EQ}: *Share price index.* Index 1990=100. IMF, *International Financial Statistics.*
- P_H: *Residential property prices.* Index 1990=100. Source: *Bundesbank.* Interpolation of annual prices in DEM 1000 of new or existing good quality "Reihenhaus" in West-Germany.
- R_S: *Three-month deposit interest rate.* In percentages. Source: *De Nederlandsche Bank, Quarterly Bulletin.*
- R_{US}: *Three-month U.S. deposit interest rate.* In percentages. Source: *De Nederlandsche Bank, Quarterly Bulletin.*
- WT: *Relevant world trade.* Volume index 1990=100. Weighted import volumes of 12 other countries in the EUROMON data set, using calculated trade weights of 1990.
- Y: *Gross domestic product.* In constant prices of 1990. Source: *OECD National Accounts.*

References

ADEMA, Y. (2003): "A Taylor rule for the euro area based on quasi-real time data," *Research Memorandum WO* 738, De Nederlandsche Bank.

ALLEN, F., AND D. GALE (2000): *Comparing Financial Systems.* MIT Press, Cambridge.

AOKI, K., J. PROUDMAN, AND G. VLIEGHE (2002): "House prices, consumption, and monetary policy: a financial accelerator approach," *Working Paper* 169, Bank of England.

BARTH, M., AND V. RAMEY (2000): "The cost channel of monetary transmission," *Working Paper* 7675, National Bureau of Economic Research.

BERNANKE, B. (1986): "Alternative explanations of the money-income correlation," *Carnegie-Rochester Series on Public Policy*, 25, 49–99.

——— (2003): "Monetary policy and the stock market: some empirical results," Remarks At the Fall 2003 Banking and Finance Lecture, Widener University, Chester, Pennsylvania.

BERNANKE, B., AND A. BLINDER (1988): "Credit, money, and aggregate demand," *The American Economic Review*, 78, 435–439.

BERNANKE, B., AND M. GERTLER (1995): "Inside the black box: the credit channel of monetary policy transmission," *Journal of Economic Perspectives*, 9, 27–48.

——— (1999): "Monetary policy and asset price volatility," in *New Challenges for Monetary Policy, Proceedings of the 19th Jackson Hole Conference*, ed. by F. R. B. of Kansas City. Federal Reserve Bank of Kansas, Kansas City.

——— (2001): "Should central banks respond to movements in asset prices?," *The American Economic Review, Papers and Proceedings*, 91, 254–257.

BERNANKE, B., M. GERTLER, AND S. GILCHRIST (1999): "The financial accelerator approach in a quantitative business cycle framework," in *Handbook of Macroeconomics*, ed. by J. Taylor, and M. Woordford, vol. 1C, pp. 1341–1393. North-Holland, Amsterdam.

BERNANKE, B., AND I. MIHOV (1997a): "Measuring monetary policy," *Quarterly Journal of Economics*, 113, 869–902.

——— (1997b): "What does the Bundesbank target?," *European Economic Review*, 46, 1025–1053.

BLANCHARD, O., AND D. QUAH (1989): "The dynamic effects of aggregate demand and supply disturbances," *The American Economic Review*, 79, 655–673.

BLANCHARD, O., AND M. WATSON (1986): "Are business cycles all alike?," in *The American Business Cycle: Continuity and Change*, ed. by R. Gordon, pp. 123–165. University of Chicago Press, Chicago.

BRAINARD, W., AND J. TOBIN (1968): "Pitfalls in financial model building," *The American Economic Review*, 58, 99–122.

CANOVA, F., AND G. DE NICOLO (2002): "Monetary disturbances matter for business fluctuations in the G-7," *Journal of Monetary Economics*, 40, 1131–1159.

CECCHETTI, S. (1999): "Legal structure, financial structure, and the monetary policy transmission mechanism," *Economic Policy Review*, Federal Reserve Bank of New York.

CECCHETTI, S., H. GENBERG, AND S. WADHANI (2002): "Asset prices in a flexible inflation targeting framework," Paper presented at the conference on "Asset Price Bubbles: Implications for Monetary, Regulatory and International Policies", Federal Reserve Bank of Chicago/World Bank, Chicago.

CHEUNG, Y., AND K. LAI (1993): "Finite sample sizes of Johansen's likelihood ratio tests for cointegration," *Oxford Bulletin of Economics and Statistics*, 55, 313–328.

CHIRINKO, R., L. DE HAAN, AND E. STERKEN (2003): "Should policymakers be concerned about asset prices?," *Mimeo*, De Nederlandsche Bank.

CHRISTIANO, L., M. EICHENBAUM, AND C. EVANS (1999): "Monetary policy shocks: what have we learned and to what end?," in *Handbook of Macroeconomics*, ed. by J. Taylor, and M. Woordford, pp. 65–148. North-Holland, Amsterdam.

Clarida, R., and M. Gertler (1997): "How the Bundesbank conducts monetary policy," in *Reducing inflation: motives and strategies*, ed. by C. Romer, and D. Romer. National Bureau of Economic Research, Chicago.

Cushman, D., and T. Zha (1997): "Identifying monetary policy in a small open economy under flexible exchange rates," *Journal of Monetary Economics*, 39, 433–448.

Dornbusch (1999): "Comments on Bernanke and Gertler," in *New Challenges for Monetary Policy, Proceedings of the 19th Jackson Hole Conference*, ed. by F. R. B. of Kansas City. Federal Reserve Bank of Kansas, Kansas City.

Eichenbaum, M. (1992): "Comments: Interpreting the macroeconomic time series facts: the effects of monetary policy," *European Economic Review*, 36, 1001–1011.

Elbourne, A., and R. Salomons (2003): "Monetary transmission and equity markets in the EU," *Mimeo*, University of Groningen.

Faust, J., and E. Leeper (1997): "When do long-run identifying restrictions give reliable results?," *Journal of Business and Economic Statistics*, 15, 345–353.

Filardo, A. (2001): "Should monetary policy respond to asset price bubbles? Some experimental results," *Working Paper* 01-04, Federal Reserve Bank of Kansas City.

Flaig, G., and C. Plötscher (2001): "Estimating the output gap using business survey data," *IFO Studien*, 47, 221–232.

Gali, J. (1992): "How well does the IS-LM model fit the postwar U.S. data?," *Quarterly Journal of Economics*, 107, 709–738.

Garratt, A., K. Lee, M. Pesaran, and Y. Shin (2003): "A long-run structural macroeconometric model of the U.K. Economy," *The Economic Journal*, 113, 412–455.

Giannone, D., L. Reichlin, and L. Sala (2002): "Tracking Greenspan: systematic and unsystematic monetary policy revisited," *Mimeo*, Free University of Brussels.

Giuliodori, M. (2003): "Essays on the transmission mechanism of monetary policy," Ph.D. thesis, University of Glasgow.

Goodhart, C., and R. Hofmann (2001): "Asset prices, financial conditions, and the transmission of monetary policy," Paper presented at a conference on "Asset Prices, Exchange Rates, and Monetary Policy", Stanford.

Hubbard, R. (1998): "Capital market imperfections and investment," *Journal of Economic Literature*, 36, 193–225.

Iaccoviello, M. (2000): "House prices and the macroeconomy in Europe: results from a structural VAR analysis," *Working Paper Series* 18, European Central Bank.

IMF (ed.) (2000): *World Economic Outlook, Spring*. International Monetary Fund, New York.

Kakes, J., and J.-E. Sturm (2002): "Monetary policy and bank lending: evidence from German banking groups," *Journal of Banking and Finance*, 26, 2077–2092.

Kim, S., and N. Roubini (2000): "Exchange rate anomalies in the industrial countries: a solution with structural VAR approach," *Journal of Monetary Economics*, 45, 561–584.

Kiyotaki, N., and J. Moore (1999): "Credit cycles," *Journal of Political Economy*, 105, 211–248.

La Porta, R., F. L. de Silanes, and A. Shleifer (1999): "Corporate ownership around the world," *Journal of Finance*, 54, 471–517.

LASTRAPES, W. (2002): "The Real Price of Housing and Money Supply Shocks: Time Series Evidence and Theoretical Simulations," *Journal of Housing Economics*, 11, 40–74.

LETTAU, M., S. LUDVIGSON, AND C. STEINDEL (2002): "Monetary policy transmission through the consumption-wealth channel," *Economic Policy Review*, Federal Reserve Bank of New York.

LUDVIGSON, S., AND C. STEINDEL (2002): "How important is the stock market effect on consumption?," *Economic Policy Review*, Federal Reserve Bank of New York.

MOJON, B., AND G. PEERSMAN (2003): "A VAR description of the effects of monetary policy in the individual countries of the euro area," in *Monetary policy Transmission in the Euro Area*, ed. by I. Angeloni, A. Kashyap, and B. Mojon. Cambridge University Press, Cambridge.

ORPHANIDES, A. (2001): "Monetary policy rules based on real-time data," *The American Economic Review*, 91, 964–985.

PEERSMAN, G. (2002): "Monetary policy and long-term interest rates in Germany," *Economics Letters*, 77, 271–277.

PEERSMAN, G., AND F. SMETS (2001): "The monetary transmission mechanism in the euro area: more evidence from VAR analysis," *Working Paper Series* 91, European Central Bank.

PESARAN, M., AND Y. SHIN (1998): "Generalized impulse response analysis in linear models," *Economics Letters*, 58, 17–29.

ROMER, C., AND D. ROMER (1989): "Does monetary policy matter? A new test in the spirit of Friedman and Schwartz," in *NBER Macroeconomics Annual 1989*, ed. by O. Blanchard, and S. Fischer. MIT Press, Cambridge.

RUDEBUSCH, G. (1998): "Do measures of monetary policy in a VAR make sense?," *International Economic Review*, 39, 907–931.

SAUER, S., AND J.-E. STURM (2003): "Using Taylor rules to understand ECB monetary policy," Mimeo, IFO.

SIMS, C. (1980): "Macroeconomics and reality," *Econometrica*, 48, 1–48.

——— (1986): "Are forecasting models usable for policy analysis?," *Quarterly Review* Winter, Federal Reserve Bank of Minneapolis.

SIMS, C., J. STOCK, AND M. WATSON (1990): "Inference in linear time series models with some unit roots," *Econometrica*, 58, 113–144.

SIMS, C., AND T. ZHA (1995): "Does monetary policy generate recessions?," *Mimeo*, Yale University.

TAYLOR, J. (1993): "Discretion versus policy rules in practice," *Carnegie-Rochester Series on Public Policy*, 39, 195–214.

WALSH, C. (ed.) (2003): *Monetary Theory and Policy, 2nd edition.* MIT Press, Cambridge.

WEBER, A. (1996): "Germany before and after unification: a structural VAR analysis," *Economic Modelling*, 13, 575–601.

WICKSELL, K. (1907): "The influence of the interest rate on prices," *The Economic Journal*, 17, 213–220.

Credibility and Transparency of Central Banks: New Results Based on Ifo's *World Economic Survey**

Sandra Waller[1] and Jakob de Haan[2]

[1] Bayerische Landesbank, Munich, Germany sandra.waller@web.de
[2] University of Groningen. PO Box 800, 9700 AV Groningen, The Netherlands and CESifo, Munich, Germany j.de.haan@eco.rug.nl

1 Introduction

Credibility of policymakers is considered to enhance the effectiveness of monetary policy in many theoretical models.[1] For instance, in a standard Barro–Gordon type of model a higher level of credibility implies that policymakers can reduce inflation at lower cost. Likewise, various theoretical models suggest that transparency of policymakers will be beneficial.[2] For instance, Geraats (2000) shows that opaqueness about economic forecasts damages the reputation of a strong central bank that is averse to inflation. Similarly, in the

---

*We would like to thank participants in the conference on the Academic Use of Ifo Survey Data, 5–6 December 2003 for their comments. Special thanks to Uli Klueh for his very helpful comments on a previous version of this paper. The usual disclaimer applies. The views expressed are those of the authors only. At the time the survey was hold, Waller was working at Ifo, where she was responsible for the World Economic Survey.

[1]Cukierman and Meltzer (1986), p. 1108 define credibility as "the absolute value of the difference between the policymaker's plan and the public's beliefs about those plans".

[2]Basically two definitions of transparency can be distinguished in the policy-oriented literature on central bank transparency. Sometimes, transparency refers to the activities of the central bank in providing information. For instance, Lastra (2001) defines transparency as the degree to which information on policy actions is available. Others use the term disclosure for this (see, e.g., Siklos (2002)). Alternatively, transparency may refer to the public's understanding of the decisions taken by the monetary authorities and the reasoning behind it (see, for instance, Winkler (2000)). In the theoretical literature transparency is conceptualized in different ways, with authors focusing on preferences, models, knowledge about the shocks hitting the economy, the decision making process, or policy decisions. Conclusions on the usefulness of transparency are sensitive to different notions of transparency (see Posen (2003)).

modified Barro–Gordon model of Faust and Svensson (2001) a high degree of transparency generally reduces the inflation bias. In the model it is assumed that the central bank controls inflation imperfectly and that the central bank has an employment target which varies over time according to an idiosyncratic component. By revealing the control error over inflation, the central bank renders its intentions for inflation observable, which results in lower inflation as it increases the sensitivity of a central bank's reputation to its actions, making it more costly for the central bank to pursue a high inflation policy (see also Jensen (2001)).

Also various policymakers think that credibility and transparency will enhance the effectiveness of monetary policy. For instance, Issing argues that "a high degree of transparency and accountability in monetary policy making reinforces the legitimacy of the central bank and consolidates the public support for its price stability mandate. In turn, this may add to the credibility and thereby the effectiveness, of monetary policy, hence facilitating the central bank's effort to attain its statutory objectives." (Issing (2001), p. 13).

Blinder (2000) mailed a questionnaire to the heads of 127 central banks soliciting their opinions on a number of issues related to central bank credibility. The response rate was 66%. The respondents were asked to answer questions relating to the importance and determinants of central bank credibility. Blinder's respondents considered credibility important "to keep inflation low". The best way for a central bank to earn credibility is to "have a history of doing what it says it will do".

In this paper we report the results of a survey among private sector economists on credibility and transparency of central banks. By using the Ifo World Economic Survey, we were able to solicit the views of private sector economists on these issues. By asking similar questions as Blinder did, we can examine whether private sector economists share the views of central bankers on these matters. Although there are some minor differences between both groups, it turns out that our respondents broadly share the views of Blinder's respondents. According to our respondents, the Federal Reserve is the most credible, transparent and independent central bank out of seven large central banks. The ECB is not perceived as highly credible or transparent, even though our respondents consider it to be very independent.

The remainder of this paper is organized as follows. The next section offers a brief review of the empirical literature on transparency and credibility. Section 3 summarizes Blinder's survey results on credibility. Our results on credibility are reported in Sect. 4, while Sect. 5 contains our findings on transparency and central bank independence. Section 6 offers some concluding comments.

2 Review of the Literature

Even though many authors agree on the importance of transparency for the efficiency of policymaking[3], this issue has received only scant attention in the empirical literature (see Posen (2003) for a discussion). One reason that transparency could matter is that communication by the central bank about its long-term inflation goal may allow the bank to be more flexible in response to shocks in the short-run. The greater trust in the central bank resulting from communication implies that deviations from the target do not indicate a lack of commitment (King (1997)). If the central bank builds greater trust by communicating its long-term inflation objective, inflation persistence will decline since there is a strong belief that inflation will return to its target level. There is some evidence in support of this view. Kuttner and Posen (1999) have examined the response of bond markets (proxying for inflation expectations) in Canada, New Zealand and the UK before and after the central banks in these countries adopted inflation targeting. They find that interest rates decreased, which is consistent with the view that the adoption of inflation targeting increases flexibility. Kuttner and Posen (2001) report similar results for a broader range of countries: inflation targeting reduces inflation persistence, in contrast to other elements of the monetary framework, like central bank independence. However, Ball and Sheridan (2003), who compared seven OECD countries that adopted inflation targeting in the early 1990s to thirteen that did not, report no supportive evidence. They find that after the early 1990s, performance improved in both the targeting countries and the non-targeters. Where targeters improved by more than non-targeters, this is explained by the fact that targeters performed worse than non-targeters before the early 1990s, and there is regression to the mean. Once regression to the mean is taken up, there is no evidence that inflation targeting improves performance.

Another reason why transparency may matter is that communication removes noise from markets (Posen (2003)). Greater disclosure will lead to greater predictability of central bank actions. The results reported by Kuttner (2001) offer support for this point of view. Changes in the Federal Reserve's disclosure policy have reduced market volatility and increased predictability.

Recently, Chortareas and Sterne (2002) have found for a sample of 87 countries that their index of disclosure, based on data taken from Fry (2000), which is based upon the details in central banks' published forecasts and

[3]Still, there is no consensus in the theoretical literature about the optimal level of disclosure (see e.g. Cukierman (2001) and Eijffinger and Geraats (2002)). Also in the Faust and Svensson (2001) model, there is a regime (called the "extreme" transparency regime) in which both the central bank's employment goal and its inflation intentions are observable. In this situation, the central bank's reputation is no longer affected by its actions and an inflationary bias reemerges resulting in a higher inflation. Some authors have pointed out that secrecy may also be beneficial under certain circumstance; see, for instance, Goodfriend (1986).

which ranges from zero to four, is negatively related to average inflation, also if various control variables are taken up.

Also empirical evidence on the importance of credibility is scarce. Cechetti and Krause (2002) also use the information provided by Fry (2000) to examine the extent to which macroeconomic performance in their sample of 63 countries is related to credibility, transparency, independence and accountability of central banks.[4] They find that credibility and, to a lesser extent, transparency is related to inflation. However, given the way that Cechetti and Krause (2002) have constructed their index of credibility, their results are perhaps better interpreted as suggesting that inflation is quite persistent.[5]

According to Issing (2001), transparency of monetary policy will enhance credibility. By providing the public with adequate information about its activities, the central bank can establish a mechanism for strengthening its credibility by matching its actions to its public statements (IMF (2000)). In the model of Jensen (2001), which in terms of its informational structure is similar to the Faust and Svensson (2001) set-up, increased transparency will increase the reputational costs of deviations from the inflation target and therefore increase the credibility of the central bank. However, the credibility-enhancing effect of transparency becomes redundant when central bank preferences are already public information. Chortareas and Sterne (2002) argue that a high degree of transparency is desirable for central banks with poor credibility but may be costly in terms of less flexibility for high-credibility banks.

Whether transparency enhances the credibility of policy makers is not investigated in the empirical studies by Chortareas and Sterne (2002) and Cechetti and Krause (2002). The latter authors report that the correlation between their index of credibility and their index of transparency is 0.31, while credibility is virtually unrelated with their measures of accountability and independence.

---

[4]The information reported by Fry (2000) is based on a survey of 94 central banks. The index of transparency used by Cechetti and Krause (2002) utilizes responses to three questions relating to the degree and frequency at which each central bank provides reports on its policy decisions, assessments about the state of the economy and public explanation of forecasts. The index is obtained as a simple average of these three criteria. Independence is determined on the basis of the responses of five questions (relating to the importance of price stability, goal independence, instrument independence, government's reliance on central bank financing and term in office of the governor). Accountability is determined on the basis of the role of government in determining the objective(s) of monetary policy and on monitoring by parliament and the government. The index of credibility used by Cechetti and Krause (2002) is determined on the basis of the difference between an assumed inflation objective of 2 percent and expected inflation, proxied by actual inflation over the period 1985–1989.

[5]This index is defined as:

$IC = 1 \quad \text{if} \quad E(\pi) \leq \pi^t$

$IC = 1 - \frac{1}{0.2-\pi^t}(E(\pi) - \pi^t) \quad \text{if} \quad \pi^t < E(\pi) < 20\%$

$IC = 0 \quad \text{if} \quad E(\pi) \geq 20\%$

Recently, some authors have presented the results of surveys among central bankers on transparency and credibility. The comprehensive survey by Fry (2000), to which we have already referred, reveals that 74% of their respondents consider transparency a vital or very important component of their monetary policy framework. The next section summarizes the results of the survey of Blinder (2000).

3 Blinder's Survey among Central Bankers on Credibility of Central Banks

Blinder (2000) mailed a questionnaire to the heads of 127 central banks soliciting their opinions on a number of issues related to central bank credibility. The response rate was 66%. The respondents were asked to select a number on a five-point scale, whereby the points have different meanings depending on the question being asked. Table 1 summarizes Blinder's findings.

The first question (Q1) is: *How important is credibility to a central bank?* In this case the points on the five-point scale were:
1 = unimportant
2 = of minor importance
3 = moderately important
4 = quite important
5 = of the utmost importance.

The average score to the first question was a stunning 4.83, with a standard deviation of only 0.37. Blinder (2000) asked the same question to a similar-sized sample of academic economists. The average score for the first question in this group was somewhat lower (4.23), while the standard deviation was higher (0.85).

The second question (Q2) is: *How closely related are the concepts of (a) a central bank's credibility and (b) a central bank's dedication to price stability?* In this case the five point scale has the following meaning:
1 = unrelated
2 = slightly related
3 = moderately related
4 = quite closely related
5 = virtually the same.

As follows from Table 1, the average score on this question in Blinder's survey among central bankers was 4.10. The academic economists gave a considerably lower score (3.31). The next seven questions focus on the issue of why credibility might be important to a central bank. Respondents were asked to express their views on a five-point scale, ranging from strongly disagree to strongly agree.

One argument – that received a score of 4.13 in the survey of Blinder (Q3) among central bankers – is that it will reduce disinflation costs. In the ranking it was even given second place, also in the survey among academic economists. Surprisingly, given this high score, the academic literature has come up with discomforting outcomes as almost all studies report that CBI worsens the trade-off. For instance, Posen (1998) finds a positive correlation between CBI and the sacrifice ratio, i.e. the cumulative increase in unemployment that is due to the disinflation effort divided by the total decrease of inflation (see Eijffinger and Haan (1996) and Berger, De Haan, and Eijffinger (2001) for extensive surveys). Still, one might argue that what really matters for disinflation costs from a theoretical point of view is credibility, which may be influenced by actual (instead of legal) independence of a central bank. So far, the unavailability of indicators for credibility has made more direct testing impossible.

Table 1 also summarizes the outcomes for the other reasons given by Blinder as to why credibility may be important. It follows that the argument "to keep inflation low" received the highest average score. Also the argument that a credible central banker may find it easier to change operating procedures – as, for instance, the Federal Reserve did under Volcker in 1982 – received a very high average.

Question 10 of Blinder's survey listed the reasons indicated in the previous seven questions on the importance of credibility and asked the respondents to rank them. The ranking is shown in parentheses in Table 1. Note that there are some inconsistencies in the average scores and the rankings.[6] For instance, the average score for the answer that credibility will allow central banks to change tactics was 4.38, only slightly lower than the average score for the argument that credibility will help to keep inflation low (score 4.39). However, the changing-tactics-argument was only ranked fifth in question 10. The argument that it is less costly to disinflate received the fifth score in terms of the average score, while it was ranked second in question 10.

The rankings of the academic economists differed somewhat from that of the central bankers. The largest difference occurred with respect to the support-for-independence argument, which was ranked seventh by the economists, and fourth by the central bankers. However, the academic economists agreed with central bankers in their number one and two rankings (i.e. to keep inflation low and less costly to disinflate).

How can credibility be earned? Questions 11 to 17 in Blinder's survey give various possible answers of which the scores are again shown in Table 1. The ranking (in this case based on average scores) is given in parentheses. The top-rated way for a central bank to establish credibility, according to central bankers (and academic economists as well), is to "have a history of doing what it says it will do". Although the economic literature is full of optimal contracts for central bankers (e.g. Walsh (1995)) and incentive-compatible payment schemes (e.g. Svensson (1997)), central bankers give these options a rather low rating, as did academic economists.

[6]We thank Uli Klüh for pointing this out.

Table 1. Blinder's (2000) Survey among Central Bankers about Credibility

Question	Issue	Average	Stand. dev.
Q1	Importance	4.83	0.37
Q2	Related to dedication to price stability	4.10	n.a.
Q3	Less costly disinflation	4.13 (2)	0.78
Q4	To keep inflation low	4.39 (1)	0.60
Q5	To change tactics	4.38 (5)	0.54
Q6	To serve as lender of last resort	4.12 (6)	0.77
Q7	To defend the currency	4.29 (3)	0.70
Q8	Public servants should be truthful	4.00 (7)	0.84
Q9	For support of independence	4.34 (4)	0.75
Q10	Ranking of Q3 to Q9 (shown in parentheses)	–	–
Q11	Importance of CBI for credibility	4.51 (2)	0.63
Q12	Importance of transparency for credibility	4.13 (4)	0.71
Q13	Importance of history of honesty for credibility	4.58 (1)	0.52
Q14	Importance of history of fighting inflation for credibility	4.15 (3)	0.67
Q15	Importance of being constrained by a rule for credibility	2.89 (6)	1.01
Q16	Importance of incentives (personal loss) for credibility	2.15 (7)	1.10
Q17	Importance of small deficit and low debt ratio for credibility	3.92 (5)	0.93

Note: rankings on questions Q3 to Q9 (=Q10) and Q12 to Q17 (ranked by mean scores) are shown in parentheses.

Source: Blinder (2000)

4 Our Survey on Credibility

We were able to conduct a survey directed towards economists in OECD countries that participate in Ifo's *World Economic Survey (formerly known as Economic Survey International ESI).* The Ifo Institute has been running this survey since 1981. [7] Its aim is to obtain the most up-to-date quarterly picture of the economic situation as well as forecasts for the important industrialized, emerging and developing nations.

The explanatory power of the World Economic Survey (WES) results has been tested in various empirical studies. The results can be summarized as follows (Brand and Lindbauer (1997)):

- The survey results represent valuable indicators for explaining global economic developments
- The survey results are also suitable for forecasting economic developments, although the forecasting power of WES indicators is naturally inferior to their explanatory power.
- The number of participants in the survey, which varies from country to country, does not seem to have any significant bearing on the quality of the survey results.

The survey was held for the first time in May 2000. More than 200 respondents filled in the questionnaire. This was a response rate of 45 %. As we have information on the respondents, we can differentiate between economists from various countries. We distinguish between economists from countries in the euro area and those from other countries. We can also differentiate between economists affiliated with financial institutions (banks, insurance companies, etc.) and those working with other firms or research institutes. Finally, the survey allows us to analyze whether the inflation experience of the country where the respondent is located is systematically related to the answers given.

Most of the questions that we asked correspond to those in the Blinder (2000) survey.[8] Our first question corresponds to Q1 in Table 1, i.e.:

Question 1: *How important is credibility to a central bank?*

The possible answers on a five-point scale are the same as in the Blinder survey. Following Blinder (2000), we did not provide our respondents with a

---

[7]See Brand and Lindbauer (1997), Haupt and Waller (2000). Haupt and Waller (2000) examined whether the incorporation of WES data in econometric models significantly improves their ability to analyze and forecast economic developments. Concentrating on the survey data on inflation, these authors found that forecasting models which incorporate WES survey data clearly outperform models which do not. This leads to the conclusion that the WES respondents have relevant information about future developments.

[8]We thank Alan Blinder for providing his survey to us.

definition of credibility. Blinder (2000) motivates this as follows: "I deliberately failed to provide a precise definition of credibility, allowing each respondent to attach his or her own preferred meaning to the term. In fact, there appears to be no generally agreed-upon definition."(p. 1422)

We also did not ask our respondents to give their definition. However, our second question asks about the relationship between credibility and dedication to price stability. The question is almost the same as Q2 in Table 1, i.e.:

Question 2: *How closely are the concepts of credibility and dedication to price stability related?*

The possible answers on a five point-scale range from unrelated (1) to virtually the same (5).

Table 2 shows the results of our survey. As far as the importance of credibility is concerned (Q1), our respondents gave almost as high a mark as central bankers, although the standard deviation is somewhat higher. Also as far as the relationship between credibility of a central bank and its dedication to price stability is concerned (Q2), the average score of our respondents is very close to those of Blinder's survey among central bankers. Professional economists apparently agree more on this issue with central bankers than with academic economists.

As we could only ask a limited number of questions, we did not ask our respondents to answer Blinder's questions Q3 to Q9. Thus, we asked the respondents to rank the seven reasons instead of using the five point answering scheme for each question.

Question 3: *Can you rank (from 1 to 7, where 1 is highest) the following reasons that are often considered as explanations why credibility may be important for a central bank?*

- A more credible central bank can reduce inflation at lower social cost
- A more credible central bank is better able to maintain low inflation once low inflation has been achieved
- A more credible central bank will find it easier to change tactics or operating procedures without upsetting markets or creating doubts about its underlying objectives or its resolve
- A more credible central bank will find it easier to act as a lender of last resort in a financial crisis (e.g., during a market crash or bank run) without creating fears that it has lost its dedication to fighting inflation
- A more credible central bank will find it easier to defend its currency in case of a speculative attack
- Central bankers are public servants, who, therefore, have a duty to be open and truthful
- Credibility is important as a way to justify public support for an independent central bank.

Table 2. Our Survey of Private Sector Economists about Credibility

Question:	Issue:	Average:	Stand. dev.:
Q1	Importance	4.66	0.49
Q2	Related to dedication to price stability	4.02	0.61
Q3	Less costly disinflation	3.31 (2)	2.09
	Keep inflation low	3.40 (3)	1.68
	Change tactics	3.26 (1)	1.72
	Serve as lender of last resort	3.74 (4)	1.71
	Defend the currency	3.96 (5)	1.91
	Public servants should be truthful	5.82 (7)	1.70
	For support of independence	4.53 (6)	1.86
Q4	Importance of CBI for credibility	1.80 (1)	1.32
	Importance of transparency for credibility	3.13 (3)	1.46
	Importance of history of honesty for credibility	2.93 (2)	1.43
	Importance of history of fighting inflation for credibility	3.70 (4)	1.36
	Importance of being constrained by a rule for credibility	4.85 (5)	1.47
	Importance of incentives (personal loss) for credibility	6.38 (7)	1.07
	Importance of small deficit and low debt ratio for credibility	5.26 (6)	1.49

The results of this question can be compared with question Q10 in Blinder's survey. Some notable differences between both surveys show up. The strongest divergence of rankings exists with respect to the usefulness of credibility for changing tactics. Our respondents gave this reason for the importance of credibility the highest ranking, whereas the central bankers in Blinder's survey ranked this reason only fifth.[9] Another interesting result is the ranking of the importance of credibility for price stability in both surveys. Whereas central bankers put this on top of their list, our respondents ranked it third. Credibility as a means to support central bank independence plays only a minor role, according to our respondents. This result is in line with Blinder's findings for academic economists, who ranked it seventh. However, central bankers gave it rank 4.

Next, we asked our respondents to rank the various possibilities given by Blinder as to how a central bank can build credibility. So Blinder's questions Q11 to Q17 are combined to:

[9] However, as pointed out before, in terms of the average score on importance, the changing-tactics-argument got rank 2 in the central bankers' survey.

Question 4: *Can you rank (from 1 to 7, where 1 is highest) the following means which have been suggested to establish or create central bank credibility?*

- The central bank should have a high level of independence
- The central bank should be open and transparent
- The central bank should have a history of doing what it says it will do
- The central bank should have a history of fighting inflation
- The central bank should be bound (whether by law or by custom) to follow a prescribed rule that constrains decision-making
- The central bank governor should suffer some personal loss (e.g. lower salary or loss of job) when inflation is too high
- Absence of high fiscal deficit and debt ratio create central bank credibility.

The rankings of our respondents are broadly in line with those of the central bankers (and academic economists) in Blinder's survey. A history of honesty and central bank independence received the highest ranking in both surveys. Personal incentives for central bankers are not regarded as an adequate means to earn credibility.

Table 3 shows the outcomes of three sub-samples of our respondents: economists from euro area countries, economists affiliated with a financial institution, and economists based in countries that had relatively high inflation rates in the past.[10] The answers from economists from banks and insurance companies as to the reasons why credibility is important and how it can be established are very much in line with the results for our total sample. The same is true for economists located in the euro area and in countries with relatively high inflation rates in the past.

Finally, we asked our respondents to rank 7 central banks with respect to their credibility. Specifically:

Question 5: *Can you rank (from 1 to 7, where 1 is highest) the following central banks in terms of their credibility?*

- Banca d'Italia
- Bank of England
- Bank of Japan
- Banque de France

[10]Using the IMF's Classification of Advanced Economies (taken from the World Economic Outlook), we calculated average inflation rates for the period from 1971 to 2000 (long-term) and from 1990 to 2000 (medium-term). For the long-term, we calculated an average inflation rate of 7%, for the medium-term of 3%. High-inflation countries had above average inflation in both periods.

- Deutsche Bundesbank
- European Central Bank
- Federal Reserve

Table 3. Our Survey of Private Sector Economists about Credibility: Economists from EMU Countries, Financial Institutions and High-Inflation Countries

Question:	Issue:	EMU based:	Financial Institutions:	High inflation countries:
Q1	Importance	4.65	4.78	4.67
Q2	Related to dedication to price stability	4.10	4.15	4.03
Q3	Less costly disinflation	3.29 (2)	2.82 (1)	3.43 (3)
	Keep inflation low	3.38 (3)	3.49 (3)	3.75 (4)
	Change tactics	3.41 (1)	3.12 (2)	3.33 (1)
	Serve as lender of last resort	3.62 (4)	3.81 (4)	3.85 (5)
	Defend the currency	3.99 (5)	4.28 (5)	3.40 (2)
	Public servants should be truthful	5.75 (7)	5.99 (7)	5.71 (7)
	For support of independence	4.57 (6)	4.54 (6)	4.57 (6)
Q4	Importance of CBI for credibility	1.89 (1)	1.75 (1)	1.75 (1)
	Importance of transparency for credibility	3.05 (3)	3.09 (3)	3.36 (3)
	Importance of history of honesty for credibility	3.01(2)	2.97 (2)	2.89 (2)
	Importance of history of fighting inflation for credibility	3.71 (4)	3.59(4)	3.88 (4)
	Importance of being constrained by a rule for credibility	4.79 (5)	5.18 (5)	4.75 (5)
	Importance of incentives (personal loss) for credibility	6.43 (7)	6.19 (7)	6.36 (7)
	Importance of small deficit and low debt ratio for credibility	5.11 (6)	5.35 (6)	5.05 (6)

Table 4 presents our findings for the credibility marks of the various central banks. It follows that our respondents gave the Federal Reserve the highest mark, closely followed by the Bundesbank. The credibility of the Bank of England and the ECB are clearly better than that of the Bank of Japan and the Banca d'Italia.

Table 5 shows the scores for economists in our sample who are affiliated with financial institutions, who are based in an EMU country, or are from a high-inflation country. As far as differences between economists located in

Table 4. Our Survey: Rankings of Central Banks in Terms of Their Credibility

Central Bank:	Average:	Standard deviation:
Banca d' Italia	6.42 (6.29)	1.02
Bank of England	3.74 (3.56)	1.19
Bank of Japan	5.48 (5.71)	1.29
Banque de France	4.86 (4.82)	1.14
Deutsche Bundesbank	1.89 (2.25)	1.12
European Central Bank	3.86 (3.52)	1.39
Federal Reserve	1.79 (1.59)	1.10

Note: The rankings in parentheses are the result of a second survey, held in October 2001.

the euro area and the rest is concerned, the most remarkable result is that economists from EMU countries give the ECB a somewhat better score. The rating of the ECB by economists affiliated with financial institutions is somewhat worse than in Table 4, while the opposite holds for economists from high-inflation countries.

Table 5. Rankings of Credibility of Central Banks: Economists from EMU Countries, Financial Institutions and High-Inflation Countries

Central Bank:	EMU based:	Financial Institutions:	High inflation countries:
Banca d' Italia	6.30	6.24	6.23
Bank of England	3.95	3.71	3.65
Bank of Japan	5.53	5.80	5.68
Banque de France	4.83	4.76	4.90
Deutsche Bundesbank	2.03	1.94	1.94
European Central Bank	3.56	4.03	3.70
Federal Reserve	1.81	1.50	1.90

To examine whether over time the credibility of the ECB has improved, we repeated question 5 in another survey held in October 2001. In Table 4 the results of this second survey are shown in parentheses. Interestingly, the score of the ECB has improved somewhat.

So far, we have only analyzed and compared the results of the total samples of both surveys. It should be noted, however that the samples do differ significantly in size – the sample of the first survey was almost twice as large as in the follow-up survey – and in their composition. Several participants took part in the first survey but not in the second one and vice versa. The answers of experts who participated in both surveys allow for a more in depth analysis of the change of assessments and opinions over time. Unfortunately, this reduces the sample to 58 participants. Table 6 shows the outcomes for the rankings of the respondents who participated in both surveys, as well the rankings based on the full samples. The results for both samples are identical: the ECB has been able to improve its position.

Table 6. Credibility Rankings over Time: All Respondents

	Respondents participating in both surveys		Whole Sample	
	2000	2001	2000	2001
Federal Reserve	1	1	1	1
Deutsche Bundesbank	2	2	2	2
Bank of England	**3**	**4**	**3**	**4**
ECB	**4**	**3**	**4**	**3**
Banque de France	5	5	5	5
Bank of Japan	6	6	6	6
Banca d'Italia	7	7	7	7

As follows from Table 7, respondents in EMU countries gave the ECB a higher rating in the follow-up survey. Although they generally consider the ECB somewhat less credible than most other respondents, among respondents from financial institutions the ECB has gained some ground, too, and has surpassed the Banque de France. In low-inflation countries the ECB also surpassed the Bank of England in terms of credibility. In the high-inflation countries, the ECB maintained its position and is still ranked fourth after the Fed, the Bundesbank and the Bank of England.

5 Transparency and Central Bank Independence

We finally asked our respondents to rank seven central banks according to their transparency and independence. Again, we did not provide the respondents with our definitions of these concepts for reasons explained earlier. The results for transparency are presented in Table 8. Two conclusions can be drawn. First, the ranking of central banks in terms of transparency is the same as for the ranking in terms of credibility. This finding can be interpreted in different ways. Our respondents may, for instance, consider the concepts to be closely related. Alternatively, they may have simply ranked central banks on the basis of their recent performance.

Second, the results on (perceived) transparency by our respondents are broadly in line with an earlier survey by Goldman and Sachs held in February 2000, in which a sample of financial market participants was asked to rate on a scale of 1 to 5 how well they understood the reasoning behind monetary

Table 7. Credibility Rankings over Time: Various Groups of Respondents

Central Bank:	EMU based:				Financial Institutions:				Low inflation countries:			
	Respondents Participating in Both Surveys		Whole Sample		Respondents Participating in Both Surveys		Whole Sample		Respondents Participating in Both Surveys		Whole Sample	
	2000	2001	2000	2001	2000	2001	2000	2001	2000	2001	2000	2001
Federal Reserve	1	1	1	1	1	1	1	1	1	1	1	1
Deutsche Bundesbank	2	2	2	2	2	2	2	2	2	2	2	2
Bank of England	**3**	**4**	4	4	3	3	3	3	**3**	**4**	**3**	**4**
ECB	**4**	**3**	3	3	**5**	**4**	4	4	**4**	**3**	**4**	**3**
Banque de France	5	5	5	5	**4**	**5**	5	5	5	5	5	5
Bank of Japan	6	6	6	6	7	6	6	6	6	6	6	6
Banca d'Italia	7	7	7	7	6	7	7	7	7	7	7	7

policy decisions of four central banks (a higher grade indicates a better understanding). In this survey the ECB did not perform well (average score of just 2.2) in comparison to the US Federal Reserve (a top rating of 4.3; see Gros et al. (2000) for further details). Likewise, in our survey the Federal Reserve and the (old) Deutsche Bundesbank are clearly perceived as more transparent than the ECB. Second, the Bank of England has a similar score to the ECB in our survey.

Table 8. Our Survey: Rankings of Central Banks in Terms of Their Transparency

Central Bank:	Transparency:
Banca d'Italia	6.17 (0.94)
Bank of England	3.33 (1.38)
Bank of Japan	5.93 (1.24)
Banque de France	4.86 (1.04)
Deutsche Bundesbank	2.63 (1.24)
European Central Bank	3.17 (1.50)
Federal Reserve	1.66 (1.21)

These results are very much out of line with the rankings as implied by various indicators of transparency/disclosure. These indicators are constructed on the basis of a list of questions on issues relating to transparency (like: does the central bank publish an inflation report, are economic forecasts published, are there press conferences during which policy decisions are explained, etc.). Table 9 gives the summary scores of the indicators of Fry (2000), Bini-Smaghi and Gros (2001), Amtenbrink and Haan (2002), Eijffinger and Geraats (2002) and Siklos (2002). Most indicators rank the ECB quite high, except for the indicator of Siklos (2002) that gives the ECB the lowest ranking of the banks under consideration here. The latter outcome is somewhat remarkable as Siklos (2002) takes many of the same issues into account as the other authors who construct disclosure indicators. On closer inspection it turns out that the low score for the ECB on the Siklos index is the result of the relatively high weight of the items "publication of minutes of central bank meetings" and "publication of committee voting record" (on which the ECB scores zero) and a low weight on items like publication of reports and regular speeches for which the ECB gets the highest score possible. [11]

How can the discrepancy between the high degree of disclosure and the public perception of the ECB's transparency be explained? A possible cause

[11] The Siklos index also includes the item "special recognition of the role of financial system stability" (on which the ECB gets a score of zero), which has little to do with disclosure. Finally, it seems that Siklos has made a mistake in his coding for the element "publication of a monetary policy strategy". In his book Siklos (rightly) states that the ECB has published its strategy, but in the coding the ECB receives a zero on this element.

for the low score on perceived transparency may be found in the quality of the information being provided. As pointed out by the IMF (2000), transparency requires more than just making information available about policy objectives, responsibilities, policy decisions, and performance results. The content of disclosure is critical for the efficient functioning of markets and its importance will only increase with the evolving changes in international trading and financing arrangements and sophistication of markets. Failure to present public statements and reports on monetary policy issues with appropriate content could undermine the credibility of central banks and result in corresponding behavior by the financial markets, thereby negatively influencing the outcome of monetary policy. The focus of disclosure should be on the materiality and relevance of the information that is being provided to the public. The objective of transparency would, for example, not be met by the release of reports that offer contradictory assessments. The same holds true for contradicting public statements by the members of the decision-making organs of the central bank, something that the ECB has been criticized for in the past and sometimes rightly so.[12]

Table 9. Transparency Indicators

Central Bank:	Fry et al. (2000)	Gros and Bini–Smaghi (2001)	Amtenbrink and De Haan (2002)	Eijffinger and Geraats (2002)	Siklos (2002)
Max. score:	1.00	30	19	15	1.00
Banca d'Italia	0.81	n.a.	n.a.	n.a.	0.43
Bank of England	0.94	24	18	12.5	0.91
Bank of Japan	0.89	14	n.a.	8	0.74
Banque de France	0.53	n.a.	n.a.	n.a.	0.22
Deutsche Bundesbank	0.70	13	10	n.a.	0.70
European Central Bank	n.a.	19	16	10	0.52
Federal Reserve	0.95	16	11	10	0.87

Often the low degree of ECB transparency is related to the monetary policy strategy of the ECB. Begg et al. (2000) find, for example, that "Our observations of ECB's deeds and words in 1999 [...] suggest that much remains to be done to communicate the precise meaning of the announced monetary policy strategy. Unless the ECB clarifies its intentions it will take time – possibly a lot of time – for outside observers to form a clear view"(p. 25)[13]

[12]Hämäläinen (2001) acknowledges this: "It is true that we have not always been very successful in our communication despite ambitious intentions. But communication is not easy in a pan-European context in which differing cultures, languages, traditions and motives affect how messages are interpreted by the different counterparties involved."

[13]See De Haan, Eijffinger, and Waller (2004) for an extensive discussion of the monetary policy strategy of the ECB.

In the second survey we also asked our respondents to rank various central banks with respect to independence. The results are presented in Table 10. It follows that the Fed is perceived to be more independent than the Bundesbank by our respondents. The ECB receives a rating similar to that of the Bundesbank. Still, in this case, the results for independence as perceived by our respondents are more in line with the rankings implied by indicators for legal central bank independence as shown in Table 11.[14]

Table 10. Our Survey: Rankings of Central Banks in Terms of Their Independence

Central Bank:	Independence:
Banca d'Italia	6.20 (0.89)
Bank of England	3.65 (1.32)
Bank of Japan	5.74 (1.30)
Banque de France	5.07 (1.14)
Deutsche Bundesbank	2.59 (1.31)
European Central Bank	2.57 (1.46)
Federal Reserve	1.95 (1.25)

[14]The index of Alesina (1989) focuses on questions like: does the central bank have final authority over monetary policy?; are there government officials on the governing board of the bank? and are more than half of the board members appointed by the federal government? Grilli, Masciandaro, and Tabellini (1991) present indices of political and economic independence. The first focuses on appointment procedures for board officials, the length of their term in office and the existence of statutory requirements to pursue monetary stability. The economic independence indicator focuses on the extent to which the central bank is free from government influence in implementing monetary policy. Generally the total score on the political and economic independence is employed as an indicator for legal central bank independence. Eijffinger and Schaling (1993) have constructed an index which centers on three items: the location of the final responsibility for monetary policy, the absence or presence of a government official on the board of the central bank and the fraction of board appointees made by government. Central bank laws under which the central bank is the final authority get a double score in this index. The number of positive answers plus one gives the total score on this index. Cukierman (1992) provides an index which is the aggregate from sixteen basic legal characteristics of central bank charters which in turn are grouped into four clusters: 1. the appointment, dismissal and legal term of office of the governor of the central bank; 2. the institutional location of the final authority for monetary policy and procedures to resolve conflicts between the government and the bank; 3. the importance of price stability in comparison to other objectives; 4. the stringency and universality of limitations on the ability of government to borrow from the central bank. The index of Fry (2000) is based on a survey among central bankers. See footnote 4.

6 Concluding Comments

We have reported the results of a survey among private sector economists about credibility and transparency of central banks. In line with the survey of Alan Blinder among central bankers, we asked participants in Ifo's World Economic Survey to answer questions on the importance and determinants of credibility. The results of both surveys are closely comparable. Credibility is considered to be important to attain price stability at low cost, while the best ways to earn credibility are a history of honesty and a high level of central bank independence. Central bankers, academic and professional economists all agree on this. According to our respondents, the Federal Reserve is the most credible, transparent and independent central bank out of large seven central banks. The ECB is not perceived as highly credible or transparent, even though our respondents consider it to be very independent.

Table 11. Central Bank Independence Indicators

Central Bank:	Alesina	G–M–T*	Cukierman	E–S**	Fry et al.
Banca d'Italia	1.5	5	0.22	2	0.88
Bank of England	2	6	0.31	2	0.77
Bank of Japan	3	6	0.16	3	0.93
Banque de France	2	7	0.28	2	0.90
Deutsche Bundesbank	4	13	0.66	5	0.96
European Central Bank	4	14	0.94	5	n.a.
Federal Reserve	3	12	0.51	3	0.92

Source: Eijffinger and Haan (1996), Eijffinger and Haan (2000)

*Grilli–Masciandaro–Tabellini **Eijffinger–Schaling

Note: the index of Fry (2000) differs from the other indicators, as the index is based on a survey among central bankers, whereas the other indicators are based on the interpretation of the central bank law by the author(s) who constructed the particular index. The index of Fry also refers to the beginning of 2000, while the other indicators refer to the situation before EMU.

References

Alesina, A. (1989): "Politics and Business Cycles in Industrial Democracies," *Economic Policy*, 8, 55–98.

Amtenbrink, F., and J. D. Haan (2002): "A Non-Transparent European Central Bank? Who is to blame?," mimeo, University of Groningen.

Ball, L., and N. Sheridan (2003): "Does Inflation Targeting Matter?," Working Paper No. 9577, NBER.

Begg, D., et al. (2000): *One Money, Many Countries – Monitoring the European Central Bank*, vol. 2. CEPR, London.

Berger, H., J. De Haan, and S. Eijffinger (2001): "Central Bank Independence: An Update of Theory and Evidence," *Journal of Economic Surveys*, 15(1), 3–40.

Bini-Smaghi, L., and D. Gros (2001): "Is the European Central Bank Sufficiently Accountable and Transparent?," Working Paper No. 7, CEPS, Brussels.

Blinder, A. (2000): "Central Bank Credibility: Why Do We Care? How Do We Build It?," *American Economic Review*, 90(5), 1421–1431.

Brand, D., W. G., and J. D. Lindbauer (1997): "Selected General Indicators of the Ifo Institute for Economic Research," in *Business Cycle Indicators*, ed. by K. Oppenländer. Aldershot, Avebury.

Cechetti, S., and S. Krause (2002): "Central Bank Structure, Policy Efficiency, and Macroeconomic Performance: Exploring Empirical Relationships," *Federal Reserve Bank of St. Louis Review*, 84(4), 47–59.

Chortareas, G., D. S., and G. Sterne (2002): "Does It Pay To Be Transparent? International Evidence from Central Bank Forecasts," *Federal Reserve Bank of St. Louis Review*, 84(4), 99–118.

Cukierman, A. (1992): *Central Bank Strategy, Credibility and Independence: Theory and Evidence*. MIT Press, Cambridge (MA).

——— (2001): "Accountability, Credibility, Transparency, and Stabilization in the Eurosystem," in *The EMU and its Impact on Europe and the World*, ed. by C. Wyplosz. Oxford University Press, Oxford.

Cukierman, A., and A. H. Meltzer (1986): "A Theory of Ambiguity, Credibility, and Inflation under Discretion and Asymmetric Information," *Econometrica*, 54(5), 1099–1128.

De Haan, J., S. Eijffinger, and S. Waller (2004): *The ECB: Centralization, transparency and credibility*. MIT Press, Cambridge (MA), forthcoming.

Eijffinger, S., and P. Geraats (2002): "How Transparent Are Central Banks?," Discussion Paper No. 3188, CEPR.

Eijffinger, S., and J. D. Haan (1996): "The Political Economy of Central-Bank Independence," *Princeton Special Papers in International Economics*, 19.

——— (2000): *European Monetary and Fiscal Policy*. Oxford University Press, Oxford.

Eijffinger, S., and E. Schaling (1993): "Central Bank Independence in Twelve Industrial Countries," *Banca Nazionale del Lavoro Quarterly Review*, 184, 1–41.

Faust, J., and L. E. Svensson (2001): "Transparency and Credibility: Monetary Policy with Unobservable Goals," *International Economic Review*, 42(2), 369–397.

Fry, M. (2000): "Key issues in the choice of monetary policy framework," in *Monetary Policy Frameworks in a Global Context*, ed. by L. Mahadeva, and G. Sterne. Routledge, London.

GERAATS, P. M. (2000): "Why Adopt Transparency? The Publication of Central Bank Forecasts," Discussion Paper No. 2582, CEPR.

GOODFRIEND, M. (1986): "Monetary Mystique: Secrecy and Central Banking," *Journal of Monetary Economics*, 17, 63–92.

GRILLI, V., D. MASCIANDARO, AND G. TABELLINI (1991): "Political and Monetary Institutions and Public Financial Policies in the Industrial Countries," *Economic Policy*, 13, 341–92.

GROS, D., ET AL. (2000): *Quo Vadis Euro? The Cost of Muddling Through.* CEPS, Brussels.

HAUPT, H., AND S. WALLER (2000): "Economic Analysis and Short-term Forecasting with Qualitative Data from the Economic Survey International (ESI)," in *Use of Survey Data for Industry, Research, and Economic Policy*, ed. by B. S. K.H. Oppenländer, G. Poser. Avebury, Aldershot, Selected papers presented at the 24th CIRET Conference, Proceedings, Wellington, New Zealand, 1999.

HÄMÄLÄINEN, S. (2001): "The ECB's Monetary Policy – Accountability, Transparency and Communication, Introduction at the Old Age," in New Economy and Central Banking Conference, organized by CEPR/ESI and Suomen Pankki, 14 September 2001, Helsinki.

IMF (2000): *Supporting Document to the Code of Good Practices on Transparency in Monetary and Financial Policies.* IMF, Washington.

ISSING, O. (2001): "The Euro Area and the Single Monetary Policy," Working Paper No. 44, Österreichische Nationalbank.

JENSEN, H. (2001): "Optimal Degrees of Transparency in Monetary Policymaking," Discussion Paper No. 2689, CEPR.

KING, M. (1997): "Changes in UK monetary policy: Rules and discretion in practice," *Journal of Monetary Economics*, 39, 81–97.

KUTTNER, K. (2001): "Monetary Policy Surprises and Interest Rates: Evidence from the Fed Funds Futures Market," *Journal of Monetary Ecoomics*, 47(3), 523–44.

KUTTNER, K., AND A. POSEN (1999): "Does talk matter after all? Inflation targeting and central bank behavior," Working Paper No. 99–10, Institute for International Economics.

——— (2001): "Inflation, monetary transparency, and G3 exchange rate volatility," in *Adapting to Financial Globalization*, ed. by M. Balling, E. Hochreiter, and E. Hennessy. Routledge, London.

LASTRA, R. (2001): "How much accountability for central banks and supervisors?," *Central Banking*, 12(2), 69–75.

POSEN, A. (1998): "Central Bank Independence and Disinflationary Credibility: A Missing Link?," *Oxford Economic Papers*, 50, 335–59.

——— (2003): "Six Practical Views of Central Bank Transparency," in *Central Banks, Monetary Theory and Policy: Essays in Honour of Charles Goodhart*, ed. by P. Mitzen, vol. 1. Edward Elgar, London.

SIKLOS, P. (2002): *The Changing Face of Central Banking: Evolutionary Trends Since World War II.* Cambridge University Press, Cambridge.

SVENSSON, L. E. O. (1997): "Optimal Inflation Targets, "Conservative" Central Banks, and Linear Inflation Contracts," *American Economic Review*, 87(1), 98–114.

WALSH, C. E. (1995): "Optimal Contracts for Central Bankers," *American Economic Review*, 85(1), 150–67.

WINKLER, B. (2000): "Which kind of transparency? On the need for clarity in monetary policy-making," Working Paper No. 26, ECB.

Printing and Binding: Strauss GmbH, Mörlenbach